His Own Counsel:

The Life and Times of Lyman Trumbull

Judge Lyman Trumbull.

His Own Counsel:

The Life and Times of Lyman Trumbull

Ralph J. Roske

UNIVERSITY OF NEVADA PRESS
RENO, NEVADA
1979

Library of Congress Cataloging in Publication Data

Roske, Ralph Joseph, 1921-
His own counsel.

(Nevada studies in history and political science; no. 14)
Includes bibliographical references and index.
1. Trumbull, Lyman, 1813-1896. 2. United States — Politics and government — 1849-1877. 3. Legislators — United States — Biography. 4. United States. Congress. Senate — Biography. I. Title, II. Series.
E415.9.T86R58 328.73'092'4 [B] 79-19409
ISBN 0-87417-055-9

University of Nevada Press, Reno, Nevada 89557 USA

Printed in the United States of America
Cover designed by Jane Brenner

CONTENTS

PREFACE

MY STUDY OF Lyman Trumbull has spanned thirty years. It began with a doctoral dissertation that covered the last thirty-one years of Trumbull's life. I then embarked on a full-scale biography of this statesman which has finally evolved into a manuscript for this series of the University of Nevada Press. Because of space limitations in this series, what originally was a manuscript three times as long has been pared down to this present size.

I have had the cooperation of several of Trumbull's descendants in sharing their material with me, most notably, Edward Trumbull, Walter Trumbull, and Mrs. Elizabeth Worrall. I greatly appreciate their help.

For ease in footnoting, I have lumped the relatively small collection of Lyman Trumbull papers in the Illinois State Historical Library with the later acquisitions of the Lyman Trumbull family manuscripts by that Library.

Many colleagues have read this manuscript and counselled me, as have readers for and staff members of the Nevada Press, most particularly Robert Laxalt. I am certain that I have produced a far better manuscript as a result of this help.

I should most particularly like to thank Mrs. Joyce Standish for her typing and editorial assistance, as well as my wife, Rosemary, who has aided me often in many ways in seeking to capture the elusive Trumbull character and personality.

For all errors, I am, of course, solely responsible.

R.J.R.

Las Vegas, Nevada
January 1979

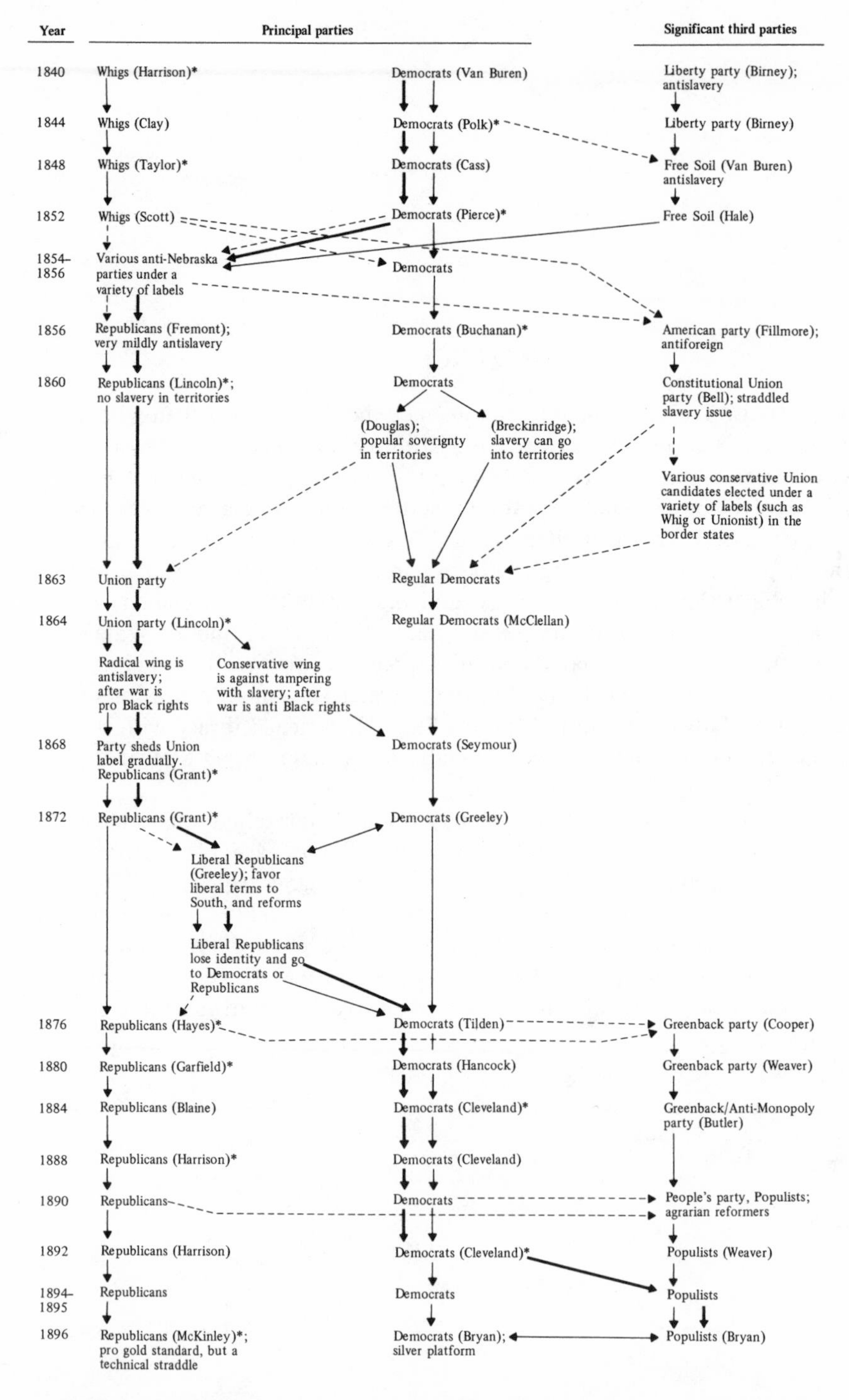

A simplified chart of Lyman Trumbull's political environment. Heavy arrows indicate Trumbull's changing party affiliations; light arrows show political direction taken by majority of party members; dashed arrows show direction taken by minority of members. Asterisks indicate winning candidates.

CHAPTER ONE

PREAMBLE TO A CONSTITUTIONALIST

LYMAN TRUMBULL was born on October 12, 1813, in the town of Colchester in New London County, Connecticut, the seventh child of Benjamin and Elizabeth Trumbull. This first Trumbull to emigrate to America settled in Roxbury, Massachusetts in 1637. In 1670, his third son, Joseph, moved to Suffield, Connecticut, where he had four sons, John, Joseph, Ammi and Benoni. John was grandfather of John Trumbull, the poet-author of "McFingal" and other works. Three governors of early Connecticut were descended from Joseph. The first was the famous Revolutionary War incumbent, Jonathan Trumbull. The painter John Trumbull also descended from Joseph Trumbull. Benoni Trumbull was grandfather of the Reverend Benjamin Trumbull, a prominent clergyman and author. He, in turn, was Lyman Trumbull's grandfather.[1]

Elizabeth Mather Trumbull, Lyman's mother, was descended from the Reverend Richard Mather, who landed in Boston from England in 1635 and was the father of the brilliant Cotton Mather.[2]

Despite their illustrious forebears, Lyman Trumbull's parents possessed only moderate means. Benjamin's practice as an attorney was modest, and he supplemented his income with produce of his medium-sized farm. Since he could not afford to send his sons to Yale College, they attended schools in Colchester.[3]

Colchester was located twenty-three miles from Hartford and twenty miles from New London. In 1800 it could boast a population of more than three thousand people. Although settled in 1701, the town had grown slowly, since it included within its forty-three square miles much stony soil unfit for farming. Located within Colchester was a free grammar school which operated for two-thirds of the year. Lyman attended this school prior to matriculation at Bacon Academy, founded in 1800, and one of the finest academies in Connecticut, which then stood in the forefront of American education.[4]

Lyman received a thorough classical education at Bacon Academy. All his life, his writings displayed his grasp of grammar, spelling and punctuation, in his day rare virtues even among public figures.[5]

Lyman attended Bacon Academy continually until he became nineteen, laboring on the family farm when not in school. Since his father was far from wealthy and the family was large, everyone worked. Years later, Lyman remembered, "If there ever was a family of children grew up loving each most tenderly, this was one."[6] When he was fifteen, his mother died. Trumbull was moved by his mother's death; nearly thirty years later he could recall every detail of her last day.[7]

At nineteen, he began grammar school teaching in a nearby town. Two years later, he obtained a better teaching post at Portland, sixteen miles from Colchester. There he met his first love, Louisa Guildersleeve. Her wealthy father scorned Lyman as a potential son-in-law and quickly broke up the romance.[8]

The winter after he reached nineteen, Lyman traveled to New Jersey to take a teaching post and to forget Louisa Guildersleeve, but he returned the following summer to Colchester. There, he heard of the demand for teachers in the South. It was supposed to be so great that they could command a salary of two hundred dollars a year.

Trumbull left on a Connecticut River schooner for Charleston, South Carolina. The rough voyage caused him to avoid ocean trips the rest of his life.[9] Arriving at Charleston, Trumbull moved inland to Georgia, where he eventually found an opening as principal of Greenville Academy.[10] The academy had a total staff of two or three, and the term "principal" meant principal teacher.[11] For three years, Trumbull successfully headed Greenville Academy.

Teaching school was not a lifetime occupation for ambitious young men in the first half of the nineteenth century. Like many of his counterparts, Lyman used it as a stepping-stone to a more lucrative career in the law. From childhood, he had desired a legal career. As an attorney he would also have ample opportunity to indulge himself in politics. Therefore, in his free hours Lyman studied law in the office of another transplanted New Englander, Hiram Warner, a prominent Georgia lawyer. Under Warner's tutelage, Trumbull developed for the law a passion which his less worldly relatives gave to theology.[12]

During this time, Trumbull boarded in the town hotel. As a Yankee teacher he found he was treated with politeness rather than warmth by white, plantation-dominated Georgia society. For his part Lyman looked with harsh eyes upon the institution of slavery, which he thought degrading to both master and slave. Yet he was no abolitionist and he felt that the slave system must be allowed in states that desired it as one of their rights guaranteed under the American Constitution.[13]

Persevering as principal of the Greenville Academy until he had completed his legal studies and had been admitted to the Georgia bar, Trumbull left Greenville in 1837 for the more congenial social climate of the Old Northwest.[14] Trumbull chose rather than Indiana, the new state of Illinois, since many of its leading citizens were transplanted Yankees.[15]

After some searching, Trumbull decided to settle at Belleville, a town four years older than the state of Illinois.[16] A contemporary who met him shortly after his arrival in Illinois wrote of him: "He was tall, well-proportioned, with a slight stoop, probably owing to his great short-sightedness, and had rather light hair and blue eyes. His complexion was very pale. His features were regular and handsome."[17]

But before actually starting to practice law in Belleville, Trumbull returned to Colchester. His hometown seemed an unprogressive place in contrast to the bustling Illinois towns, and he was convinced he had made the correct choice in emigrating to Illinois.[18]

In August 1837, upon his return from the East, he was admitted to the bar in Belleville. A lawyer in frontier Illinois occupied a position of some status. He was better paid than the schoolteacher and considered more knowledgeable in worldly matters than the local minister. He was almost always a community leader. For three years, Trumbull was the law partner of a razor-sharp but folksy-appearing lawyer, John Reynolds. Reynolds was widely known about the state, having been governor; and he made an excellent senior partner for Trumbull.[19]

In 1840, the Reynolds-Trumbull partnership was dissolved when Reynolds was elected to Congress and Trumbull claimed a seat in the state legislature. Lyman was then joined by his brother George, who, with the easy informality of the times, joined him as partner after a short time spent in studying law under his older brother.[20]

Lyman was now successfully handling a wide variety of cases, criminal and civil. A fellow-lawyer explained his phenomenal success, writing: "For so young a lawyer, he was a very good one, and his addresses to the court and jury were logical and impressive. . . . On occasion his smile was sneeringly sardonic. While for lack of a strong imagination, he could not be called an orator, he was a powerful and successful debator. He was a man of indomitable industry. . . ."[21]

Trumbull always had a lively interest in politics. A Jacksonian Democrat, he had cast his first vote in 1836 for Martin Van Buren.[22] The 1840 campaign brought him his first opportunity for public office. Nationally, it was the occasion of the log-cabin campaign of the Whigs, pitting their William Henry Harrison against Martin Van Buren and the Democrats. Fighting desperately, the Whig speakers in Illinois were led by a rising lawyer, Abraham Lincoln, who made an engaging speech, well-suited to his audience. As a Harrison elector, he stumped the state, bringing new luster to his name.[23] Fearing a Whig victory, the Democrats in Trumbull's home county of St. Clair nominated their strongest ticket, which included Lyman as a nominee for the legislature.

Trumbull made speeches throughout his district and was aided by two effective Democratic orators, James Shields and Gustave Koerner. Shields, an Irish immigrant with a smooth platform delivery, would in time emerge as a rival within the Democratic party. The other, Koerner, was a leader of the important German element in southern Illinois. Koerner became a life-long friend and supporter of Trumbull. Both men would play important roles in Trumbull's future career.[24] Then, in the election for the lower house of the legislature, held on August 3, 1840, Trumbull led all the candidates, winning his seat.[25]

At twenty-seven, Trumbull was the youngest member of the state legislature, which met in November 1840, in the new capital of Springfield.[26] At this time, there was a galaxy of political stars in Springfield such as was perhaps never exceeded anywhere, at any time, in state politics. These included Abraham Lincoln, Stephen A. Douglas, David Davis, Richard Yates, E. D. Baker, Sidney Breese, James Shields, O. H. Browning and William A. Richardson.[27] Trumbull could hold his own in debate with any of them.[28]

Gustave Koerner explained Trumbull's rise to eminence in Illinois politics. He believed that Trumbull succeeded because he set but two goals in life for himself — to succeed in law and rise in political circles.[29]

During the special session and the regular session which followed it, the Illinois legislature faced urgent problems. A crisis gripped the state, resulting from the Panic of 1837, which had adversely affected the state banks, as well as the Illinois internal improvement system. In the 1830's, Illinois had chartered banks and created a heavy state debt to finance an elaborate system of internal improvements. In December 1836, the legislature had authorized further expansion of the banks, and they had just begun this pleasant maneuver when the Panic of 1837 burst upon them. Despite charter provisions to the contrary, the banks suspended payment of specie in exchange for their bank notes. To keep them solvent, Governor Thomas Carlin called this special session.[30]

The Illinois Whigs generally favored the banks to be consistent with their national party stand. The Democrats had two opinions. One Democratic faction favored a lenient attitude toward the banks as the best way out of the state's difficulty.[31] The other Democratic group, with Trumbull as one of its leaders, adamantly opposed further concessions to the banks.[32] In the legislature, Trumbull worked zealously to embarrass the banks. He used every parliamentary trick. He tied crippling amendments to favorable measures, and when these moves failed, fought the passage of the bills.[33] Meanwhile, he sought acceptance for his own anti-bank proposals.[34]

The banks' friends nonetheless pushed through a bill to allow the banks to suspend specie payment without loss of their charters, but Trumbull and the anti-bank Democrats wrote a stiff protest into the House *Journal*.[35] Tied to the bank issue were the state debt and the internal improvement program. Being caught up in the national trend to have the state provide extensive public works, the Illinois legislature had voted the construction of roads, railroads, and canals.[36] In order to involve as many parts of the state as possible, a given public works project was worked upon in widely separated places. Thus, when construction was suspended, the completed portions of a canal or railroad were useless. The result was a grievous waste of money. The Illinois state debt reached fifteen million — a staggering sum for that time.[37]

Convinced that the internal improvement scheme was futile, Trumbull unsuccessfully proposed that all workers on the program be discharged at once.[38] Then Trumbull vainly fought for a bill repealing all legislation authorizing the public improvement system.[39] In the course of the debate over the internal improvement system, Trumbull crossed verbal swords with the Whig spokesman, Abraham Lincoln.[40] The two men were almost always on opposing sides of these questions.[41]

Trumbull's most important contribution in this legislative session was his sponsorship of a bill[42] which as enacted provided that any free black could register his status with the current court clerk of his county. This registration would serve as *prima facie* evidence in case his free status was ever questioned in court.[43] In several court cases where he had represented blacks, Trumbull had seen the pressing need for this law.[44]

Lyman's unprecedented activity and his strident opposition to banks and the internal improvement system drew adverse comment from more conservative Democrats. They claimed that Trumbull was a dangerous demagogue.[45] Yet this image of Trumbull should be modified by his strong opposition to a law which aided debtors whose property was sold under auction.[46]

At this time, a dispute arose concerning the right of removal of the secretary of state by the governor. In 1838, Governor Carlin had removed Alexander P. Field and appointed John A. McClernand in his place. The issue was taken to the courts and the four-man Illinois Supreme Court, dominated by Whigs, reversed the lower decisions for McClernand and decided for Field.[47]

This decision was not the only anxious moment given the Democrats by the Whig-dominated court. As a result, in the 1840 legislative session, Trumbull and McClernand, aided by Stephen A. Douglas' lobby, rammed through a measure to pack the court by allowing five additional justices to be appointed. Some Democrats opposed the bill, but Trumbull and McClernand made the measure a test of party loyalty. The revamped court did not have to reverse the Field decision, because early in the session when the state senate confirmed the governor's new choice of Douglas as secretary of state, Field, bowing to the inevitable, surrendered his office.[48]

When Douglas resigned after only a few months to take an Illinois Supreme Court seat,[49] the governor nominated Trumbull for the place. Trumbull had not sought the post. He wrote his brother, "The new Governor never consulted me about the appointment, &, in fact, I was but slightly acquainted with him & how he came to make the appointment the Lord only knows."[50] Actually, Carlin had become disenchanted with McClernand and had appointed Trumbull so as to build a rival to McClernand within the party. Now the bitter McClernand joined James Shields to mobilize their friends against state senate confirmation of the Trumbull appointment.[51] But the effort was in vain; the illinois senate confirmed Trumbull as Douglas' successor as secretary of state, 22 to 14.[52]

CHAPTER TWO

POLITICS, COURTS, AND COURTING

THE EIGHTH MAN to serve as Illinois secretary of state, Trumbull found his chief function was keeping the governor's records. By statute or custom, he also performed a wide variety of other tasks, most of which he thought "trifling." To free himself from the drudgery of his official duties, he employed a reliable clerk, his brother Benjamin, who came from the East for this purpose.

Thus, Lyman could leave Springfield to tend his extensive law practice centered in St. Clair and adjacent counties. Trumbull felt the perquisites of his office were excellent — $1,500 and additional fees, but he knew that he could not hold the post of secretary of state indefinitely; he needed his law practice.[1] Then, as a result of the gubernatorial election of 1842, he found himself not serving under the easy-going Carlin, but rather Governor Thomas Ford, who scornfully referred to members of Trumbull's wing of the Democratic party as "ultras."[2]

The enmity between Trumbull and his new superior surfaced during the 1842-1843 legislative session. The great legislative issues then revolved about the state banks' method of termination. Ford urged that the banks be allowed to end their operations under the most favorable terms possible. The legislature listened to Ford and authorized him to act together with the state auditor to draft terms for the banks. Ford fashioned a compromise settlement whereby these institutions would surrender their state bonds in return for bank stock held by the state, on a dollar-for-dollar basis.[3] Trumbull felt that Ford's attitude toward the banks was treasonous to the tenets of the Democratic party. In conjunction with Illinois Supreme Court Clerk Ebenezer Peck, Trumbull opposed the governor's bank policy. He openly, but unsuccessfully, fought Ford's program in the legislature.[4]

Nevertheless, Ford was bitter because of Trumbull's opposition and, on March 4, 1843, summarily removed him. After a difficult struggle, the state senate approved the governor's choice for his replacement, Thompson Campbell.[5] The vote was close, 20 to 19, since Trumbull's Democratic friends joined forces with the Whig minority to resist his removal.[6]

Leaving Springfield for Belleville was more difficult for Trumbull than the political situation alone might have warranted. Lyman had fallen in love with Julia Jayne, one of the belles of Springfield society. It had all begun when Trumbull joined a Springfield literary organization which included many aspiring politicians. At his first society meeting, Trumbull met Julia Jayne, daughter of Springfield's earliest physician.[7] Julia was lithe, tall, dark-haired, and blue-eyed. She was seventeen and had attended the "leading young ladies seminary" in the state. Trumbull recognized in her the fine intellectual capacity which can be discerned from her existing letters.

Lyman had produced as great an impression upon Julia. After meeting him, she reported to her mother that the other young men at the party had talked "nonsense" to her, while Lyman had "talked sense." Conscious of his position as secretary of state and being naturally dignified, Lyman was not a person to make trifling talk, even on social occasions; also, being nearly thirty, he was older than most Springfield swains.[8]

At this time, Julia Jayne and another young Springfield socialite, Mary Todd, were good friends. Mary Todd may, in fact, have been a short-lived rival for Lyman's affections. In June 1841, Mary wrote her friend, Mercy Levering, in reference to Trumbull: "Now that your fortune is made, I feel much disposed in your absence, to lay my *claims* as he [Lyman] is talented and agreeable & sometimes *countenances* me."[9]

In November 1842, when Mary Todd married Abraham Lincoln, Julia was one of her bridesmaids.[10] Weddings and talk of weddings absorbed Springfield society. Trumbull wrote his sister Julia about Julia Jayne, "Whether because she looks a little like you . . ., or for some reason I know not but . . . I think her a very fine girl." Lyman escorted Julia to many events on Springfield's crowded social calendar.[11]

Lyman's romance with Julia Jayne suffered a temporary setback when he was removed as secretary of state and left Springfield. But Lyman pressed his courtship in person when his legal business permitted, and with a stream of letters to Julia when it did not. Julia and Lyman were married on June 21, 1843, at the First Presbyterian Church. The "groomsmen" included George Trumbull and a political crony, Norman B. Judd.[12] After a visit to Lyman's relatives in Connecticut, the Trumbulls returned to Illinois in late September, 1843. Then, while visiting the Jaynes in Springfield, Lyman contracted a fever which confined him to his room for ten days. Doctor Jayne tenderly cared for him until he recovered.[13]

Illness and sorrow continued to trouble the young Trumbulls. Julia left their home in Belleville in April to return to Springfield for the birth of their first child. The baby, a son, was born on May 4, 1844. While journeying to see his wife and son, Lyman fell ill in Carlinville with a severe fever and chest pain. Dr. Jayne travelled to Carlinville to tend Lyman. When Lyman was able to travel, he was taken by his father-in-law to Springfield in a carriage. The pain in Lyman's right side continued and he was "bled" again and frequently blistered. This treatment caused Lyman to recover only slowly. In June, he was still so weak that he was confined to his room for days.[14] Heartbreak complicated this troubled scene when the baby, Lyman Jr., died of an undiagnosed illness on August 27.[15]

In the 1840's Illinois burgeoned. The state debt of fifteen million dollars seemed lighter as the wealth of Illinoisans increased and the state's population nearly doubled to 851,000 in the decade 1840-1850. The air was filled with schemes for large-scale railroad building, some of which became reality with federal aid in the 1850's. In this time of building and growing, the memory of the Panic of 1837 faded.[16]

In the 1840's, Trumbull played a prominent role in eradicating slavery from Illinois. Ostensibly, the Northwest Ordinance of 1787 had banned slavery from Illinois. In practice, the law was ignored. When it had been passed by the Confederation Congress in 1787, some lawyers had argued that the ordinance could not be retroactively applied to slaves held in Illinois by the French inhabitants. These slaves, they contended, had been guaranteed as property in 1763 and 1783, when the Illinois country passed first from the French to the English, and then to the Americans.

As Southerners moved into the Northwest Territory, they had brought their slaves with them. To give a semblance of legality to their actions, they enacted a territorial law permitting a black indenture system, only one step from slavery. The Indiana territorial indenture act of 1807, which had applied to Illinois when that area was part of the Indiana Territory, was enacted by the Illinois territorial legislature in 1812.

When Illinois became a state in 1818, the territorial act remained on the statute books. This toleration of slavery proved unsatisfactory to ardent pro-slavery men. They demanded a new constitution openly allowing slavery.[17] Their effort to call a new constitutional convention failed by sixteen hundred votes.[18] Then, the pro-slavery forces had to switch to a defensive position; yet black bondage was so deeply entrenched in Illinois that recourse to the courts was the only available avenue to those who would free the blacks still in servitude under the indenture act.[19]

Lyman Trumbull had long advised any black servant who consulted him that slavery in any form was illegal in Illinois. This position was a courageous one for Trumbull to take, since slavery was most common in southern Illinois where he then sought a political career. His hostile attitude toward slavery involved him in the Borders Case. Sarah Borders and her three children, held to bondage under the Illinois indenture law, escaped from their master, Andrew Borders, of Randolph County. Captured in Peoria County, Sarah Borders and her children were arraigned as fugitive servants before a justice of the peace. Sarah Borders argued that she and her children had been retained as servants beyond the maximum time set by the law. Although the justice court ruled that the fugitives were free, when their master appealed the decision, the county court ruled in his favor. The Borders servants appealed to the Illinois Supreme Court and retained Lyman Trumbull and Gustave Koerner, for only nominal fees, to represent them. At the December 1843 session of the court, the two lawyers contended that in Illinois any form of slavery was illegal since the Northwest Ordinance. The court rejected their arguments and decided for the master.[20]

This victory for the pro-slavery forces was short-lived. Two years later, in 1845, Trumbull argued against the legal existence of slavery in the prairie state before the Illinois Supreme Court in the case of *Jarrott* v. *Jarrott*. In this case, a descendant of a slave, held in the Illinois country while it was a French possession, instituted a suit against his former master for wages. Arguing for the black, Trumbull insisted that the sixth article of the Northwest Ordinance of 1787 banning slavery was retroactive in its application and thus, applied to all slaves in the territory. A reconstituted supreme court adopted many of Trumbull's arguments. Its decision in this suit wrote a legal end to Illinois slavery, although masters were slow to heed the court's decision.[21]

Trumbull continued his interest in politics after leaving the post of secretary of state. Indeed, as soon as he returned to Belleville, he was mentioned as a congressional candidate.[22] As a result of the 1840 census, Illinois gained four additional representatives. Thus the legislature had created a new district, which included Trumbull's home county. This necessitated a special election in 1843.

Trumbull found his path to the new congressional seat barred by two rivals, his former law partner, John Reynolds, and his old rival, James Shields.[23] At the congressional district nominating convention, Trumbull quickly canvassed the delegates and discovered that Shields had a majority. Turning to John Reynolds, with whom he remained on friendly terms, he suggested an alliance against Shields. Reynolds agreed. Still, their combined forces were a minority. They decided upon a stratagem to defeat Shields. There was a successful businessman, Robert Smith of Madison County, who dreamed of a political career. As a gesture, Smith had persuaded his county delegation, which really preferred Shields, to tender him a complimentary vote on the first ballot. Learning of this arrangement, Trumbull and Reynolds had their delegates vote for Smith, once Madison County had announced its complimentary vote. Thus, to Smith's delight and Shields' anger, the Madison County businessman was nominated.[24] Smith, a capable campaigner, easily won in the general election.[25]

The next year, the regular congressional election was held. Again, Trumbull coveted the Democratic nomination. His chances seemed improved, since the "Springfield clique," as Governor Ford's and Shields' supporters were termed, suffered from internal dissension.[26] Although Smith allegedly had pledged himself not to seek re-election, he avidly sought a second term. At the district Democratic nominating convention, Reynolds and Trumbull cooperated in a stop-Smith movement. The effort failed; Smith was easily renominated. With Trumbull's support, Reynolds ran against Smith in the general election as an independent candidate. But Smith, running as the party regular, was an easy winner.[27]

Although once again the congressional seat had eluded Trumbull, he remained undaunted. His independent stand had attracted support for him as an 1846 gubernatorial candidate in opposition to Ford's statehouse faction. Trumbull authorized the Randolph County *Record* to hoist his name to its masthead as the newspaper's choice for the Democratic nomination.[28] His campaign had begun.

Trumbull's prospects brightened when the split within the ranks of the "Springfield clique" widened. William Walters, the senior editor and publisher of the state Democratic official newspaper, the *Illinois State Register,* died of an illness and was succeeded by his junior editor, Charles Lanphier. Lanphier reversed the newspaper's long-standing policy and commented sympathetically on Trumbull's political ambitions.[29] By aggressive campaigning, Trumbull garnered enough support to alarm Governor Ford. The incumbent governor might be too controversial to hope for a second term for himself, yet he strove to get a nominee of whose record he approved.[30]

Before the gubernatorial convention began, Trumbull was considered the front-runner. Yet, he had made too many enemies. By hard political maneuvering, his opponents coalesced a majority of the convention behind an obscure dark-horse, eastern Illinoisan Augustus French.[31] After French's nomination, Trumbull won over many of the opposition delegates when he made a stirring address, asking for party unity.[32]

A tireless campaigner, Trumbull, after his defeat in the gubernatorial convention, again turned his attention to the congressional district nomination.[33] Reynolds, foreswearing his own political ambitions, actively aided Trumbull against the incumbent Smith. Although Trumbull's forces controlled the district nominating convention, Smith and his supporters bolted the meeting, bellowing, "Fraud!" The remaining delegates promptly nominated Trumbull as the Democratic congressional candidate.[34]

Smith accepted an independent Democratic nomination by the bolters of the convention and then ran with Whig support in the general election. Trumbull rigorously stumped his district, but found himself on the defensive, answering questions about his intra-party quarrel with Governor Ford.[35] On election day, August 3, 1846, Trumbull received only forty-one percent of the vote to Smith's fifty-eight percent.[36] In his home county of St. Clair, however, he received almost three-quarters of the vote cast.[37]

Trumbull's defeat is easily explained. He was successfully painted by Smith as an "ultra" Democrat whom no independent or Whig could support. Also, Ford, in his last months as governor, had managed to siphon off considerable Democratic support from Trumbull.[38]

If 1846 was a year of political disappointment for Trumbull, it brought personal satisfaction. His second son, Walter, was born on February 21, 1846. Although handicapped by poor health all his life, Walter, the eldest of Trumbull's surviving sons, shared his father's enthusiasm for politics. The infant son whom Lyman held in his arms in 1846 became an important political lieutenant of his father.[39]

CHAPTER THREE

JUDICIAL REVIEW

ALTHOUGH TRUMBULL'S POLITICAL prospects had dimmed, his growing legal practice served as balm to his injured pride. Unwilling to sway a jury with passionate pleas, Trumbull was at his best in arguments before a judge alone. He became widely respected by his legal colleagues for the meticulous research and the logic of his briefs.[1]

While Trumbull's practice in the St. Clair County courts was varied, much of his legal business was in defense of those charged with petty crimes. He usually won by finding procedural errors in the prosecution.[2] Yet civil suits were the backbone of his practice. In the beginning, Trumbull's fees had been modest, only about twenty-five dollars for the average case; but as he grew in legal stature, his fees rose proportionately. By 1847, he and his brother George together were earning $2,300 — a very respectably annual wage for the times.[3]

Between 1839 and 1848, Trumbull argued eighty-seven cases before the Illinois Supreme Court, nearly ten percent of the total cases decided by the tribunal. He won fifty-one of them, or almost sixty percent of the cases argued. Trumbull's opponents in these cases included many of the most successful practitioners of the Illinois bar, Gustave Koerner, Stephen T. Logan, James Shields, and Lincoln's future Attorney General, Edward Bates. Trumbull held his own with all of these attorneys, but lost all three of his appearances against Abraham Lincoln.[4]

By 1848, Trumbull had been in political retirement for two years. His retirement might have continued except for Governor Augustus C. French. French had not known Trumbull before the gubernatorial convention of 1846, when Trumbull's grace under pressure had captured French's attention. In the next two years, as Trumbull visited Springfield often on legal business, French came to know him. French was also impressed that Trumbull's large personal following remained loyal to him even during his retirement from the active political scene. French also believed that Trumbull had a judicial temperament and so the governor encouraged him to seek a seat on the supreme court under the new constitution of 1848.[5]

This constitution provided for a bench of three justices, each from a division of the state. French suggested that Trumbull run for a place on the new supreme court. Flattered, Trumbull sounded out the opinions of other influential politicians. Even after these proved to be favorable, Trumbull waited to see who his opponents might be.[6] When only David J. Baker, a rather obscure Whig politician, and a so-called "independent," John Dougherty, a perennial congressional candidate surfaced, Trumbull entered the race.[7]

With the power of the statehouse behind him,[8] Trumbull easily routed his two opponents in the election on September 4, 1848.[9] Trumbull continued his close association with Governor French and the governor awarded him the patronage of his portion of the state.[10]

Trumbull's fellow supreme court justices were John Dean Caton and Samuel H. Treat. Caton, Trumbull had never known, but Treat had been Lyman's political ally against the state bank five years earlier. As provided in the constitution, in December 1848 they drew lots to determine their length of term. Caton drew the longest term and served as chief justice. Trumbull was ambivalent about drawing the shortest term, only three years, since he did not know if he would enjoy his new position.[11]

Although Lyman previously had considered moving to either St. Louis[12] or Chicago,[13] he now decided to move to a larger city within his judicial district, Alton, only twenty miles from Belleville. Alton was growing more quickly than Trumbull's hometown, it had a larger population of former New Englanders, and it had a better water supply than Belleville. This last consideration was important, since Belleville's polluted water seemed a reason for the Trumbull family's poor health.[14]

Since Alton rents were high, Trumbull rented a house for only a year before buying a dwelling for $2,500 in cash, which he frugally had saved. It was a comfortable-sized dwelling with three acres of garden and an orchard.[15] Not long after this house purchase, a third son was born to the Trumbulls, on April 8, 1849. This infant was named Lyman Perry. He was always sickly, and despite the best medical care the time afforded, died of "cholera infantum" at the age of fifteen months on July 21, 1850, in Springfield at the Jaynes' home.[16] Another son, Perry, was born January 26, 1851. Perry would survive his father, the only one of Lyman's children to do so.[17]

The civil cases to come before the Illinois Supreme Court varied widely from breach-of-promise suits brought by jilted fiancées to the most complicated trust and purchase agreements involving many thousands of dollars. Trumbull's legal knowledge was enhanced by his handling of such diverse and difficult legal problems.[18]

In *Hone* v. *Ammons,* Trumbull cast the deciding vote and concurred in an opinion of Justice John Caton that the sale of a slave in Illinois was void. In a scathing concurring opinion Trumbull showed his anti-slavery feelings when he wrote, "I would as soon think of enforcing a contract to carry into effect the African slave-trade as that under consideration. . . ."[19]

As a state supreme court justice, Trumbull voted more often with John Dean Caton than with his former political crony, Samuel H. Treat. With Caton and Trumbull often in agreement, Treat had to go along also or dissent alone. Still, Trumbull and Treat joined in decisions more often than did Treat and Caton. Trumbull dissented only five times in over five hundred and fifty cases decided while he was active on the supreme court bench. Yet he spoke for the court in less than one quarter of the cases decided. This phenomenon can be explained by Trumbull's many absences because of his own illness and that of members of his immediate family.[20] Trumbull remained on excellent terms with both his judicial colleagues during his supreme court service.[21]

The Illinois Supreme Court convened in three widely separated Illinois cities — Ottawa, Springfield and Mount Vernon. Trumbull traveled a great deal, but was excused from having to ride the circuit, as earlier Illinois Supreme Court judges had been required to do. Because of his sober dress and solemn manner, he was, at times, mistaken for a clergyman.[22] Occasionally, he was accompanied by his family; more often, he went alone. Since this was before the era of extensive railroads in Illinois, Trumbull's time-consuming trips were made mainly by stage, carriage, and horseback over roads which were clouds of dust in summer and muddy bogs in fall and spring. When possible, Trumbull preferred to take a river steamboat to his destination. While Lyman was away in Ottawa and Mount Vernon, Julia, as was her custom, visited her parents in Springfield, taking the children with her. When court met in Springfield, Lyman, along with Julia and the children, stayed with his in-laws.[23]

In 1852, when Trumbull's three-year term was expiring, even the Whig press had only kind words for his judicial performance.[24] As a result, Trumbull was unopposed when he ran for re-election for a full nine-year term.[25]

Trumbull's standard of living was high. Beside maintaining a large house in Alton, his travel expenses for himself and his family were heavy. Moreover, he was much visited by relatives who remained as guests for long periods of time. He employed three servants to perform household chores for Julia. The salary of an Illinois Supreme Court judge, as set by the constitution, was only $1,200.[26] Since as a supreme court justice he had curtailed his private legal practice, Trumbull turned to other pursuits for an increase in income.

In May 1851, he was elected president of the Alton & Jersey Plank Road Company.[27] In June 1852, it contracted for two miles of toll road.[28] Until the coming of a competing railroad, the company prospered. As late as May 1855, Trumbull was re-elected for another term as a director of the company at the same time at which a dividend of five percent of the value of its stock was declared.[29] Also, between 1851 and 1855, Trumbull served on the board of directors of the Illinois Mutual Fire Insurance Company.[30]

All these activities together did not yield enough financial return. Therefore, in the early 1850's, Trumbull became a partner in a real estate business with George T. Brown. Brown, who never lost the burr in his speech, had been born in Jedborough, Scotland in 1820. Migrating to Canada as a youth, he left there to settle in Alton, Illinois. Although a lawyer by training, he preferred business as a vocation. In addition to his very active real estate partnership with Trumbull, Brown, in May 1852, founded the Alton *Daily Morning Courier*. For the next few years, the *Courier* was second in influence only to the Springfield papers in downstate Illinois. Brown, a bachelor, was noted for his generosity; he gave liberally of his time and money to civic enterprises. He dabbled in politics, serving one term as mayor of Alton, and in 1852, was a strong contender for lieutenant-governor. A free spender, an open-hearted extrovert, Brown made a good business and political partner for Trumbull for eighteen years.[31]

In the spring of 1853, when his second term as a supreme court justice barely had begun, Trumbull decided to resign.[32] His troublesome health and the inadequate salary, he indicated, were factors in his decision.[33] Yet another reason for his resignation which Trumbull may have experienced difficulty in articulating to his political contemporaries was his desire to spend more time with his family. Unlike Abraham Lincoln, he never relished the rough masculine company of the judicial circuit. Trumbull was no yarnspinner, and the evenings around the pot-bellied stoves in taverns seemed dull. He missed his comfortable home and garden. Julia was a confirmed gardener and had interested Lyman in this hobby.[34]

Trumbull had hoped to complete his judicial business gracefully during the summer of 1853, but ill health hampered his efforts. He was stricken with a severe attack of pneumonia at his home in Alton. The local doctors were baffled by his illness, and he summoned his father-in-law, the physician, to attend him.[35] Trumbull's condition took a turn for the worse and the Alton *Courier* published daily bulletins on his condition.[36] Late in June, he began to improve, but since he had resigned as of July 4, 1853, he could not take his place on the bench for the last supreme court session.[37]

Trumbull was proud of his service on the bench, and the rest of his life his intimates called him "Judge." Forty years after Lyman left the bench, the then Illinois Chief Justice commented that no lawyer could read Trumbull's opinions "without being satisfied that the writer of them was an able, industrious and fair-minded judge."[38]

Still weak from his illness, upon the advice of his doctors Trumbull decided to tour the East. Nineteenth-century physicians believed travel to have curative effects. Accompanied by his wife and older son, Walter, his mother-in-law, and her daughter, Ellen, he left for the Atlantic coast. They went by way of Chicago, where, while walking upon a crowded sidewalk, the still-weak Trumbull stumbled off the pavement into the gutter a foot below. Although he did not fall flat, to avoid a spill, he spun, shifting his weight; a sharp pain told him unmistakenly that he had twisted his spine badly. Shrugging off the pain and calling it only a minor mishap, Trumbull continued his trip, traveling by train and stage-coach to Connecticut. The jarring and bouncing of the trip convinced Trumbull that he had been seriously injured. He consulted doctors in the East. They maintained that he had not been injured, but was only suffering from the symptoms of rheumatism. If indeed it were rheumatism, they could not relieve his pain, and for the remainder of his trip, he suffered extreme discomfort.

He found there were few young people left in Colchester; they had migrated either to the West or to the great cities of the East in search of greater economic opportunities. His own family, with the exception of a sister, all had left the place. His brothers had migrated to Illinois or Michigan. His father had joined his sons in Michigan before dying there in 1850.[39]

From Colchester, Trumbull's party journeyed to Saybrook Point, Connecticut, where they visited the family of a Captain Ingraham, who had married Lyman's cousin. While there, Walter Trumbull and his young aunt, Ellen, played with the Ingraham's daughter, Mary, only a few years older than they. She was a blue-eyed, fair-haired girl who loved to romp with the other children and joined them in their games.[40] Years later, after the death of Julia Trumbull, Lyman would take Mary as his second wife.

Lyman returned to Illinois in the early fall. By this time, he was in excruciating pain; the Jaynes convinced him to spend the winter with them, so that Dr. Gershom Jayne could care for him. Scorning the opinions of the Eastern physicians, Gershom Jayne diagnosed Lyman's trouble as an inflammation of the spine caused by his accident in Chicago.[41]

Slowly, animated by a flinty determination, Lyman grew better. It was a lengthy journey back to health. At last, months later, he emerged from his sick-room and, heavily leaning on a cane, was able to walk downstairs to the parlor. Weak and shaken, Lyman was recovering more in spite of his medical treatment than because of it. His ability to walk was impaired for several years, and he moved only with the aid of a cane. But Trumbull refused to be treated as an invalid and continued to strengthen his back muscles with exercises.[42]

By mid-1854, Lyman returned to Alton, resuming the practice of law. Then he demonstrated that he had lost none of his courtroom verve.[43] Also, he opened a law office over a prominent bookstore in downtown Alton and advertised regularly in the local press.[44]

Trumbull had recovered for more than the practice of law. While he had lain ill that fall and winter, the newspapers' banner-black headlines screamed the story of the Kansas-Nebraska Bill's progress through Congress. This bill, which repealed the Missouri Compromise and threw open to slavery the twin territories it created, shattered the uneasy truce between the sections which had existed since the Compromise of 1850.[45] The political consequences of this bill were enormous. Stephen A. Douglas had skillfully guided the bill through Congress to quiet the slavery issue. Instead, old parties disintegrated, political careers were ruined, and the dreaded specter of civil war hovered ever nearer.[46]

CHAPTER FOUR

ANTI-NEBRASKA TIDE

THE EVENTS FOLLOWING the passage of the Kansas-Nebraska Act provided a favorable climate for the regeneration of the political careers of Trumbull and Lincoln. Both men had been checked. The traditional account is that Lincoln's ill-received opposition to the Mexican War had caused him temporarily to retire as an elective office-seeker. The Whigs' practice of rotating the congressional nomination of his district may have been more important in relegating him to the sidelines. He had been biding his time from 1849-1855, seeking a return to the political arena.[1] Now, Whig Lincoln and Democrat Trumbull joined others who felt that the repeal of the long-standing Missouri Compromise, and the resultant opening of the territories of Kansas and Nebraska to slavery, was intolerable.

In Douglas' Illinois, many Democrats rejected the Little Giant's lead in championing popular sovereignty for slavery in the western territories. These Democrats regarded Douglas' vaunted principle, letting the settlers of the territory vote upon the lawful existence of slavery, as a trick whereby an area once closed to slavery had been reopened to it. In Illinois, in the northern part of the state, many Democratic elements were greatly disturbed by Douglas' action.[2]

In Trumbull's section of the state — heavily Democratic southern Illinois — revolt proved more difficult. The backbone of the party consisted of men who had migrated from the border states. By changing their residence, they had rejected a slave society; yet, they were, at best, indifferent or even hostile to freedom for the blacks. Most were small farmers who were deeply convinced of the Jacksonian dogmas concerning "gut" issues. Opposition to banks and monopolies, an aversion to a protective tariff and a suspicion of the industrial East were of greater concern to them than whether slavery did or did not spread to the Kansas prairies. Birth was not everything: Douglas came from Vermont and Lincoln from Kentucky; but it is noteworthy that a trio of Kentucky-born Democratic leaders — James C. Allen, Orlando B. Ficklin, and William A. Richardson — never wavered in their support of Douglas.[3] An urbane New Englander such as Trumbull, who long had possessed a tender conscience upon slavery, reacted very differently. All his life, he would carry among his intellectual baggage the Jacksonian Democratic outlook upon economic issues; nonetheless he was disturbed by the spread of slavery in the West and he was willing to challenge his party's leadership on this issue.

Trumbull quickly decided that the Kansas-Nebraska Act represented a wrong principle, and that he must resist it. Yet he hoped to fight the issue within the Democratic party. In 1848, with a great effort, he had supported the Democratic presidential candidate, Lewis Cass, over the Free Soiler, Martin Van Buren. In 1854, Trumbull still hoped to wrest control of the Democratic party away from Douglas. To join the Whigs, then the only viable opposition to the Democrats, was unthinkable to him. He viewed the Whigs as exponents of a "big government," which he abhorred.[4]

Still feeble from his illness, Trumbull began to rally the Democratic opposition to Douglas in his section of Illinois. Lyman easily convinced George T. Brown, his business associate, to follow him. Other Democratic leaders in the Eighth Congressional District, perhaps the staunchest Democratic stronghold in the state, hesitated to join Trumbull until they could see the future more clearly.[5]

This controversy over the Kansas-Nebraska Act continued into the political campaign of 1854. Nativism and the internal improvement question also competed in Illinois with Kansas-Nebraska for a place in the debate on the stump. At stake in 1854 were all the seats in the federal House of Representatives, as well as control of the legislature which had great significance that year, since that body would choose the successor to federal Senator James Shields, Douglas' supporter in the fight for the Kansas-Nebraska Bill.

Fighting to control the Democratic organization, the Douglasites stigmatized as traitors any party members rejecting the Kansas-Nebraska Bill. The Illinois Whigs were elated by the Democratic schism; however, they were such a decided minority that even with the split in Democratic ranks, a Whig victory was uncertain. In addition, most dissident Democrats maintained their identity, cooperating only with the Whigs as allies.

Eventually, the diverse opposition groups made an agreement against the Douglasites. In Illinois, where the Whigs were strongest, the Anti-Nebraska Democrats agreed to support them for office, under the title of Whigs or as Independent Republicans. The label "Republican" was used at this time by ardent extremists. Although they used the name "Republican," they were not yet the future Republican party in Illinois. For their part, in southern Illinois, the Whigs, there a minority, agreed to support Anti-Nebraska Democratic candidates.[6]

In Trumbull's own Eighth Congressional District, the political situation was particularly confused. There was no incumbent congressman. Trumbull, with his eye on the available congressional seat, began wooing the dissident Democrats of the district. One bloc Trumbull needed to win was the German vote. In St. Clair County alone, there were eighteen thousand Germans.[7] The Germans were skeptical about the Anti-Nebraska movement, since so many nativist Whigs were active in that movement. Yet, the St. Clair Germans were unfriendly to slavery, and with the help of two local German leaders, Frederick Hecker, an impulsive lawyer-politician, and Lyman's old friend, Gustave Koerner, now lieutenant-governor, Trumbull won most Germans to the Anti-Nebraska cause.[8]

In Trumbull's congressional district, the local Democratic party was so divided that a district convention meeting at Carlyle never did agree on a nomination.[9] Unofficially, the Anti-Nebraska Democrats selected Trumbull as their nominee.[10] The Whigs also enthusiastically supported Trumbull.[11] Philip B. Fouke (or Foulke) came forward as the Douglas-regular Democratic nominee. Foulke seemed a formidable opponent. A native Illinoisan, he had been a civil engineer, newspaper publisher, and lawyer. He also had enjoyed a political career, having been elected a county prosecuting attorney and a state legislator.[12]

Trumbull campaigned with important newspaper support. In the 1840's, his opponents, through their control of the press, had painted a portrait of him as an irresponsible radical. Trumbull grimly resolved this should not happen again. Under the editorship of George T. Brown, the Alton *Courier* steadily sang his praises. The influential Chester *Herald* proved an enthusiastic Trumbull newspaper. The Alton *Telegraph* supported him, as did the Whig press of Springfield and Chicago. Yet, these newspapers were a mixed blessing, since some displayed an abolitionist tinge which irked conservative southern Illinoisans.[13]

Trumbull spiritedly campaigned across the nine counties comprising his congressional district. He held a series of one-day stands in the more important towns. Although Trumbull still leaned heavily upon his cane for support, he surprised observers with his physical energy and spirit. With his personal campaign progressing well, Trumbull accepted an invitation to speak at Springfield during the state fair. In rural Illinois, the state fair, held the first week in October, was the social highpoint of the year. In 1854, heightened political excitement won spectators from the more mundane features of the fair to the political programs arranged by the contending parties to ensnare their votes.[14]

Fighting hard to hold Illinois within the ranks of the regular Democratic party, Douglas also journeyed to Springfield during state-fair week. Since the adjournment of Congress the previous summer, he had been campaigning steadily in his home state. Tough, hard-bitten Douglas was an excellent stump speaker. Standing only slightly over five feet tall, he had the head and torso of a larger man, hence, his sobriquet, "Little Giant." His deep bass voice, unaided by mechanical amplifiers, still rang out clarion-clear, captivating his listeners. Yet, even Douglas, for all his oratorical skills, was not always able to gain a hearing. In Chicago, he was howled down by a mob.[15] Undismayed, Douglas continued his tour. Lincoln, originally drawn into the campaign to aid Richard Yates, the Whig congressman from his district, expanded his speaking engagements. Lincoln trailed Douglas around the state, hitting at the Little Giant's record and enlarging his own reputation.[16]

On October 3, the day the state fair opened, Stephen Douglas defended the Kansas-Nebraska Act, varying his theme with a savage attack on the nativists with their anti-foreign platform.[17] It had been planned that Trumbull and Lincoln both answer Douglas on the next afternoon, but because of the caprices of the primitive trains, Trumbull arrived from Chester too late to speak. Lincoln alone answered.[18] He delivered his most telling address of the campaign, flaying the principle of popular sovereignty.[19] Lincoln had invited Douglas to reply if he wished, and the Little Giant did so for nearly two hours, again insisting that only local government could keep slavery out of the western territories.[20]

The late-arriving Trumbull spoke that evening to over 2,500 people. For two hours, Trumbull harangued the crowd. And the auditors, to whom Judge Trumbull the man was no stranger, had looked expectantly to candidate Trumbull, the dissident Democratic leader, whose opening shot in his congressional battle had startled the Democratic bigwigs "like a clap of thunder in a clear sky."[21] Trumbull, however, delivered his usual address, a little more cadenced and polished, to the effect that the Kansas-Nebraska Act had shattered the sectional peace and allowed slavery to spread into the vast western territories.[22]

Simultaneously with the state fair, there was a convention of a group calling themselves "Republicans." Generally, these men were abolitionists and held views greatly beyond those of plain foes of slavery extension.[23] Seeking new recruits, these men tried to draw Lincoln into their party, but he skillfully avoided their political embrace.[24] Nor was Lincoln the only Anti-Nebraska leader that they assiduously wooed; they formed a potent source of discomfort for Trumbull. Attending all the speech-making sessions, they played the role of an embarrassingly noisy claque for him. He had to be circumspect in his dealings with them. Riding a possible wave of the future, they were not to be totally rejected; yet their proffered hand of friendship had to be brushed aside, since Trumbull, in common with the mass of his constituents, viewed them as noisy troublemakers. Trumbull continued stumping his district throughout October and into November, although he was safely ahead according to all the impartial observers.[25]

On election day, November 7, Trumbull was not disappointed. That election the Anti-Nebraskans made a strong showing. The month before, in the October election states, the Democrats lost thirty-one congressional seats in Pennsylvania, Ohio and Indiana. Because of Douglas and his well-knit organization, the Anti-Nebraskans did not fare as well in Illinois as in many other Northern states. Yet even in Illinois, five of the nine Anti-Nebraska congressional candidates won over their regular Democratic opponents; overall, the regular Democrats lost control of the next House of Representatives and only seven of forty-two Northern congressional Democrats who voted for the controversial act were returned to Washington.[26]

Trumbull had run very strongly in his congressional district, which in 1852 had given Franklin Pierce a majority of over one thousand votes in his race for the presidency.[27] Trumbull had so reversed the regular Democratic trend that he was the victor by more than 2,600 votes in a total of 13,000 cast.[28]

This election was a milestone in Trumbull's life, marking the start of his national political creer. Then an excommunicated Democrat, he maintained for more than a year longer that not he, but the renegade Douglasites who had captured the party were the disloyal Democrats. He had cast his first vote for Martin Van Buren in Georgia in 1836 and had ardently supported the Jacksonian dogmas, particularly the tenet that government should be "small." As the issue of slavery extension had become paramount, Trumbull reluctantly reassessed his political ties. Then he decided to break with the regular organization. For this he was branded by the Douglasites a traitor. There would be no turning back — the sweep of events would ultimately push him into the new anti-slavery party.[29]

After the Anti-Nebraska election victory, interest at once turned to speculation as to who would win the United States Senate seat, held the previous term by ardent Douglasite James Shields. At that time, before the adoption of the Seventeenth Amendment, United States Senators were chosen by the state legislature. Party lines had become so blurred that control of the legislature was in doubt. The diverse elements of the Anti-Nebraska coalition were the prototype "Republicans," the Anti-Nebraska Democrats, and the Whigs. The Whigs were particularly an unknown quality, since so many of them had equivocated on the Nebraska question.

At that time, the Illinois legislature consisted of one hundred members — twenty-five senators and seventy-five representatives. Since the terms of the state senators were staggered, twelve of them had been elected in 1852 for a four-year term, and the other thirteen had been chosen at the recent election in 1854. Included within the latter thirteen were three Anti-Nebraska Democrats — John M. Palmer, Burton C. Cook, and Norman B. Judd. In addition to these three Anti-Nebraska Democrats, the senate was composed of nine Whigs and thirteen regular Democrats. Complicating the picture, one Whig, J. D. Morrison of Monroe and St. Clair counties, was suspected of pro-slavery sympathies. His vote in the United States senatorial question was uncertain. Since the entire membership of the lower house had been elected in 1854, there the Anti-Nebraska coalition possessed a majority.

There was no law requiring the two houses to meet in joint session. Consequently, Anti-Nebraskans feared that rather than see an opposition member elected to the United States Senate, the senate Democrats would prevent a joint convention and any selection.[30] The regular Democrats were pledged to the re-election of James Shields,[31] but secretly they were prepared to jettison Shields in favor of the popular Governor Joel A. Matteson, who was unsullied by association with the Kansas-Nebraska Act.[32]

The opposition suffered no dearth of candidates. Lincoln, ever since the polls closed, had been actively importuning Whig legislators to vote for him.[33] At first, Trumbull felt reluctant to seek the senatorship. Since the Whigs were more numerous a group in the Anti-Nebraska coalition, it was believed that surely the senatorial election would be claimed for their candidate. He yielded, however, to his three Anti-Nebraska friends in the Illinois Senate and allowed them to nominate him.[34]

Meanwhile, many Democrats felt confident that a joint convention could be prevented. If the legislature failed to elect a senator, the governor would fill the vacancy; he would select a Douglas Democrat.[35] For a time, the Democrats seemed excellent prophets. For after the legislative session began in January 1855, time after time, the Democratically-controlled senate voted against going into a joint session with the Anti-Nebraska-dominated house.[36] Meanwhile, the Anti-Nebraskans had organized the house, electing the speaker and other offices. Then, in the senate, in a surprise move, the Anti-Nebraskans also organized that chamber, electing its permanent officers. This success occurred because a Nebraska Democrat, Uri Osgood, bolted his regular party ranks because of the patronage promises. As an excuse, he argued that although he had been elected as a regular Democrat two years earlier, his district in 1854 had been carried by the Anti-Nebraska Democratic forces. In a rare act of self-abnegation, the Whigs allowed Osgood and three Anti-Nebraska Democratic senators to name the senate officers. Thus, the Whigs hoped to obligate these four dissident Democrats to accept Lincoln for senator. The Democrats accepted the Whigs' generosity, but denied any commitment to Lincoln. The senate officers chosen then included Trumbull's old crony, George T. Brown.[37]

On February 5, the Anti-Nebraskans got the state senate to agree to a joint session of the legislature three days later.[38] On February 7, the regular Democratic caucus endorsement went to the incumbent, James Shields. At that time, five Anti-Nebraska legislators refused to join the Democratic caucus. Similarly, these men spurned the meeting of the Whigs and Republicans, the Anti-Nebraska caucus, which named Lincoln as its nominee. Instead, they hoped to hold the balance of power and elect their own candidate, Lyman Trumbull. At three o'clock on a wintry February 8, the Illinois legislature convened in joint session. The legislators balloting for senator totalled ninety-nine, with one unaccountable absentee. Fifty votes constituted a choice.[39]

The first ballot showed Lincoln in the lead with forty-five votes, to forty-one for Shields and a mere five for Trumbull. Eight votes scattered.[40] Confusing shifts occurred. A Whig, Morrison, and the Nebraska Democrat, Osgood, who had helped the Anti-Nebraska coalition organize the senate, supported the regular Democrats throughout the balloting. Several members of the lower house, elected as Anti-Nebraska Democrats, voted for Shields or Lincoln.[41]

On the second ballot Lincoln continued in the lead, although he had slipped to forty-three votes; Shields held steady with forty-one; Trumbull had six; and nine votes scattered. On the third ballot, Lincoln dropped into a tie with Shields at forty-one votes; Trumbull remained at six, with the rest scattered.[42] The Lincoln forces, perturbed that their champion was slipping, tried to recess the joint session. All the other candidates' supporters combined to defeat this motion.[43]

Shields took an undisputed lead on the fourth ballot with his steady forty-one votes; Lincoln slumped to thirty-eight; and Trumbull rose to eleven; eight votes went to minor candidates.[44] On the fifth ballot, Shields reached his peak — forty-two votes; Lincoln dropped to a new low of thirty-four votes; Trumbull's total slumped to ten; and twelve votes scattered.[45] The sixth ballot provided little change.[46]

Between the sixth and seventh ballot, the Democratic leaders arranged a switch which seemed a well-rehearsed move. The regular Democrats dropped Shields and brought forth Matteson as their choice. The Democratic leaders now displayed an assured air; they believed that Matteson would prove to be an irresistible senatorial candidate.[47] Besides his availability, Matteson thought that he could claim support from two Republican representatives, John Strunk and Erasumus O. Hills. These men, elected from Matteson's home district, would support him as his friends. In the case of Strunk, he was correct. Strunk deserted the Anti-Nebraska coalition on the seventh ballot, voting steadily afterward for Matteson. Hills was different; he refused all overtures to support Matteson. He voted for Lincoln on the first three ballots, feeling bound to that extent by the Anti-Nebraska caucus, and then he backed Trumbull.[48]

On the seventh roll call, the vote for the major candidates stood: Matteson, forty-four; Lincoln, thirty-eight; and Trumbull, nine.[49] On the eighth ballot, the Lincoln strength ebbed, and Matteson made a small gain; however, Trumbull picked up additional Anti-Nebraska support as the roll call revealed a vote of forty-six for Matteson; twenty-seven for Lincoln; and eighteen for Trumbull.[50] Trumbull's gains were made directly at Lincoln's expense.[51]

Lincoln faced a cruel dilemma. His strength had declined from the first ballot. The eighth roll call had revealed that Matteson was close to success, while his own declining support had virtually eliminated him. His sole choice lay between the slowly-gaining Trumbull or the almost-victorious Matteson. Lincoln still would not ask his supporters to vote for Trumbull, despite the latter's Anti-Nebraska principles, so the balloting continued.[52] On the ninth vote, Matteson reached a peak strength of forty-seven ballots, garnering the support of every regular Democrat, the Whig Morrison, and Strunk of Kankakee. Trumbull forged into second place with thirty-five votes, while Lincoln's support collapsed to fifteen die-hard Whigs.[53]

The decisive moment was at hand. Joseph Gillespie, an oddly- and untidily-dressed Whig leader, slouched over to Lincoln for instructions. Lincoln had received word from the wife of a staunch supporter who had learned of a plot to deliver some of Trumbull's support to Matteson if the balloting continued.[54] Lincoln probably had heard similar rumors from other sources.[55] Therefore, he told Gillespie to support Trumbull for the sake of the Anti-Nebraska cause.[56]

The tenth ballot proved decisive. Acting on Lincoln's instructions, the Whigs voted for Trumbull, and he was elected with fifty-one votes to forty-seven for Matteson, with one ballot cast for a minor candidate.[57] At Trumbull's election, thunderous cheers echoed through the hall.[58] Amid the jubilation, Lincoln, despite his deep disappointment,[59] took his frustration with grace.

The very evening of the election, there was a reception, according to one version, at the home of Nicholas H. Ridgley, Springfield's leading banker. The Mattesons, the Lincolns, and the Trumbulls were all invited. Matteson and his wife never appeared. Lyman and Julia Trumbull caused a stir as they beamingly swept into the drawing-room. They were the center of an admiring throng when Abraham and Mary Lincoln entered. Quickly, the hostess remarked that she had been disappointed at Lincoln's defeat, but rejoiced with him that the Anti-Nebraska principle had triumphed. Gracious in defeat, Lincoln smiled, moved toward Judge Trumbull, saying, ''Not too disappointed to congratulate my friend Trumbull,'' and shook him warmly by the hand.[60]

Lincoln, shrewd and worldly, could accept his defeat gracefully; others became more rancorous. Mary Todd Lincoln and Julia Jayne Trumbull had remained friends over the years, although after their marriages and ensuing family responsibilities they had not been as close as previously. At the time of the senatorial election, Mary Lincoln seemed to accept her husband's defeat with resignation.[61] Yet William Jayne, Julia's brother, later claimed that from then on the two women's friendship cooled.[62] Each woman was politically ambitious for her husband, so that rivalry between the two men for leadership in the Republican party further chilled the wives' friendship. After Lincoln's presidential election, patronage squabbles added to social rivalry, further straining the ties between the former Springfield belles. No dramatic break occurred, but there was a steady deterioration of their relations.[63] After Lincoln's assassination, their relationship touched bottom, as Mary Lincoln, then visiting in Chicago, wrote of Julia, "Mrs. Trumbull has not *yet* honored me with a call; should she ever deign, she would not be received. She is indeed 'a white sepulchre.' "[64]

Lincoln's political friends were also bitter about Trumbull's victory. David Davis vowed that he never would have allowed the Anti-Nebraska Democrats to dictate the senatorial choice.[65] Other Whigs were also disgruntled,[66] and the hard feelings engendered at this time divided the new Republican party until Lincoln's presidential nomination.[67]

As for James Shields, deeply chagrined at his treatment at the hands of a party he had served so long, he migrated to Minnesota. Shields later won some distinction when he served for short periods in the United States Senate, representing first Minnesota and then Missouri, becoming the only senator from three different states.[68]

Trumbull himself broke precedents. He was the first senatorial candidate elected over the regular Democratic nominee since the rise of the Whig party.[69] Also, he refused to continue the time-hallowed custom of celebrating his victory with a grand ball. The balls had so grown in splendor that Douglas had spent over fifteen hundred dollars on one. Trumbull thought the custom foolish.[70]

CHAPTER FIVE

GIANT KILLER

IF TRUMBULL SUPPOSED that his election settled his right to a Senate seat, he was quickly disabused. The regular Democrats, furious at his election, decided to harass him. On February 21, 1855, the *Illinois State Register* printed a letter from "an able lawyer," arguing that Trumbull was ineligible to be a senator under the Illinois Constitution. That document declared that state officers were ineligible for any other office during their terms plus one additional year. Therefore, since Trumbull had been elected as a state judge for a nine-year term in June 1852, he would not be eligible for another office until 1862.[1]

Democratic attacks on Trumbull's eligibility did not slacken, so, in April 1855, Trumbull wrote a letter to the chairman of the Senate Judiciary Committee, South Carolina Senator A. P. Butler, in which he argued the merits of his claim to a Senate seat.[2] Butler answered promptly, but evaded a statement on Trumbull's eligibility.[3] Hedging his political bets, Trumbull did not resign his House seat. Realizing that the Anti-Nebraska coalition would control the House of Representatives, he felt certain he could be seated in that body, even if the Democratically-controlled Senate turned him out.[4]

Meanwhile, smarting over his recent defeats in Illinois, Douglas decided to tour the state, rebuilding his prestige. The Illinois Anti-Nebraska coalition, fearing that Douglas might reestablish his ascendency by default, importuned Trumbull to undertake a state-wide tour of his own. In the summer of 1855, Trumbull and the other Anti-Nebraska leaders met in Chicago to plot strategy. They decided to keep Douglas on the defensive.[5]

In late summer, Trumbull undertook a speaking tour to counter Douglas' whirlwind campaign. On September 26, 1855, the two men met face-to-face by chance in Salem. At that time, Douglas suggested a joint platform appearance. After much haggling, a rough agreement was negotiated. Taking alternate turns, one man would open and the other reply. This format would be used at most places advertised as Douglas' speaking engagements. The series would begin that afternoon at an outdoor meeting in Salem.

September dusk came early, and Douglas speaking first, far exceeded the time limit. He declared that as Trumbull and he represented divergent views, they could not both truly represent Illinois in the Senate. To determine whose views prevailed, Douglas called for both Trumbull and him to resign and seek an immediate re-election. Suddenly, the Little Giant finished speaking and bolted from the platform, taking many of the crowd with him. The sun sank low in the west as Trumbull spoke. He branded Douglas' proposition a trap, pointing out that should Douglas and he resign, there would be no election, but only an interim appointment by Democratic regular, Governor Joel Matteson. As darkness rapidly settled over the grounds, Trumbull briefly summarized his Anti-Nebraska position and the meeting adjourned.

On his return to town, Trumbull unsuccessfully searched for Douglas to clarify the rules of their subsequent appearances. Trumbull then wrote out the terms of their oral agreement, sending these by messenger to Douglas' lodging; he received no answer. The next morning, Douglas hailed Lyman on the street as the Little Giant jolted by in a carriage bound for Mount Vernon. Douglas shouted out that he would complete an answer to Trumbull after his arrival at that town.[6]

When Lyman reached Mount Vernon, he could not locate Douglas until arriving at the outdoor meeting. There, Trumbull discovered that Douglas again had preempted the first speaking period. Douglas talked incessantly until darkness. In the cold, fading light, Trumbull announced that he considered their debate agreement to have been repudiated by Douglas. (Douglas denied that he had actually accepted the debate proposal.) Therefore, Trumbull announced his resumption of independent campaigning.[7] Within the next several weeks, Trumbull addressed giant rallies at Alton[8] and Chicago.[9]

As bad weather closed over the state, active campaigning ended for 1855. Despite charges that he was a turncoat, Trumbull vowed that he would not relinquish his membership in the Democratic party. Indeed, when Owen Lovejoy, the "Republican" leader, requested that Trumbull attend a state convention to unite the opposition to Douglas, Trumbull refused. He was unwilling to surrender the Democratic party label to the Douglasites.[10]

In November 1855, Lyman, accompanied by Julia, left for Washington. For the next eighteen years, over half of Trumbull's time was passed in the nation's capital. He habitually took his wife with him, an arrangement that was extraordinary, since most congressmen journeyed to Washington alone. This action was indicative of their personal closeness.

Julia's interest in politics exceeded that of the average mid-nineteenth-century woman. She attended the meetings of both branches of Congress regularly.[11] She also read widely in the press — not just Illinois papers — but the important New York and Washington sheets as well.[12] But Julia also took part in the Washington social whirl and did charitable work.[13] The Trumbulls, finding no rental in Washington where children were welcome, left their pre-school-aged child, Perry, with the Jaynes in Springfield. Walter was placed in a Connecticut boarding-school.[14] These modest arrangements were a blow to the Trumbull purse, since congressmen had only just been raised to a salary of three thousand dollars a year.

On December 3, 1855, the first session of the Thirty-Fourth Congress began. The Senate, an exclusive club with a maximum then of sixty-two members, met in a small chamber which it occupied until 1859, when it became the Supreme Court room.

John J. Crittenden of Kentucky, the kindly but undemonstrative leader of the variegated Senate opposition to the Democrats, presented Trumbull's credentials to the Senate. Meanwhile, the Illinois Democratic press had continued its opposition to Trumbull's seating.[15] Governor Matteson had refused the customary election certificate. As a result, all Trumbull possessed was a statement of the legislative vote as certified by the Illinois Secretary of State. When Trumbull's credentials had been presented to the Senate, Lewis Cass of Michigan offered a protest to Trumbull's seating signed by forty-two members of the Illinois legislature. The legislators alleged that Trumbull was ineligible under their state constitution.[16] In accordance with normal procedure, the protest was tabled, and Trumbull was sworn in pending further investigation.

Having entered the Senate under a cloud, Trumbull was soon placed in further jeopardy. Senator Lewis Cass asked that the protest be referred to the judiciary committee for action.[17] To emphasize Trumbull's probationary status, he was awarded no committee assignments. Custom forbade Trumbull's engaging in any Senate business, except when his own right to a seat was questioned. He did, however, take care of his constituents by introducing a number of petitions which had been sent to him.[18]

Finally, on February 27, 1856, the judiciary committee reported that it was hopelessly divided on the question of Trumbull's eligibility. Its chairman, Butler, asked that the entire Senate decide Trumbull's case. The Senate speedily agreed to this procedure. Then, George Pugh of Ohio, a small and youthful crony of Douglas, announced that he would propose a resolution unseating Trumbull.[19] Before Pugh could frame a resolution, Crittenden introduced a proposal of his own, declaring Trumbull to be properly seated.[20] The Douglasites blocked immediate action, but on March 3, Crittenden steered his pro-Trumbull resolution to the floor. Two of Douglas' friends, Pugh and Charles E. Stuart of Michigan, declared Trumbull's election a nullity.[21]

Behind the scenes, Douglas' lieutenants assiduously worked for Trumbull's expulsion. Even if Douglas personally had not felt uncomfortable with Trumbull as his colleague, the Little Giant's friends in Illinois repeatedly demanded that Lyman be unseated so as to weaken Anti-Nebraska prestige within the state.[22]

On March 5, the Crittenden resolution confirming Trumbull's right to a seat passed by the towering majority of 35 to 8. Douglas, who was ill, did not vote. The 8 nay votes were evenly distributed between Douglas' Northern friends and die-hard Southern Democrats.[23] Trumbull, who had continued to advertise as a lawyer in Alton, now closed his law office. The House of Representatives also declared Trumbull's House seat vacant after he had been confirmed as a senator.[24]

Meanwhile, Kansas had become a land of turmoil after the passage of the Kansas-Nebraska Act. Northern free soilers and Southern pro-slavery advocates rushed to settle and control it. The pro-slavery group, largely Missourians who had crossed the border to vote, had swamped the free soilers in March 1855, gaining control of the new territorial legislature. In quick succession, the territorial legislature accepted a slave code, and in retaliation, the free soilers organized a rival governmental organization. On January 24, 1856, President Franklin Pierce sent a special message to Congress which generally defended the pro-slavery position in Kansas.[25]

The presidential message was referred to the committee which endorsed Pierce's message; whereupon, the sturdily Anti-Nebraska Whig, Jacob Collamer of Vermont, decided to issue a minority report. Trumbull volunteered to help him. To mute the trumpet of Collamer's protest, the committee's majority quickly produced a report. On March 14, Trumbull made his maiden speech, protesting their action as an attempt to distribute the majority report before the minority views could be heard.[26]

Using the report as a point of departure, he extemporaneously (believing senatorial set speeches to be an affectation) declaimed against the Kansas violence. Trumbull emphasized that the Kansas-Nebraska Act was interpreted very differently in the North and in the South. There was confusion, he said, over when self-determination could be applied to a territory in regard to slavery. Northerners held that slavery could be banned during the territorial period, whereas Southerners believed that the people of a territory could bar slavery only when they prepared a constitution for admission to the Union. Ending his speech, Trumbull declared, "As a remedy for existing evils if Congress will not restore the Missouri Compromise, it ought to annul the present territorial acts, and give the actual settlers an opportunity to elect a Legislature for themselves. . . ."[27]

In quick reply, Douglas made acid remarks about the company, abolitionists and worse, that Trumbull was then keeping in the Anti-Nebraska coalition. Thereupon, Douglas sat down, vowing that he soon would make a formal reply to Trumbull's oratory. The junior senator from

Illinois had the last word, saying, "I shall never permit him [Douglas] . . ., to make an assault upon me personally without meeting it. . . ."[28]

Illinoisans reacted strongly when they heard that their two senators had clashed on the Kansas-Nebraska question. The freshman senator, in the opinion of Anti-Nebraskans, had successfully withstood the famous Little Giant.[29] Meanwhile, the Illinois Democratic press predicted that Douglas, in his formal reply, would rout Trumbull.[30] On March 20, Douglas' expected "boom" was only a mild "pop" when he replied to Trumbull. In the main, he followed his extemporaneous argument that he had already delivered at the conclusion of Trumbull's speech. After defending his record upon the Kansas question, Douglas charged that Trumbull was an apostate Democrat.[31] A friendly biographer declared of Douglas' speech, "Nothing that he said shed any new light on the controversy."[32] After Douglas finished, Trumbull again replied. Illinois could not doubt that Trumbull would continue to play gadfly to Douglas.

In late March, after Lyman's right to a Senate seat had been assured, Julia left Washington for Illinois. Her primary mission was to take their lonesome son, Perry, back to live with them in the capital. Julia, a capable person — very unlike the stereotype of a helpless Victorian lady — transacted much personal business for Lyman. She also sounded the murky waters of Illinois politics, reporting that Lyman was very popular with the Anti-Nebraska leaders. There was one jarring note during Julia's visit home. It was the growing bitterness of Mary Lincoln toward her former friend. In a chance meeting after church, Mary refused to catch Julia's eye, appearing not to see her. In an attempt to repair the breach, Julia caused her mother to invite Mary to a party. Mary refused the invitation, sending word that she was too ill to attend.[33] Finally, during Julia's visit to Springfield, she by chance came face-to-face with Mary Lincoln. As Julia later described it: "I have shaken hands with Mary. Her lips moved but her voice was not audible. I think she was embarrassed."[34] In May, accompanied by Perry, Julia returned to Washington.[35]

CHAPTER SIX

THE BLACK REPUBLICAN

BY THE SPRING of 1856, the dust obscuring the political landscape since the fall of 1854 had settled. In Illinois, the old Whig and Democratic parties had split and recombined. Anti-Nebraska Democrats such as Trumbull derived most of their support from former Whigs and had the active adherence of only a minority from their old party.[1] On the other hand, Douglas, who claimed most Illinois Democratic support, had received a heavy accretion of Whig strength.[2]

During the winter of 1855-1856, many Illinois Anti-Nebraskans, such as John M. Palmer, felt restive outside the old party of Jackson. Trumbull tried to placate them. He argued that a new, mild anti-slavery extension party would appear. This new party would be an acceptable vehicle to receive Whig recruits without letting them dominate the organization. Out-and-out abolitionists such as the so-called "Republicans" of 1854 in Illinois would be allowed only in the back benches of such a new party. It would provide a political base for refugees from the party of Jackson who would be spared begging to be taken back into the Democratic party as their only viable alternative.[3]

Actually, Trumbull, as an important Democratic defector, could not rejoin his former party on terms other than that of surrender. Yet, many Anti-Nebraska Democrats, such as Kentucky-born John A. McClernand, did manage a return to Democratic orthodoxy. The Whigs had less conscience-wrestling to perform; their party had slowly dissolved. Their choice lay between the regular Democrats, the mildly anti-slavery group, soon to be called nationally the Republicans, or a third group, the American party. This last political grouping tried to ignore the slavery question, emphasizing instead nativism.[4]

The heterogeneous opponents of the Pierce administration received a boost in February 1856, when after months of balloting they organized the House of Representatives. Actual control of the chamber remained precarious as the House membership was split between three groups, the regular Democrats, the anti-slavery Democrats and Whigs, and the nativist Whigs and American party members.[5] On the national scene, the new Republican party gradually emerged. In February 1856, a preliminary conclave at Pittsburgh laid the groundwork for a national Republican nominating convention at Philadelphia.[6]

Simultaneously, in Illinois the party realignment also progressed. In February 1856, the Anti-Nebraska newspaper editors' convention at Decatur planned a state meeting in May at Bloomington.[7] Many conservative men such as Trumbull were unhappy about events in Decatur. They felt that the abolitionist element had predominated at this conclave. Therefore, they acted to swing Illinois Republicanism into the right-center of the political stream. Trumbull, to strengthen the conservative wing of the party, ''franked'' political tracts to a carefully-pruned list of his Illinois supporters. Most responded enthusiastically,[8] but there were Anti-Nebraskans who had followed Trumbull this far, but now returned to the regular Democrats. The Republican tracts proved too rich for their political palates.[9] During this phase of Trumbull's career, he made many lasting friendships with leaders just below the top management of the new party. These leaders, in time, were his greatest political asset. This group included David L. Phillips, Jesse W. Fell, William I. Conkling, and John J. Bryant. Also, Trumbull consistently fed government publications to friendly newspapers in the prairie state.[10]

Local organization of the new, but as yet unnamed anti-slavery extension party, moved quickly across Illinois. The name ''Republican'' never appeared in the pre-convention publicity of the party lest it drive off conservative recruits. First, county conventions knitted the diverse opposition groups together. Trumbull corresponded tirelessly to ensure that the Bloomington political convention have a conservative aura.[11] Also, Trumbull worked indirectly, through his crony George T. Brown, who tirelessly crisscrossed the state, planning with political leaders for the state convention.[12]

Trumbull and other conservative Republican leaders had laid their plans well. The convention was under a tight rein from the moment George T. Brown gavelled it to order on May 29. As Brown had forecast, a conservative former Democrat, William H. Bissell, was chosen as the gubernatorial candidate. Appropriate resolutions condemning Douglas and praising Trumbull were adopted.[13]

In addition, Trumbull wanted the national Republican party to nominate a presidential candidate who could carry Illinois. John C. Fremont, the colorful pathfinder, was often suggested, although there was doubt concerning his political strength.[14] Personally, Trumbull was much smitten by the prospects of Justice John McLean of the United States Supreme Court. Trumbull knew McLean professionally and socially,[15] and he liked the Supreme Court Justice's conservative views.[16] McLean had two obvious handicaps: He was well past seventy, and as a Supreme Court Justice, he could be criticized under the mores of the time for seeking elective office.

Trumbull wished to avoid the Republican national convention, but he attended in response to Lincoln's plea.[17] His mission was to insure the adoption of a conservative platform and national candidates.[18] After reassessing McLean's chances, Trumbull changed his mind and left Washington for Philadelphia, a confirmed Fremont supporter.[19] Fremont was an easy winner over McLean for the presidential nomination. Since Fremont was a former Democrat, the ticket was balanced, as became the Republican custom, with an ex-Whig, William L. Dayton.[20] This taste of national convention machinations left Trumbull disgusted. Contemptuous of open place-seeking and horse-trading delegates, he never again attended another national convention until after he had left public life.

Meanwhile, in Congress it was "politics as usual." Douglas had framed a bill conferring statehood on Kansas. However, it slumbered in favor of more pressing business. During this lull in the Kansas imbroglio, Senator Charles Sumner stepped into the forefront of the crisis. On May 19-20, he delivered a speech entitled, "The Crime Against Kansas." In his speech, the Massachusetts solon unjustifiably attacked the aged South Carolina Senator A. P. Butler. On May 22, after the Senate recessed, a Butler relative, Representative Preston Brooks, injured Sumner by attacking the Massachusetts senator with a cane upon the very floor of the Senate Chamber. The assault electrified the nation. To Northerners, this brutality was indefensible; to Southerners, it seemed an act of retribution.[21]

On May 23, the Senate met in an atmosphere of tension. Some Northern and Southern congressmen were armed in anticipation of violence, but not Trumbull. Lyman supported a Seward-sponsored resolution for an investigating committee. The resolution speedily passed. Its effectiveness was vitiated when none but regular Democrats were elected to it.[22] In due course, the committee reported that the Sumner incident lay beyond the Senate's jurisdiction. The House could never muster the two-thirds majority needed to expel Brooks. The South Carolina congressman resigned, only to be triumphantly re-elected. The injured Sumner became a Northern hero and was later returned to his Senate seat by a nearly unanimous vote of the Massachusetts legislature.[23]

Trumbull tried to end the Kansas violence which had continued on May 21 with a pro-slavery sack of Lawrence. This action heightened tension, since it had happened almost simultaneously with Sumner's caning. Trumbull's action was predictable — a piece of legislation. His bill would have abolished Kansas and merged its territory with that of Nebraska, thus ending the struggle with a free soil victory.[24]

At once a general debate broke out. Trumbull again charged that the principle of the Kansas-Nebraska Bill was interpreted differently, North and South, as to when and how a territory could exclude slavery.[25] Lyman later reported to Lincoln that he hoped to pin Douglas on this point, but the Little Giant had evaded a reply.[26] In 1858, Lincoln questioned Douglas on this point in the course of the Lincoln-Douglas debates and he elicited a Douglas reply known as the "Freeport Doctrine."[27] But in 1857 the best Trumbull could accomplish was to have his bill printed, yielding valuable publicity. As he expected, the bill was referred to the committee on territories, where it died.[28]

After the Republican national convention, the Democrats, stung into counteraction, produced the Toombs bill. Introduced by the senator from Georgia, it offered a fair solution of the Kansas imbroglio. At this time, the Democrats wished to quiet the Kansas strife, since violence there manufactured Republican votes in the North. The Toombs bill provided that after a census had established the number of actual settlers in Kansas, an election was to be held for delegates to a state constitutional convention.[29] Douglas quickly reported the Toombs bill from his committee on territories as the majority report. To prevent this bill from being printed before the minority report could be heard, Trumbull forestalled Douglas with a well-timed objection.[30] Trumbull, in the debate which followed, called the Toombs bill a denial of the self-determination promised by the Kansas-Nebraska Act. As revised by the committee on territories, the Toombs bill contained no provision to refer the completed state constitution to a vote of the Kansas people.[31]

The Senate Republicans proposed a number of unsuccessful amendments to the Toombs bill.[32] The bill then passed 33 to 12.[33] The House gave the Anti-Nebraska answer to the Toombs bill, a frankly partisan measure which admitted Kansas with a constitution previously drawn up by the free soil shadow government.[34] In the Senate, the House bill was referred to Douglas' committee, which quickly substituted the Toombs bill for it.[35] This version of the Toombs bill passed the Senate for the second time 30 to 13.[36] It was wasted motion; the House never accepted the Toombs bill.

The slavery-in-Kansas issue now reached Congress in a new convulsion. The House passed a version of the Army appropriation bill forbidding use of the military to enforce acts of the pro-slavery Kansas legislation. The Pierce administration prevailed upon the Senate Finance Committee to prune this clause when it reported the bill to the Senate floor. Despite energetic Republican opposition, led by Trumbull, the Democratic majority jammed the amended bill through the Senate.[37]

As the last day of the session arrived, Trumbull gained inches of space in the *Congressional Globe* for the House position, when he lectured the Senate on the merits of the House bill.[38] But neither chamber would give way, and Congress had adjourned with the Army appropriations bill still unpassed.[39] After Congress had adjourned, Trumbull addressed a giant mass meeting in Philadelphia in behalf of the Fremont cause,[40] in the interval before the President called Congress into special session. In this short session, Trumbull championed the House version of the Army appropriation bill in the Senate debates; but vainly, as eventually the House, by a three-vote margin, wearily accepted the Senate-administration position.[41]

The session of 1855-1856 revealed Trumbull's pattern of senatorial conduct. He was a keen debater on the Senate floor;[42] he never avoided an encounter with more experienced Senators.[43] He was a "small government" man,[44] interested in federal economy,[45] but in a partly contradictory stance favored most internal improvement projects.[46] He displayed an independence of party restraint. Thus, though William H. Seward was the acknowledged leader of the Republican minority, Trumbull never hesitated to differ publicly with him.[47]

Unlike many members of the minority, Trumbull often attended President Pierce's social gatherings. He believed that partisan differences should not be allowed to limit social contacts between political leaders.[48] He had scruples about dancing, but he loved to argue politics politely at social gatherings. Julia, who thought Lyman worked too hard, encouraged his attendance at social functions.[49]

In Washington, during the last days of the session, Trumbull anxiously scanned Illinois political developments. As many correspondents reported faithfully to him, he was fully informed of moves on the political chessboard.[50] By the summer of 1856, the Illinois political picture settled into the following perspective. In the northern part of the state, the Republicans were clearly in the majority; in the south, they were a distinct minority; and a no-man's-land existed in the central portion. There, the balance of power lay with former Whigs who might be lured from the moribund American party ticket headed by former President Millard Fillmore.[51]

Trumbull stumped Illinois beginning September 11, concentrating upon the central and northern parts of the state.[52] Opening in Chicago with a talk on the Kansas problem, Trumbull worked his way south.[53] On September 20, Trumbull and Douglas were both scheduled to speak at Olney in Richland County. The Republican committee on arrangements promptly challenged Douglas to share the same platform with Trumbull. Douglas refused, and the Republicans raised the cry that the Little Giant had dodged a forensic encounter with his senatorial colleague.[54]

After campaigning in the Springfield area, at the beginning of October, Trumbull returned to Alton for a gigantic rally, where the enterprising local committee also had scheduled Abraham Lincoln. Lincoln and Trumbull had made an informal arrangement whereby they agreed to avoid joint appearances, ostensibly to cover more ground, but actually so that the latent rivalry between their followers would not be fanned.[55] Having finished their Alton speeches, the surprised Lincoln and Trumbull found that they had agreed separately to address a crowd on the north side of the Peoria Courthouse.[56] Afterwards, Lyman traveled to his next speaking engagement at Jerseyville, speaking to six hundred Republicans.[57]

Although the Democrats carried the October election states of Indiana and Pennsylvania, the Republicans had yanked pivotal Ohio from under the Democrats, giving them new incentive for a November victory.[58] Trumbull hit the hustings hard. Once more, he shared a platform with Lincoln at his former home, Belleville. Trumbull tried hard to give a good stump speech on the Kansas question, and the audience was not unappreciative. Yet, the local reporter observed, "The palm, however, belongs to Mr. Lincoln; his was the speech of the day."[59] Trumbull filled several more engagements on his way to Alton to vote, and the campaign was over. He had traveled over eleven hundred miles by rail, carriage, and river-boat during this campaign.

In November, as the national returns trickled in, the Republicans found a silver lining in defeat. Buchanan had garnered 174 electoral votes to 114 for Fremont and a pathetic total of 8 for Fillmore. In popular vote totals, the new party had done well, despite a void in the South, gathering seventy percent as many votes as the well-entrenched Democrats.[60] In Illinois, it was much as the Republicans had anticipated. Their state ticket, headed by William Bissell, won by a shadow-thin margin, whereas Democratic presidential electors had been chosen by 9,000 ballots.[61] When the Trumbulls made the long trip back to Washington in late November 1856, it was with the confidence that, politically, the future seemed bright with hope.[62]

When Congress met in early December 1856, it became clear that the Kansas question remained paramount. President Pierce had appointed a new Kansas governor, John W. Geary, who brought peace to that brawling territory. Thus, Pierce proudly reported in his state-of-the-union message that a "peaceful condition" existed in Kansas.[63] A debate exploded in the Senate immediately after Pierce's message. During this exchange, several senators stated that the Congress had no authority to ban slavery from the territories. In answer, Trumbull declared that the Supreme Court had ruled that Congress did possess the authority to exclude slavery from the territories.

Then Lyman was interrupted by petulant old Lewis Cass of Michigan, who asked why the Illinoisan had said that Congress had the same legislative power over a territory that a state legislature possessed over its citizens? Flush-faced, Cass demanded the exact legal reference. Confidently, Trumbull retorted, "Certainly." Turning to a Senate page, Lyman asked the boy to bring him the first volume of the *Peters Report* of Supreme Court decisions. When the boy brought it, Trumbull, without hesitation, turned to the proper place and cited one of John Marshall's decisions, *American Insurance Company* v. *Canter*. Trumbull then read from it that "Congress in legislating for the territories has the combined power of the General Government and a State Government." Then, Lyman asserted that if the Michigan legislature could keep slavery out of Michigan, Congress could bar the institution in a territory. At this, Cass sat dejectedly, while the galleries guffawed and his fellow-senators snickered. For eight years Cass had spoken and written on slavery in the territories without being aware of this Supreme Court pronouncement.[64]

Six days after the session opened, on December 8, the Democratic majority composed the list of Senate committees for the new session. Trumbull was allotted a place on the same committee as he had eventually been given at the last session — a seat on the relatively inactive committee on manufactures. Since the Republicans had few important committee assignments, they openly groused over the committee slots. Trumbull asked for the ayes and nays on the committee assignments so that the country could see them for a partisan maneuver. Predictably, the Senate accepted the committees' composition by a vote of 34 to 12.[65]

Trumbull parted company with his Republican colleagues of Whiggish origins when he enthusiastically supported the further reduction of the mild tariff of 1846. The resultant tariff of 1857 was the lowest such tax law the country was to enjoy.[66] On March 4, the Thirty-Fourth Congress expired and the new president, James Buchanan, was inaugurated. In company with most of his Republican senatorial colleagues, Trumbull boycotted the Buchanan inauguration ceremonies.[67]

Trumbull's work in Washington had not ended, since President Buchanan called a special session of the Senate immediately, so that the upper house might confirm the new administration's appointees. As a result of Republican successes in Northern states, the new party's Senate strength reached twenty. Two of the new Republicans were to play leading roles in Trumbull's political future. The first, James Rood Doolittle of Wisconsin, had been born a New Yorker and was two years younger than Trumbull. Of conservative principles, industrious, an excellent orator, Doolittle was widely regarded as a man of granite integrity.[68] The other Republican was tall, powerfully-built Zachariah Chandler of Michigan. Chandler, a New Hampshire Yankee by birth, was about as old as Trumbull. At age twenty, the canny Zachariah had accepted one thousand dollars from his father in lieu of the classical but to him impractical college education given to his brothers. Moving to Detroit, he had amassed a fortune in the dry-goods business. Because of his wealth, he became first the financial backer of the Whigs and later the Republicans. Chandler forged ahead in politics as he had in business by operating in a cynical, pragmatic fashion. Nevertheless, for years Trumbull valued Chandler for his unblinking Republicanism and frankness.[69]

In the new Senate, when committee assignments were distributed, the Republicans, befitting their augmented strength, fared much better than previously. Trumbull drew an assignment on the important judiciary committee as well as a lesser place on the committee on patents.[70] Trumbull's attention shifted from the national scene to scan the Minnesota political picture. The previous session of Congress had passed an act enabling Minnesota to form a state constitution. While slavery was not an issue in the territory, there was a political need for the Republicans to control the new state. Minnesota Republican leaders asked Trumbull to canvass their territory. Prominent among this group of party leaders was the good-hearted, near-sighted George A. Nourse, the son of a former senatorial colleague of Trumbull's from Maine. Nourse pleaded that Trumbull spend May campaigning for Republican candidates to the constitutional convention.[71] Trumbull decided to go in the early part of May.

Republican leaders also asked Abraham Lincoln to assist them. Lincoln himself could not come, but he wrote of Trumbull, ''You will find him a *true* and an *able* man.''[72] By this time, Trumbull had recovered completely from the illness which had almost cost him his life, and his face again showed the faint pink sheen of health.[73]

Spreading the gospel of Republicanism, Lyman toured the cities and towns of Minnesota. Although heavy spring rains marred Trumbull's speaking tour, he drew large enthusiastic crowds. Since hotels were almost non-existent in the territory, the Trumbulls usually stayed in the private homes of dedicated Republicans. Meeting these friendly people provided a pleasant experience which the Trumbulls remembered all their lives. In particular, they formed a fast friendship with the Nourses, which lasted long after George A. Nourse had left Minnesota to eventually become the first attorney general of Nevada.[74] Trumbull's tour paid political dividends as well; the Republicans edged the Democrats in the election of delegates to the constitutional convention.[75]

Upon Trumbull's return to Illinois from his Minnesota visit, he found that the task of recruiting third-party voters for the Republicans had become more difficult. Democrats had skillfully spread reports that Republicans favored equal rights for blacks, including the right of intermarriage with whites. In mid-May, Trumbull delivered a speech in Edwardsville to calm conservative fears that the Republicans were in fact ''amalgamationists.'' In this speech, Trumbull flayed the Democrats for being ''soft'' on slavery; yet, he spent most of his time stressing that the Republican was ''the white man's party.''[76]

Late in June, Trumbull delivered an address at Springfield in the chamber of the Illinois House of Representatives. Despite the steaming atmosphere inside the packed hall, Trumbull, in calm, assured tones, indicted the Democratic party for fostering those twin relics of barbarism in the territories — slavery in Kansas and polygamy in Utah. Trumbull made the latter charge because the Democratic party had been friendly to the erection of the Mormon colony on the shores of the Great Salt Lake. And the Mormons were abhorrent in prim Springfield because of that sect's attitude toward polygamy. Turning to the recently-decided Dred Scott case, Trumbull had no qualms about denouncing the opinion seemingly rendered by the

Supreme Court majority that slaves as property could be taken into any territory.[77] Many Illinois politicians wrote Trumbull, praising his speech effusively.[78] Gustave Koerner, a harsh realist who seldom bothered to flatter anyone, favorably compared Trumbull's effort with a speech recently made upon the same subject by Lincoln. Koerner termed Trumbull's oration to be better, saying, "Lincoln's speech is too much on the old conservative order."[79]

That summer Trumbull began a custom he practiced for many years of spending July and August vacationing in New England and visiting his relatives there.[80]

Meanwhile, Stephen A. Douglas was having political troubles. He had been as grievously gored by the Dred Scott decision that March as had been the Republicans. For if Congress could not bar slavery from a territory, could the people there by a popular vote do so? Douglas admitted that Congress could not ban slavery, but he pointed out that the right of a master to take his slaves into any territory was worthless unless positive police regulations were enacted there by the people to protect this right.[81] In June 1857, under authorization of the pro-slavery Kansas territorial legislature, an election was held for delegates to a state constitutional convention. The free soilers boycotted the polls, and the result was a pro-slavery electoral avalanche. As a consequence, a frankly pro-slavery state constitution was constructed by the resultant convention.

The convention decided against submitting the entire constitution to the Kansas electorate. Instead, the delegates proposed a vote merely on the constitution's slave clause. While seemingly fair, such a referendum would be meaningless, since even if the slavery clause were voted down, other provisions in the constitution would protect slaves already in Kansas, and only the future importation of slaves would be barred from the proposed state.[82]

By the fall of 1857, many Northerners, including Douglas, were horrified by what they saw in Kansas. The question became, would Douglas accept the Lecompton Constitution (as the Kansas organization law was dubbed from the town where it was framed) as a fair sample of popular sovereignty? In this atmosphere of political uncertainty, Trumbull, in the early fall, returned to Illinois. He held a series of private, heated conferences with Republican leaders. As a result, he left earlier than usual for Washington to observe the events there.[83]

Trumbull now looked for more permanent quarters in Washington. He rented a house at 451 Eighth Street from Pennsylvania Democratic leader John Forney. Here, the Trumbull family lived for the next six years. The house served as a Republican island in the Democratic sea that was social Washington. Lyman's home served as a social center for the hospitality-starved Republican congressmen.[84]

When Congress convened, Buchanan had his state-of-the-Union message read on December 8. The paper had its statesmanlike aspects; however, on the paramount question, the Lecompton Constitution, Buchanan had adopted the pro-slavery position. He lauded the Kansas constitution-making process and concluded with the ringing statement that the forthcoming election on the slavery clause of the new constitution was a fair expression of popular sovereignty.[85] Douglas scathingly replied to Buchanan's message the next day, December 9.[86] With much drum-beating, Douglas had arrived in Washington a week before. Relations between Douglas and Buchanan already had cooled as a result of squabbles over patronage.[87] Douglas quickly called at the White House, where he warned the President that if he backed the Kansas Constitution, he, Douglas, would denounce him. Buchanan retorted that if Douglas rebelled, his dire fate would be that of two Democrats who had tried unsuccessfully to buck Andrew Jackson. Douglas retorted: "General Jackson is dead!"[88] War between Douglas and Buchanan ensued.

Even before Douglas formally broke with Buchanan, there had been pressure from Eastern Republicans to force Illinois party leaders to support Douglas for reelection in 1858. The shouts that Douglas was fighting a Republican battle were led by the erratic editor, Horace Greeley.[89] Trumbull and Lincoln had felt the sting of Douglas' biting invective for too long to ally with the Little Giant, even if far-off Eastern Republicans could forgive and forget. Trumbull's attitude was clearly stated in his personal mouthpiece, the Alton *Courier,* which editorialized, "We do not see, however, that he [Douglas] is any better entitled to our support than before."[90] When panicky Illinois politicians begged Trumbull to illuminate the dark recesses of the Douglas-Buchanan controversy,[91] Trumbull took time from his Christmas dinner to outline his views to the harassed Lincoln. Trumbull declared that Douglas himself did not know ultimately where his rebellion might lead him. Trumbull again argued the view that Douglas' schism with the Buchanan administration might well prove to be temporary, and hence, Republicans would do well to stay out of alliances with the Little Giant.[92]

Before Lincoln got Trumbull's Christmas-Day missive, he had written Lyman, anxiously inquiring if the east-coast Republicans were determined to sacrifice the Illinois party in order to gain Douglas' adherence.[93] Soon after New Year's, Trumbull, seated in his study, penned a reply to Lincoln, while Julia offered helpful comments as she sat sewing a few feet away. Incorporating Julia's suggestions into his letter, Lyman assured Lincoln that he thought Republican adulation of Douglas was ephemeral and engendered by the shock of his spectacular break with the administration. In any event, Trumbull pledged himself to work unswervingly for Lincoln's election to Douglas' place.[94] Trumbull wrote similar letters to other Republican leaders.[95] Due in part to Trumbull's restraining influence, Illinois Republican leaders met in Springfield and resolved, as far as Douglas was concerned, "to *Keep Cool* for the present."[96]

Soon, the drama over the Kansas state-making absorbed congressional attention. The balloting upon the slavery clause of the Lecompton Constitution on December 21, 1857, with free soilers boycotting the polls, resulted in the approval of the pro-slavery clause.[97] After some hesitation, Buchanan accepted the election as a bona fide expression of Kansas sentiment.[98] He therefore submitted the Lecompton Constitution to Congress with a message in which he argued that Kansas had voted to become "as much a slave state as Georgia or South Carolina."[99]

On March 17, Trumbull made one of his rare prepared speeches in the Senate. Meeting the Southern argument for equality in the territories head-on, Trumbull argued that this equality only meant that any territorial law should apply equally to a former citizen of Massachusetts or one from South Carolina who moved West. To Trumbull it never meant that slavery must be carried there. Trumbull's speech was widely published in Illinois.[100] On March 23, the Senate voted 33 to 25 to accept the Lecompton Constitution for the new state of Kansas.[101] But the House, despite severe administration pressure, voted a total substitute for the Lecompton measure, 120 to 112; the Douglas Democrats supplied the vital votes.[102] Ultimately, a conference committee of representatives from the two Houses of Congress met to work out the differences. Alexander Stephens of Georgia and his political lieutenant, William H. English, readied a report that would salvage the maximum possible from the wreckage of the original Lecompton measure.[103]

This report is known in history as the English Bill, although technically, it was an amendment. It provided for a re-balloting on the Lecompton Constitution by the Kansans. The devious method used was to have the Kansas settlers vote upon accepting a federal land grant with the implication that if the grant were accepted, the Lecompton Constitution with its slavery clause would take effect. If Kansas rejected the land grant, its entrance into the Union would be indefinitely postponed.[104]

This compromise posed an agonizing choice for the Douglas Democrats. In the House, enough of them buckled under administration pressure to pass the measure there.[105] Trumbull's attitude toward the compromise measure was ambivalent. As an administration measure, he opposed it as a matter of course; privately, he expected that the Kansas free soilers would vote in the election and so defeat the Lecompton Constitution. Therefore, he perfunctorily opposed it by voice and vote while it was winning approval 31 to 22.[106] Since the vexatious problem had been settled in Congress, the Kansas settlers, with the free soil element voting, wrote the final chapter in the Lecompton saga by spurning the land grant and with it the slavery constitution.[107]

Trumbull displayed an impatience of party discipline in this session. On one occasion, when the dour William Pitt Fessenden of Maine promised in the name of the Republican minority that it would allow an early adjournment on that particular day, Trumbull snapped waspishly, "I do not consider myself committed by the remarks of any Senator made upon this floor, unless I state that I concur with them."[108] Building a record for the constituents in Illinois, Trumbull voted to build a Pacific railroad,[109] favored a bill to give public land to the states for agricultural colleges,[110] supported a drive to remove the tariff duty on sugar,[111] championed a homestead bill,[112] and secured Senate approval of funds to improve the Chicago harbor.[113]

As the session continued into June of an election year, Congress grew restive. There were growing demands for night sessions to allow an earlier adjournment. Trumbull equated night sessions with hasty, ill-drawn legislation.[114] In the course of the Senate stampede for adjournment, Trumbull uttered a principle he never entirely forgot once he became a leader of the Senate majority. In a debate, he declared, "I believe rules are made for minorities. . . . Majorities need no rules."[115]

During the session, his fellow-Republican James Rood Doolittle wrote his wife: "Trumbull sits at my left. We together constitute the Democratic right wing of the party."[116] Doolittle considered Trumbull and himself conservatives opposed to lavish federal spending and central government power. They viewed the former Whigs in the Republican party suspiciously as "big government" men who seemed almost as bad as Buchanan Democrats. In the latter half of June, Congress adjourned, and most congressmen hurried out of Washington and out on the hustings. The record had been written; the interpretations, defenses, and apologies lay in the campaign ahead.

CHAPTER SEVEN

A BATTLE OF TITANS

IN THE SPRING OF 1858, while Eastern Republicans gloated at Douglas' defiance of the Buchanan administration, Illinois Republicans grappled with the agonizing difficulties raised by his stand. Although the state's Republicans eventually rejected Douglas, the Illinois Democratic party enthusiastically embraced him. Republicans who had hoped that the Buchanan supporters would challenge the Little Giant at the Illinois Democratic state convention were bewildered at the solidarity behind Douglas.[1] Yet Prairie State Republicans expected that the "Buchaneers" or National Democrats would run candidates at the November election, siphoning off enough Democratic strength for the Republicans to control the legislature.[2]

In June, at Springfield, the National Democrats nominated a full slate of candidates.[3] Although they knew themselves to be hopeless candidates, they hoped to split the Democratic vote so as to defeat Douglas. Illinois federal officeholders were the movement's hard-core.[4]

Lincoln himself claimed to be aloof from the National Democrats, rendering them only moral support,[5] but many Republican leaders went much farther to bring Douglas down. George T. Brown was involved in the Republican-National Democratic plots. With Trumbull's approval, Brown had arranged for some Democrats to declare for Douglas. Then, after the National Democrats had entered candidates in their districts, these men announced that as Douglas had become a hopeless candidate, they were switching to Lincoln. For months, Trumbull had been recommending anti-Douglas Democrats to the Buchanan administration for Illinois federal patronage positions. He tried to obtain Senate confirmation for these nominees.[6] Douglasites whispered that former Democrats in the Republican party wished to supplant Lincoln as the party senatorial candidate with Chicago Mayor John Wentworth.[7] Therefore, the Republican state convention took the unprecedented step of designating Lincoln as the party's "first and only choice" for senator. The convention also endorsed Trumbull for his "ability and fidelity."[8]

After Congress adjourned in June, most members rushed back home to campaign; but despite frantic pleas from Illinois politicians,[9] Trumbull remained in the East. With his own political fortunes not at issue, Julia and he shrank from the heat of a midwestern summer.[10] Finally, with the campaign growing in tempo, Trumbull returned, arriving in Chicago on August 6. The next day, five thousand people gathered to hear him as he spoke from a hotel balcony. In this speech, Trumbull recalled the Toombs bill of 1856. He charged Douglas, as chairman of the committee on territories, with the responsibility for omitting a clause in that original bill which provided for the submission of a state constitution to a popular vote of the Kansans, a reversal of Douglas' later stand on the Lecompton Constitution.[11] Trumbull's speech was hailed by the Republican press as putting Douglas on the defensive.[12] As a result of conferences in Chicago, Ottawa,[13] and Springfield,[14] Illinois Republican leaders arranged an itinerary which would carry Trumbull throughout the state.

At a speech at Beardstown in mid-August, Douglas aimed a retaliatory punch at Trumbull for Lyman's Chicago address. He called Trumbull a "miserable craven-hearted wretch" who would never dare repeat in Douglas' presence his charges concerning the Little Giant's part in the Toombs bill.[15]

Meanwhile, the chief combatants in the senatorial struggle were already touring Illinois. Lincoln's strategy was to follow Douglas about the state, speaking on the heels of the Little Giant.[16] Nevertheless, Lincoln found himself overshadowed in the press by the Trumbull-Douglas feud over the Little Giant's complicity in the framing of the Toombs bill.[17] Lincoln foresaw this development, and it was partly the reason for his challenging Douglas to debate. Douglas, with a national reputation, had little to gain from these appearances, whereas Lincoln, by attaching himself to Douglas, would capture the attention of the state and nation.[18] Upon Lincoln's challenge, Douglas proposed seven debates in the seven congressional districts where the two of them had not yet appeared. Lincoln accepted the terms, and debates were scheduled from late August until October.[19]

The first of the celebrated Lincoln-Douglas forensic debates was held on August 22, in Ottawa. Despite the historical prominence of the Lincoln-Douglas debates, no issue was discussed in them unless it bore in some manner upon the slavery controversy. Trumbull and his accusations against Douglas constantly were mentioned in the debates by the Little Giant, although Lincoln would have preferred to ignore Lyman's campaign role. So, despite Lincoln's desire to focus on his own views, he was compelled to defend Trumbull.

In the Ottawa debate, Douglas repeated his charge that Lincoln and Trumbull had struck a bargain in 1854 to allow Lincoln to claim Shields' Senate seat and that Trumbull had then betrayed Lincoln by taking the place for himself. Also, Douglas charged Trumbull and Lincoln with having been members of the old abolitionist Republican party in 1855. Blending fact with fiction, he declared that Trumbull had been ''bred'' in Connecticut as a Federalist and then had moved to Georgia, where he had become a nullifier. While in Georgia, Douglas sneered, Trumbull had been a typical Yankee peddler of clocks! Only after leaving Georgia for Illinois had Trumbull turned lawyer-politician. He added that Trumbull had been a repudiationist of the Illinois debt, hating Douglas ever since the Little Giant had frustrated his unsound schemes.[20] Lincoln denied Douglas' charges concerning Trumbull and himself.[21]

Shortly thereafter, speaking in Alton, Trumbull attacked Douglas' misstatements in Ottawa. Commenting on Douglas' recent remark at Beardstown that Trumbull would rather have his ears cut off than face Douglas and repeat his charges concerning the Little Giant's part in framing the Toombs bill, Trumbull dismissed the remark as a statement that ''would disgrace a loafer in the filthiest purlieus of a fish market. . . .''[22] Hurrying on to Jacksonville, Trumbull repeated his campaign speech with such deadly effect among the Douglas Democrats that John A. McClernand rushed there to reply to Trumbull's charges.[23] Trumbull's Toombs bill charges were so successful that an old friend of Lincoln urged him in the second Lincoln-Douglas debate to follow Trumbull's approach. He wrote: ''You ought also in the opinion of your friends to ring in the Trumbull argument on to him. . . .''[24] Lincoln, however, always claimed that he had no first-hand knowledge of the Toombs bill, and so he refused to discuss it.[25]

In the Freeport debate, Lincoln, after defending Trumbull's and his own record of aloofness from the 1855 Republican party, in his turn posed four questions for Douglas. Three were minor, but the fourth stung Douglas and may have lessened his presidential chances in 1860. He asked how Douglas could square the Dred Scott decision with his doctrine of popular sovereignty.[26] Lincoln knew what Douglas' answer would be, since Douglas, goaded by Trumbull upon the Senate floor, had several times given a reply. These Douglas responses, entombed in the *Congressional Globe,* had not received much publicity. At Freeport, Douglas repeated that despite any Supreme Court decision, the people of a territory could eliminate slavery if they refused the institution its necessary legal protection.[27] Before the next debate, Trumbull advised Lincoln to make the Little Giant elaborate upon his Freeport answer, as one Southern newspaper had interpreted it as favoring a slave code for the territories. Trumbull urged Lincoln to query Douglas further, being certain that the Little Giant, not having seen the article, would attack this interpretation. If he did, Trumbull believed that it ''would effectively use him up with the South & set the whole pro-slavery Democracy against him.''[28]

At the third debate at Jonesboro, Lincoln took Trumbull's advice and asked Douglas if he would vote for a congressional slave code for the territories.[29] Douglas equivocated, and so, the trap failed.[30] In the fourth debate at Charleston, on September 18, Trumbull's Toombs bill charges against Douglas consumed most of the encounter. Douglas forced the issue upon Lincoln by claiming that since Lincoln had vouched for Trumbull's word, he must accept responsibility for Lyman's Toombs bill attacks. In reply, Lincoln stated that he "believed him [Trumbull] to be a man of veracity. . . ."[31] Then, nettled by Lincoln's quips and queries, Douglas sneered at Lincoln for retailing Trumbull's stale charges and not making a speech of his own.[32]

In his rejoinder, Lincoln asked if it were not strange that while Douglas claimed the political statute of limitations to have run out upon the Toombs bill of 1856 he nonetheless constantly recounted ancient history about both Trumbull and himself. Lincoln ended with a resounding endorsement of Trumbull, saying, "[Not] in all the years that I have known Lyman Trumbull, have I known him to fail of his word or tell a falsehood, large or small."[33]

Meanwhile, Trumbull had been canvassing the small towns in southwestern Illinois. There, Trumbull's meetings were not advertised as "Republican" assemblies, since that label was abhorrent to its inhabitants. Instead, Trumbull's gatherings were advertised under the heading "Free Democracy." Douglas violently attacked this misuse of the Democratic label.[34] On October 7, despite the cold, the fifth Lincoln-Douglas debate at Galesburg drew the largest crowd of the joint debates.[35] By then, Douglas had decided that attacks upon the junior senator from Illinois had reached the point of diminishing returns. He launched only a lackluster assault upon Trumbull for showing false colors as a "Free Democrat."[36] In response, Lincoln contented himself with defending Trumbull by relating that during Douglas' career, he himself had campaigned under various labels.[37]

In the sixth debate at Quincy, on October 13, 1858, Trumbull's name cropped up only in Lincoln's opening remarks when he mentioned Trumbull's charges concerning the Toombs bill and defended Trumbull and himself against Douglas' allegations of a conspiracy concerning the senatorship in 1855.[38] For the first time in the debates, Douglas ignored Trumbull.[39] At Alton, on October 15, the final passage at arms occurred between the two senatorial aspirants. Since this was Trumbull's home town, Douglas wasted no time attacking him, and Lincoln did not bother to defend him.[40] Returning from his own political tour, Trumbull feted Abraham and Mary Lincoln and their son at a special dinner at the Franklin Hotel. By design, Julia was out of town, and Lyman entertained the Lincolns at the hotel.[41]

While figuring so prominently in the Lincoln-Douglas debates, Trumbull himself remained busy on the stump. He campaigned not only in Illinois but crossed into Indiana. In all, he made over twenty major speeches and dozens of smaller oratorical efforts. Despite his late start, he traveled over two thousand miles across the state, outdoing his 1856 efforts by over nine hundred miles. Trumbull's herculean effort was not an unselfish gesture, because if Lincoln were not elected senator in 1858, there were many Republicans who would favor him rather than Trumbull as the Republican senatorial nominee in 1860. And Trumbull's speeches were invariably only anti-Douglas, and ungenerously, little pro-Lincoln.[42] Trumbull's course in 1858 was indicative of his attitude toward Lincoln, a condescending one, since he had defeated Lincoln in 1855 and possessed, at least until the campaign of 1858, a larger national reputation. It was also motivated by apprehension of Lincoln's position as a leader of the more numerous former Whigs in the Illinois Republican party. Lastly, Trumbull's attitude toward Lincoln reflected an envious appreciation of Lincoln's superior oratorical ability.

In the Illinois election on November 2, the popular vote was virtually a dead heat. The Democratic victory in electing more Douglas legislators resulted largely from the collapse of the National Democratic effort. The "Buchaneers" did not have the necessary leaders to stand against Douglas.[43] Because of the large number of holdover Democratic senators, Lincoln needed to win decisively in the popular vote to control the legislature.[44] On a joint ballot, that body, in January 1859, re-elected Douglas, 54 to 41.[45]

The last session of the Thirty-Fifth Congress was a study in futility. Neither the North nor the South could attain its objectives, while each possessed the strength to frustrate the other. Most issues were economic, since Kansas' rejection of the Lecompton Constitution had made slavery there moot. The House of Representatives had a Yankee outlook; the Senate remained securely in the hands of the Southern Democrats. President Buchanan had drifted into the Southern camp. By the veto Buchanan blocked any action of which he disapproved.[46]

One major issue during this congressional session was the route of the proposed Pacific railroad. Both sections of the country, North and South, wanted a route west that was most advantageous to their interests. In the course of the debate, Trumbull attacked the notion that Republican ascendency must spell the end of the Union. He stated that the Republican party "had placed itself on the Constitution, and on the doctrines of Jefferson, Washington, and Monroe, and Madison, and Jackson in regard to the slavery question. . . ."[47] Trumbull vainly fought for a northerly route for the proposed Pacific railroad,[48] as the whole project floundered.[49] Trumbull assisted a bill to establish land grant colleges.[50] This action also proved futile, as Buchanan successfully vetoed the proposal.[51]

During this session, Trumbull and Douglas did not clash on the Senate floor. Douglas was relentlessly hounded by Buchanan supporters, even being removed from his position as chairman of the committee on territories. With the Little Giant thus badgered by his former allies, Trumbull turned to other targets — Mississippi's Jefferson Davis and Georgia's Alfred Iverson.[52] During the session's last days, Trumbull became more passive; the strain of the long Senate days coming soon after the campaign of 1858 tired him.[53] Despite his weariness, he dutifully stayed to the regular session's end and the short special Senate session that immediately followed it.[54]

Following the Senate's adjournment, and after only a brief rest, Trumbull plunged into the maelstrom of politics. Republican congressmen designated Trumbull as chairman of a committee which supervised "political education." The strategy called for authors to write articles contrasting the Republican and Democratic stand on the tariff, homestead legislation, and slavery extension. After these pieces had appeared in Republican journals, they were reprinted as pamphlets and circulated in politically doubtful areas. Even after his return to Alton in April 1859, Trumbull supervised the details of the committee's work.[55] Then the Massachusetts Republican party had taken nativist action which endangered the Republican appeal in the Middle West to vital immigrant groups such as the Germans. In an effort to placate the immigrants, Trumbull issued in May a statement in which he roundly condemned nativism.[56]

After this action, he left for the summer, taking his family to a pleasant cottage at Lakeside, in northwest Connecticut. Over the next decade, this place became the Trumbull family's summer retreat. As 1859 was an off-year, Trumbull hoped to enjoy a long, leisurely summer with his family. Yet when the political cauldron seethed in Illinois and Ohio, he returned earlier than he had planned to the Middle West.[57]

Ohio, a pivotal state, had both a gubernatorial and a legislative election in the fall of 1859. To win, both the Democrats and the Republicans sought outside help.[58] Plans were announced for Douglas to speak in September 1859, at Columbus, Cincinnati, and Wooster.[59] The Ohio Republicans then importuned Lincoln and Trumbull to reply to Douglas. Lincoln responded, speaking at Columbus, Cincinnati, and Dayton.[60] For a time, Trumbull equivocated about appearing in Ohio, but when he realized that he must return early from New England to campaign in Illinois, he added Ohio to his itinerary.

Douglas recently had published an article in *Harper's New Monthly Magazine,*[61] expounding on popular sovereignty. At Sandusky, Ohio, Trumbull answered Douglas' article. He dismissed popular sovereignty as an "unmeaning phrase" cloaking an ambiguous principle.[62] Trumbull's Ohio appearance added to his national reputation when the Republicans swept the October election, capturing both the legislature and the governorship. The Republicans were fortunate, since the election occurred prior to John Brown's ill-starred raid.[63]

From Ohio, Trumbull proceeded to Illinois, which posed its own political problem in 1859. The Sixth Congressional District seat fell vacant in 1858 when the Democratic incumbent died. A special election was held in the fall of 1859.[64] Trumbull feared that the district election might go by default, so he pushed John M. Palmer into making the race.[65] Palmer's opponent was John M. McClernand, briefly an Anti-Nebraska Democrat in 1854. McClernand soon established himself as the front-runner. A desperate Palmer asked Trumbull for help. With it, Palmer seemed to be gaining ground when John Brown and his small abolitionist band made an abortive raid at Harpers Ferry, Virginia. Realizing the enormous political consequences to their party, prescient Republicans cursed John Brown almost as heartily as did the enraged Southerners.[66] Trumbull kept Republicans working in support of Palmer by issuing optimistic statements.[67] Nonetheless, McClernand won handily. In a letter to Lincoln, Trumbull complained that the John Brown raid was only part of the burden the Illinois Republican party had to bear. Trumbull grumbled that many former Whigs in central Illinois had chosen the Democrats over the Republicans.[68]

Returning to Washington in November 1859, Trumbull was admitted to practice before the United States Supreme Court. Since he spent so much time in Washington, his Illinois law practice had dwindled away, and his senatorial income needed supplementing.[69] In Washington, as the new Congress gathered for the long session, Trumbull found the atmosphere more tense than before. Southern fears had been quickened by the Harpers Ferry raid. When the Senate convened, James Mason of Virginia demanded an investigation into the John Brown raid. To blunt Mason's maneuver, Trumbull moved to couple the Virginian's resolution with an inquiry into an arms seizure from a federal arsenal by pro-slavery men in 1855 at Liberty, Missouri, on their way to attack Kansas free-soil settlers.[70]

Mason branded Trumbull's amendment as irrelevant. Lyman replied that both acts of aggression concerned slavery. According to Trumbull, the difference between the two affairs was that Brown and his band had been punished, whereas the Missouri raiders had been "rewarded by office." Also, Trumbull claimed that the 1856 affair should be investigated, as the genesis of the Kansas disorder which had spawned John Brown.[71]

Trumbull's statement touched off a far-ranging debate in which Northern and Southern Democrats alike slashed at him.[72] Then, Florida's David Yulee proposed questions to Trumbull, ostensibly to define the Republican position on slavery. In answering them, Trumbull declared that the Republican party opposed slavery only in the territories and not within states where it already existed. Clement Clay of Alabama asked him if he believed that the Declaration of Independence and the Constitution applied to Negroes? Trumbull retorted that although a black had the same natural rights as himself, it was "not a crime, under all circumstances to hold a negro in slavery." Trying to define the Republican position further, he proclaimed:

> When we say that all men are created equal, we do not mean that every man in organized society has the same rights. We do not tolerate that in Illinois. I know that there is a distinction between the two races because the Almighty himself has marked it upon their faces; and, in my judgment, man cannot, by legislation . . . produce a perfect equality between these two races, so that they will live happily together.[73]

Strange words from the future author of the Civil Rights Act, but they underscore Trumbull's conservative thinking in 1859. In closing, Trumbull pleaded for the colonization of the free black population in tropical America, saying, "I fear the consequences which Jefferson so eloquently prophesied unless it is done."[74]

Reaction by Southern congressmen predictably was negative to Trumbull's speech. Yet Trumbull had been talking over their heads to the Northern people. In this attempt he was more successful. One Illinoisan so appreciated Trumbull's pronouncements that he named his son Lyman Trumbull Hay.[75] Lincoln commented that Trumbull's speech was "admirably made."[76] Nevertheless, Trumbull had displayed so conservative a mien that one indignant abolitionist woman termed his remarks "abominable."[77] When the Senate voted, Trumbull's amendment to investigate the arms seizure in Missouri four years earlier died 22 to 32. The Mason resolution was gavelled through as unanimous.

Trumbull's amendment and his subsequent exposition of Republican doctrine had, in the opinion of many observers, drawn the sharpest tooth from the Mason resolution.[78] The Senate could afford the digression of the Mason resolution debate, because the House was unorganized, having deadlocked in the choice of a speaker. Finally, in January 1860, William Pennington of New Jersey, a Whig of hazy current political affiliation, was elected speaker.[79] Then the legislative mill began, but it ground out only a meager product. Trumbull battled vigorously to pass a liberal homestead measure.[80] It was to no avail; Buchanan vetoed the bill.[81] Trumbull strongly supported the attempt in the Senate to override the presidential veto, but the vote fell well below the necessary two-thirds.[82] At this session, Trumbull and Douglas clashed, their first conflict in two years. Douglas attacked the Illinois Republicans as exponents of black equality. Trumbull refuted this charge. From there, they boxed the compass of political issues. The debate ended when Douglas suddenly left the chamber, leaving Trumbull in possession of the battlefield,[83] an achievement not lost upon Trumbull's constituents.[84]

The 1860 presidential campaign cast a long shadow over the Senate's deliberations. Trumbull had a stake in the selection of a strong presidential candidate who could carry Illinois so handily that a Republican legislature would be assured. He incessantly penned letters to his Illinois correspondents, asking which Republican presidential aspirants would run the strongest in crucial legislative districts.[85] There was no dearth of candidates. A leading contender, Salmon P. Chase of Ohio, was well known to be in fact as radical as Seward appeared to be.[86] In Trumbull's eyes Chase would therefore not do. As to more conservative candidates, there were several. Edward Bates of Missouri might be presidential timber. Bates, an old-line Whig, had an agreeably bland position on slavery. Trumbull thought well of Bates' possibilities,[87] until Koerner reported to him that the German Republican press had taken a strong stand against Bates because of his nativist taint.[88] Then there was Lincoln, but Trumbull refused to take the tall Illinoisan seriously as a presidential candidate.[89]

Many Republican politicians in the North and the border states considered Trumbull to be of a sufficiently conservative anti-slavery hue and offered him support for the presidency.[90] Facing the necessities of politics, Trumbull did not lose his balance. He realized that if he became an active candidate for the national ticket, he would face the implacable resistance of Lincoln's friends. They would wreck the party in Illinois before they would allow Trumbull to steal any of Lincoln's support in the Prairie State delegation. Without his home state's solid backing, Trumbull's presidential chances were non-existent. Therefore, in a prudent, self-denying gesture, Trumbull forbade his vociferous supporters to mention him in connection with the presidency.[91]

While Trumbull did not oppose the Lincoln candidacy, the more he thought about it, the less likely it seemed to him that presidential lightning could strike the Illinoisan. He underestimated Lincoln's meteoric rise to national prominence, as well as the effort he could command from his friends at the Chicago convention.[92] Dismissing Lincoln's chances, Trumbull searched for a conservative standardbearer who could defeat Seward for the nomination. The ideal candidate, Trumbull believed, might be Justice John McLean of the United States Supreme Court. McLean, then in his seventies and only a year away from the grave, had been appointed to the Supreme bench by Andrew Jackson. A perennial presidential candidate, McLean had enhanced his availability since 1856, when he had been Trumbull's first choice, by a Northern-oriented opinion in the Dred Scott case.[93] Trumbull's judgment was colored by his professional and social ties with McLean.[94]

When Trumbull suggested McLean to Lincoln, the latter correctly sensed that the Justice was an anachronism.[95] He diplomatically replied that McLean was universally considered too old and that as a Supreme Court Justice he should be above partisan politics.[96] While touting McLean, Trumbull carefully added that he was "first & foremost for Lincoln."[97] Yet his equivocal attitude was known among Lincoln's friends.[98] Therefore, Lincoln warned Trumbull that the senator should write no letters that could be "distorted" into opposition to his candidacy. Lincoln added that there were men on the outlook "for such things out of which to prejudice my peculiar friends against you."[99]

In the spring of 1860, Norman Judd, with Trumbull's close support, sought the Republican gubernatorial nomination. Judd's principal rivals were the former Whigs Leonard Swett and Richard Yates.[100] At the state convention, Judd broke into an early lead, but the Swett forces threw their support to Yates and he was nominated.[101] The Republican presidential nomination had become a greater prize because the Democratic party had split at its earlier Charleston convention. At Chicago, Seward was side-tracked in favor of Lincoln by a hard-working, hard-promising Illinois delegation. The hard fact was that Seward could not carry the doubtful Northern states but Lincoln could. In the end, geography and the prevailing political climate dictated Lincoln's nomination.[102] Trumbull had shunned attendance at the Republican convention, remaining at his senatorial post. Along with millions of others, he was surprised by Lincoln's nomination, but he sent his "warmest congratulations." In a rare burst of enthusiasm, he added, "I look upon Ills. as now safe to the Republicans in all its departments, & upon your election as a fixed fact — Glory to God the country is safe."[103]

Trumbull went up from Washington to a ratification meeting in Philadelphia. His association with Lincoln made him the logical choice for the main speaker. In a speech in the pouring rain, Trumbull declared that Lincoln was "committed to nobody except to the great principles which he has advocated all his life. . . ."[104] Except for this foray to Philadelphia, Trumbull remained in the Senate until its final adjournment. But he chafed impatiently to campaign in Illinois, where the Republicans awaited his return "with much anxiety."[105]

A four-way race for the presidency developed in 1860. The regular Democrats had reconvened at Baltimore, naming Douglas as their choice; the bolting Southern Democrats selected John C. Breckinridge of Kentucky. Meanwhile, the surviving Whig organization, under the label of the Constitutional Union party, nominated John Bell of Tennessee. Despite the distractions of three rival presidential tickets, the Republicans concentrated upon the four vital Northern states which Fremont had failed to carry in 1856, New Jersey, Pennsylvania, Indiana, and Illinois. Just before the Senate's adjournment, the Buchanan newspaper, the Washington *Constitution,* growled that Trumbull was the "representative of the Republican candidate for the Presidency. . . ." Trumbull replied on the Senate floor, saying, "I am no more his representative than is any other Senator . . . who agrees to the principles of the Republican party."[106]

Trumbull's disclaimer that he was not Lincoln's personal spokesman was more true than he wished it to be. His letters to Lincoln after the latter's nomination teemed with advice about what course of action to take.[107]

Lincoln, in his letters, handled Trumbull cleverly, reassuring him in general terms, but taking him only moderately into his confidence.[108]

Late in June, Congress having adjourned, Trumbull hastened back to Illinois. He found the Illinois Republicans organized as never before. The lion's share of the credit belonged to meticulous Norman Judd, who, despite his fussy mannerisms, was a shrewd politician.[109] After stopping off at Chicago for some quick decisions with Judd as to political geography,[110] Trumbull set to work immediately. On his way from Chicago to Alton, he detoured to Macon County, where he spoke to a wildly partisan crowd.[111] Then Trumbull pressed on to Springfield for a few moments of hurried conversations with the Jayneses, followed by more speeches; then, he continued to Alton.[112]

While Trumbull rested at his Alton home, the legislative slate-making in the crucial central counties was completed. In the vital fifteenth state senatorial district comprising the counties of Sangamon and Morgan, Dr. William Jayne was selected to make the race. This was no act of nepotism, since William Jayne, a doctor with political ambitions, had earlier defeated a popular Democrat for the post of Springfield mayor.[113] Generally, potent votegetters had been dragged from retirement to run as Republican legislative candidates.[114] Having taken a quiet but decisive role in the slate-making from his home, Trumbull resumed his campaign. Crossing the Mississippi River, he supported the successful congressional campaign of Frank P. Blair, Jr., who became the first Republican congressman from a slave state.[115] Answering a plea from David Davis of Bloomington, he joined Owen Lovejoy in a joint debate with two Democratic leaders.[116]

Early in August, the Republican state convention reconvened at Springfield. It met again because the Republican candidate for lieutenant governor, who was German-born, had resigned from the ticket because of nativist pressure. Instead of dropping him, the Republicans triumphantly re-nominated him. The party grasped this occasion to stage a great rally in Springfield. After a parade, speakers harangued the crowd from five or six stands. Lincoln emerged for one of his rare public campaign appearances. The custom of the time decreed that a presidential candidate should not actively seek the position. Therefore, Lincoln made only a brief, non-political speech. Many orators picked up the political slack left by Lincoln. In the place of honor, the first platform, Trumbull and Senator J. R. Doolittle of Wisconsin shared time with O. H. Browning. Trumbull fanned the burning issues of free homesteads and Democratic corruption into a Republican victory fire.[117]

That evening, an overflow crowd packed a temporary building, the Wigwam, to hear more speechmaking. Trumbull was a featured orator. He accused Douglas of gross inconsistency in regard to popular sovereignty. He contrasted Douglas the "dodger" with Lincoln, the man of many virtues.[118] Two days later, Trumbull traveled to western Illinois, where he stumped every town and hamlet. In these speeches, he flayed the Democratic opposition and generated a waxing Republican optimism.[119]

The pace of the campaign quickened in early September, when Orlando Bell Ficklin proclaimed himself the Democratic senatorial candidate and challenged Trumbull to debate. Although he was only fifty, Ficklin was a politician whose officeholding career already lay behind him. Born in Kentucky and a graduate of the Transylvania College law school, he had migrated as a young man to Illinois. Three times he served in the state assembly. Beginning his political career as a Whig, he had shifted to the Democrats, winning four congressional terms under their banner. While he seemed a strong candidate, in reality, he was an inept political thimblerigger. Consequently, when Ficklin challenged Trumbull to four debates, the latter confidently accepted.[120]

After agreeing to the details, Ficklin and Trumbull released the schedule to their newspaper supporters. The Republican organs joyously trumpeted the news. Not so the Democratic press, which remained mute. The Democratic leaders were chagrined at Ficklin's bold claims. Rumors soon flew that Ficklin would be pressured by the Democratic chieftains to cancel the debate schedule.[121] Nonetheless, the first debate was held the afternoon of September 20 at Mendota. A crowd estimated at fifteen or twenty thousand people came to hear. Because of the silence of the Democratic press, the crowd consisted overwhelmingly of Republicans. Both speakers were allowed one-hour speeches and then half-hour rebuttals.

In a rambling speech, Ficklin branded the Republicans as a party of amalgamationists who favored black equality. He then propounded a lengthy list of twenty questions for Trumbull to answer. When Trumbull ascended the rostrum he was greeted both by the crowd's cheers and a sudden heavy rain shower. Ignoring the raindrops, he termed Ficklin's amalgamationist arguments "pointless." Declining to answer Ficklin's tortuously worded questions, whose reading had consumed ten minutes, Trumbull blisteringly attacked Douglas as a false champion of homestead legislation. To Trumbull's slashing attacks, Ficklin proved to be an inept respondent; he was so confused by Trumbull's sarcasm that when a heckler asked how Ficklin knew that blacks were incapable of intellectual elevation, he blurted out, "I know it by having mixed with them." The audience rocked with laughter; Ficklin never regained his poise.[122]

At Pittsfield, the next stop, several dozen Republican leaders enthusiastically greeted Trumbull, whereas only a single sheepish Democrat came to welcome Ficklin. To cap his misfortunes, Ficklin discovered that the Democratic newspapers had denied the existence of a debate, labeling it a Republican trick to increase Trumbull's crowd. As a result, at the afternoon debate the crowd was almost exclusively Republican. Trumbull, speaking first, castigated the Democrats for their surly attitude toward Ficklin's candidacy. For his part, Trumbull sarcastically declaimed, he would never stifle free speech and Ficklin could always have half the time of his rallies. Finally, Ficklin, after a few embarrassed remarks, withdrew from the platform. Shortly thereafter, as a hopelessly deflated candidate, he withdrew from the senatorial race.[123]

While Trumbull remained on the hustings, his fifth son, Arthur, was born on October 9. After receiving a few reassuring telegraphic reports, Trumbull pressed on with his campaigning.[124] Although the Democratic prospects in Illinois, except for the legislature, seemed dim, there, the Democratic leaders still saw a chance of victory, denying Trumbull a re-election. They threw speakers and money into the battle to defeat him.[125] Lincoln keenly appreciated this fact, and when Republican internecine strife threatened to lose the assembly seat in Vermilion County, he wrote a letter commanding unity, since, "to lose Trumbull's re-election . . . would be a great disaster."[126] Vice-presidential candidate, Hannibal Hamlin, offered Trumbull any help he needed, since if he and Lincoln were elected and Trumbull defeated, "it will be no victory at all."[127]

In the campaign's early stage, Trumbull felt confident and asked for nothing. When he realized that the Democratic leadership was concentrating upon defeating him, he did not hesitate to accept the aid the national Republican leaders had tendered him. Through Illinois Congressman Elihu B. Washburne, he appealed for aid from the Republican national committee. The committee promised him unlimited assistance.[128] As a result, Senators Doolittle of Wisconsin,[129] Grimes of Iowa,[130] and Seward of New York[131] clamorously campaigned for Trumbull. Senator Chandler of Michigan, one of the Senate's most acid tongues, not only shared several platform appearances with Trumbull,[132] but substituted for several engagements in the October stretch when gubernatorial candidate Yates fell ill.[133]

Nor did Trumbull's campaign lack money. The oleaginous machine politician Senator Simon Cameron wrote Trumbull, "To assist in getting out voters you will receive from a friend in New York $800 which I have furnished at his suggestion."[134] This eight hundred dollars was probably in addition to five thousand dollars which the Illinois Republican state committee obtained from New York sources to enable Dr. William Jayne to run more swiftly in his vital state senate race.[135] R. M. Blatchford of New York later maintained that he had contributed three thousand dollars of this fund and thereby successfully claimed a political appointment.[136] Trumbull's campaign was also financed by one-half of a two-thousand-dollar fund distributed by the Chicago *Tribune*.[137]

On November 6, election day, a bone-tired Trumbull, who had made over fifty major speeches, cast his ballot in Alton. He left for Springfield almost immediately thereafter to receive the election returns with Lincoln. On election night, Lincoln, with a small group of friends, went to the telegraph office where the vote totals from the Eastern part of the nation clicked in. The Republicans piled up impressive vote totals throughout the Northern states. The national news remained good, and it soon appeared that, except for New Jersey, the Republican bandwagon had rolled to victory. The Southern and border states, as expected, rejected the Republicans — but no matter. After midnight, when the pattern of national victory had been clearly cut, the Lincoln party adjourned from the telegraph office to a victory feast prepared by Mary Lincoln and the Springfield ladies.[138] It was a carnival atmosphere, but the gaiety sounded hollow to Trumbull, and his smile remained thin while his own election remained in doubt. The Illinois returns trickled in slowly.[139]

Finally, the night's tumult died away, and the anti-climactic day after the election dawned in Springfield. By then it appeared that the legislature's lower house seemed safely Republican, but Trumbull's anxiety about his party's grip on the state senate remained. Since half of the upper house's membership carried over, the Republicans needed to register a net gain of one seat to grasp control. The pivotal seat lay in the Springfield area where William Jayne carried the Republican standard. Early returns were indecisive. Jayne's election seemed doubtful, since the district was normally Democratic, and in the presidential race, Lincoln himself had lost Sangamon County by almost fifty votes to Douglas.[140]

As the hours of Wednesday ticked by, Jayne's election totals remained stubbornly incomplete. On Thursday, final Sangamon County returns showed that Jayne trailed there by one vote. Morgan County remained Jayne's last thin hope. That afternoon, a telegram arrived with the cheering news that Jayne had eked out an eight-vote majority in that county, making him the victor in the two-county district by seven votes.[141] With his brother-in-law's triumph, Trumbull's own re-election was assured. While the booming of the ''Little Joker,'' a cannon manned by Republican volunteers celebrating Jayne's triumph, still reverberated in his ears,[142] Trumbull's thoughts already turned to his country's future, which seemed both promising and ominous.

CHAPTER EIGHT

SECESSION CRISIS

IT WAS IMPOSSIBLE for Trumbull to savor the Republican triumph in 1860, since secession appeared to be a fact. Defiantly, South Carolina prepared to leave the Union. The initial Northern reaction was incredulity. As other deep-Southern states also threatened secession, the clamor rose in the North that Lincoln reassure the would-be secessionists. Lincoln at first claimed that his previous statements should suffice. At last he bowed to the outcry, using Lyman Trumbull as his sounding board. He composed two paragraphs for the senator to include in his Springfield Republican victory address on November 20, 1860.[1] The correspondents in Springfield covering the President-elect reported that Trumbull would act as an administrative spokesman.[2]

In Lincoln's statement, he clarified and explained, but he was not ready to make concessions to the South. Lincoln implied that Southern politicians had impugned Republican intentions from base motives. Lincoln's second paragraph, which expressed his pleasure at the "military preparation in the South" as calculated "to suppress any uprising there," was so patently a whistling in the dark that Trumbull declined to use this phrasing.

The victory festivities were held in a building dubbed the "Wigwam," which had served as Republican headquarters. Trumbull appeared as the evening's main speaker.[3] Trumbull included the reassurance desired by Lincoln, but he broke up Lincoln's statement and scattered parts in three places. The President-elect's second paragraph, with the optimistic expressions, Lyman had recast. As he expressed it, he hoped that Southern disunion sentiment had been exaggerated and that a loyal reaction would soon appear. Finally, Trumbull forecast that the Republicans' deeds would reveal how foolish had been their detractors' dire predictions.[4] In the press reaction to the speech, although there was some positive reaction from Northern and border moderates,[5] the deep-South newspapers dismissed the address as "meaningless."[6] On the other hand, Republican journals worried that Trumbull's speech presaged Lincoln's abandonment of party policies.[7] In the upshot, the President-elect soon realized that his trial balloon had exploded, and refused to make further pronouncements.[8]

On November 21, the day after Trumbull's speech, he and Julia entrained for Chicago with the Lincolns. For the Trumbulls, it was the first stage of the journey to Washington for Congress' December meeting; the Lincolns were bound for Chicago, where Abraham would confer with Vice-President-elect Hannibal Hamlin.[9] At Chicago, the Lincoln-Trumbull party quietly detrained and journeyed to their rooms at a local hotel. The next day, a travel-stained Hannibal Hamlin appeared in Chicago. He was well-known to Trumbull, as they had occupied adjacent Senate seats. On the first day of talks, Lincoln and Hamlin met alone, but on the second day, they included Trumbull.[10]

The early talks had concerned policy, but in the next two days, they concerned Lincoln's cabinet. Lincoln told the two senators that they would act as his agents in the formation of the cabinet.[11] As a result of this conference, the press widely predicted that Trumbull would serve as the administration Senate spokesman.[12] The Lincolns returned to Springfield, and Hamlin and the Trumbulls entrained for New York.[13]

Lincoln had admitted to the senators that he was seriously considering Seward for secretary of state. He also hinted that the treasury post choice lay between the rabid anti-slaveryite, Salmon Chase, and the spoilsman, Simon Cameron. The other cabinet posts, Lincoln indicated, were open, with many aspirants.[14] Trumbull strongly expressed his aversion to Seward and his preference for Chase. Trumbull was irritated by what he felt to be Lincoln's evasiveness about the cabinet's composition.[15] The cabinet's membership was of transcendent importance since by his choices, Lincoln, a comparative newcomer to the national scene, could retain the support of the autonomous state political machines which had won his victory for him. The sprawling Republican party was far from an integrated organization, and it was imperative that Lincoln solidify the diverse groups behind his administration. Being a doctrinaire, Trumbull insisted that only able men with unblemished political records should hold cabinet places. In Trumbull's judgment that meant a cabinet seat for his friend Norman Judd.[16] Trumbull had not dared to push Judd's appointment at the Chicago meeting,[17] but later he backed Judd energetically. The Judd drive for a cabinet post became part of a furious power struggle.

While in New York on his way to Washington, Trumbull received the distinguished poet-editor William Cullen Bryant and two political associates, who desired to exclude Seward from the cabinet.[18] Trumbull reported these men's sentiments about Seward's unsuitability, so as to leave no doubt of his sympathy with the callers' purposes.[19] But Lincoln had already decided that the controversial New Yorker must be tendered a cabinet post. Now Lincoln communicated this fact to Trumbull. The President-elect had addressed notes to Seward, sealed them and sent them to

Hamlin for delivery to the New York senator. However, he had enclosed copies so that Hamlin would know their contents without Seward's realizing that fact. Also, Lincoln had instructed Hamlin to consult with Trumbull. If they agreed it was propitious, they were to deliver the notes to Seward. It was meant to be a gesture. Lincoln had cautioned the Vice-President-elect to deliver the notes only if it seemed probable that the New Yorker would decline. At that moment, Lincoln yet hoped for a cabinet free of both Seward and Cameron.[20] In the outcome, after Trumbull agreed and Hamlin had made Lincoln's left-handed offer to him, Seward accepted.[21]

Meanwhile, Cameron also wrung from Lincoln the offer of a cabinet position. Cameron clung tenaciously to this offer all that winter. Lincoln had avoided a specific commitment of a particular post to Cameron.[22] That Cameron should be considered for any cabinet place was distasteful to Trumbull, who wrote several angry letters of advice to Lincoln.[23] Their tenor can be summarized, "There is an odor about Mr. C. which would be very detrimental to your administration as our best friends think."[24]

Trumbull had a further motive in his opposition to Seward and Cameron, hoping that their posts would go to his favorite cabinet candidates, Chase and Judd. At one time, Lincoln seriously considered giving Judd a place,[25] but as the opposition to the proposal snowballed, Lincoln grew hesitant. A great clamor arose that no cabinet officer should be appointed from Illinois, Lincoln's home state.[26] Judd's candidacy sank into deeper trouble when ten Cameron Pennsylvania politicians entered the lists against him. In retaliation for the opposition to Cameron, they joined forces with the anti-Judd group in Illinois, the former Whig element in the state's Republican party.[27] Caleb Smith's Indiana supporters also grew to be anti-Judd, since they realized that if Judd were successful, their man would be left without a place. As Smith had been promised a cabinet post at the Chicago convention, the engineers of that deal, Leonard Swett and David Davis, vociferously insisted that this arrangement be honored.[28] To make the odds on Judd longer, he was disliked by Mary Lincoln, who used against Judd whatever influence Abraham permitted her in political matters.[29]

Trumbull's great activity in behalf of Judd earned him additional enemies in Illinois, as George T. Brown warned him.[30] Unmoved, Trumbull continued to support Judd.[31] Later, Trumbull wrote the President-elect urging Judd as a cabinet member with whom he would have more in common than with his other advisors.[32] This was a lame argument, as Lincoln readily perceived that a confidential advisor would shatter the cabinet's unity. Therefore he grew very cool to a cabinet position for Judd.[33] Yet Judd marshalled such impressive senatorial support that Lincoln deferred a final decision on his case until after his own arrival in Washington.

Meanwhile, a personal worry plagued Trumbull. With Republican control of the legislature, his own re-election had seemed certain. Then, John Wentworth, an old enemy, tried to detach sufficient Republicans to elect a

Democrat in Trumbull's place.[34] Further, Wentworth attempted to use Governor Yates or Owen Lovejoy to defeat Trumbull in the Republican legislative caucus. When this effort failed to attract support,[35] Governor Yates hastily proclaimed his backing for Trumbull.[36] Then an effort was made by anti-Trumbull Republicans to obtain support for Leonard Swett in the Republican legislative caucus.[37] But this move stalled, and the anti-Trumbull revolt collapsed, so that no name was presented to the Republican legislative caucus except Trumbull's, and the Republicans voted for him in the joint legislative session. Thus he was elected by a 54 to 46 margin over a nominal Democratic candidate.[38]

Amid politics-and-patronage-as-usual, the worsening secession crisis persistently nagged at Trumbull for attention. Seven Southern states were seceding and forming a new confederacy. The magnitude of the crisis dawned only slowly upon most Republican leaders. Trumbull's preoccupation with politics and patronage was not atypical. After years of Southern bluster, many Northerners thought that the South was bluffing. As late as early December, the biggest concern seemed to Trumbull that his party had not won a clear majority in either house of Congress.[39]

The second session of the Thirty-Sixth Congress was irritating to a Northern such as Trumbull. Southern senators, especially Louis T. Wigfall of Texas, would cry "Cotton is King!" and bring down the Senate galleries with applause.[40] On December 20, the day South Carolina seceded, Trumbull hotly answered Southern senators who asserted that the Union "had no right to coerce a state." Trumbull declared that while no one believed in coercing a state, loyal men did believe in suppressing a rebellion.[41] In this respect Trumbull differed from Seward, who was busy formulating peace proposals to the South.[42] Trumbull's personal feeling concerning the secession of South Carolina was starkly revealed when he attended a Republican conference in the rooms of the old Jacksonian Francis P. Blair, Sr. Largely through Trumbull's efforts, this conference resolved that the Union should be preserved at all cost.[43]

The Trumbulls, that secession winter, had a personal problem. Their oldest son, Walter, then a teenager, had always been in precarious health. To improve it, he sought a beneficial sea voyage. He wheedled a family friend, Samuel Phillips Lee, a captain in the navy, to take him as a "companion-guest" on a two-year cruise of the Far East. Walter sailed aboard the *Vandalia* early in December 1860. Partly to fill the void left by Walter's leaving, the Trumbulls threw themselves into the Washington social whirl which went on much as usual during the secession crisis.[44]

On January 10, Trumbull made a major address, replying to Senator Jefferson Davis, the soon-to-be president of the Confederacy. Using his most searing invective, Trumbull bristled that the essence of the Mississippian's speech was that "He dreads civil war; and he will avoid it by a surrender of the federal government!"[45] He turned to the Crittenden Compromise, advanced as a possible solution of the secession crisis by the elderly senator from Kentucky.[46] Trumbull scorned it as a bogus restoration of the Missouri Compromise. He closed by asking the South to await an act of Republican aggression. If it would do so, it would never secede, since the new administration would not trample Southern rights.[47] Matching his deeds to his words, Trumbull voted on several occasions to prevent discussion of the Crittenden Compromise on the Senate floor.[48] This tough stand proved extremely popular to Trumbull's Republican constituents.[49]

On January 21, several senators from the lower South, whose states already had seceded, withdrew after speaking elaborate farewells.[50] The spectacle of those Southerners coolly saying goodbye to the Senate and leaving to erect a rival government was a sight as maddening as it seemed wicked to Trumbull. This experience greatly colored his attitude toward the South for the next decade. Meanwhile, Trumbull was concerned that Lincoln be formally declared elected and regularly installed in office. Therefore, he moved that the Senate's presiding officer appoint a committee of three to meet with a House group to specify the method of counting the electoral votes. Despite some Democratic foot-dragging, under Trumbull's relentless prodding, the Senate passed his resolution. As appointed, the committee included Trumbull as one of the Senate representatives.[51]

Having been elected as chairman of the Senate committee, after a conference with the House group, Trumbull set February 13 as the date for the canvass of the electoral votes. The remaining Southern senators did not try to block Lincoln's inauguration as Trumbull had feared they might.[52] Exactly on schedule, Lincoln and Hamlin were formally declared elected.[53] Meanwhile, on February 11, Lincoln started from Illinois to Washington. A roundabout trip, it included public appearances and speech-making by Lincoln. Trumbull soon growled that Lincoln was talking too much, but since he had not consulted Trumbull recently, the Illinois solon was probably expressing his bitter feelings.[54]

After traveling to New York and then to Harrisburg, Pennsylvania, Lincoln, upon the advice of his associates who feared an assassination plot in Baltimore, slipped away ahead of schedule, arriving in Washington early in the morning of February 23.[55] He went directly to Willard's Hotel, taking a suite hastily vacated by a wealthy citizen.[56] Trumbull and other Republican congressional leaders had agreed that Lincoln should take a furnished residence until he moved into the White House, and already had selected one for him.[57] With Lincoln's hurried arrival, these tidy plans had been scrapped. At Willard's, a cloud of office-seekers prowled night and day, and it was not lost upon Trumbull that in his new quarters, Lincoln would be surrounded by pro-Cameron and anti-Judd politicians — chief among them the portly David Davis.[58]

Trumbull slowly grasped the hard fact that Judd had been excluded from and Cameron included in the cabinet. This realization, plus an exasperation that the President-elect no longer confided in him, caused Trumbull to dispatch a coldly formal note to Lincoln, informing him that, as chairman of a congressional committee, it was his duty to notify him formally of his election. Trumbull suggested the next evening for this ritual. He sent copies of Senate journals in order that Lincoln could ascertain, as Trumbull frostily put it, "what had been the usual course on such occasions."[59] The notification ceremonies were performed at the appointed time in a formal manner.[60]

Talk of a compromise between the incoming regime and the lower South continued, but it sounded more hollow with each passing day. Yet "peaceable" Americans pinned their hopes on a conference called by Virginia. The Old Dominion had been shocked by secession. Early in 1861, it had asked all the states to send delegates to a national peace conference on February 4 in Washington. However, attendance at the conference was incomplete.[61] Trumbull airily dismissed it, writing to Governor Richard Yates, "I do not expect any good to come from this meeting."[62] Trumbull's anti-compromise attitude was again evident when a senator proposed to postpone other business in favor of the Crittenden Compromise: the proposal to take up Crittenden's suggestions was voted down by the paper-thin margin of 23 to 21, Trumbull voting an emphatic *No*.[63]

Meanwhile, compromise advocates had a new proposal when the Washington peace conference drafted a report roughly similar to the Crittenden Compromise.[64] In the Senate, the report was sent to a select committee consisting of the aging Crittenden of Kentucky; Buchanan's spokesman, Bigler of Pennsylvania; the rather obscure Thomson of New Jersey; the crafty Seward of New York; and the stubbornly uncompromising Trumbull himself.[65] Trumbull seized the opportunity, as he saw it, to stiffen Seward's spine. Along with other congressional Republicans, he viewed the New Yorker's tergiversations as a simple lack of resolution.[66] Seward appeared to be devious and insincere to many unblinking Republicans.[67]

After much argument, the next day a majority of the select committee pronounced the peace convention proposal to be the basis for a constitutional amendment which would ameliorate the crisis.[68] Seward had been pushed by Trumbull to disagree with the majority report. Although the two Republicans were not allowed to submit a minority report, Seward expressed their sentiments to the Senate. They embodied a toothless proposal that the states hold a national convention to propose constitutional amendments.[69] But events moved so rapidly that the Seward-Trumbull proposal was never seriously considered.

When the Senate convened on March 2, time was running out. The day following was a Sunday, and on the fourth of March, the terms of the Representatives, a third of the Senate, and of President Buchanan would expire. In an obstructionist mood, Trumbull fought all attempts to have the Senate sit that Sunday.[70] Compromise-minded senators proposed that Senate rule twenty-six be suspended to facilitate the passage of conciliatory constitutional amendments. Rule twenty-six forbade two readings of a constitutional amendment on the same day. Trumbull objected, saying that it was "exceedingly dangerous to change a rule, for a particular purpose, in this way."[71] Unmoved, the Senate suspended the rule.[72]

Immediately, the Senate debated House Resolution No. 80, a thirteenth amendment to the Constitution which forbade any future constitutional revision permitting Congress to interfere with slavery in the states. Trumbull opposed consideration of the amendment at every step.[73] Then the Senate adjourned until the next day at seven in the evening.[74] When it reconvened, Trumbull aired his views. His speech was a far cry from his mellow discourses of December 1859. He labeled the compromisers misguided men and scored the Buchanan administration for its failure to discharge its duty.

Having fired a blast at the Buchanan administration, Trumbull allowed himself a diversionary attack. He assailed Republican Senator Edward Baker of Oregon. The occasion for the attack was the Oregonian's public pronouncement favoring a constitutional amendment permitting perpetual slavery in New Mexico. Baker, a polished orator, refused to back down. The two influential Republican senators treated the country to a war of words on the Senate floor. Piqued by the Oregonian's burgeoning influence with Lincoln, who was Baker's old personal friend, Trumbull had seized the first pretext to lash out at him. After his exchange with Baker, Trumbull called the House-proposed constitutional amendment "superfluous," since the Republicans would not tamper with slavery within states. Trumbull's solution for the crisis: couple a strong stand by the federal government against the rebellion with an avoidance of any overt act against any legitimate Southern right.[75]

In the voting which followed his speech, Trumbull supported all Republican efforts to scuttle the proposed constitutional revision.[76] The compromise-minded majority passed the constitutional amendment by the necessary margin of 24 to 12.[77] Since the House already had acted upon it, the measure went out to the states for ratification. But the swift march of events reduced it to a nullity; when a thirteenth amendment was added to the Constitution, it contained very different wording on slavery.

With this action completed, the Senate doggedly turned to other compromise solutions. The Crittenden Compromise failed to pass by the shadow-thin margin of 19 to 20; all the Republicans, including Trumbull, voted *No.*[78] As the Senate droned toward adjournment, it considered a bill to incorporate a new gas company in the District of Columbia. Bright of Indiana filibustered the last hour so that this bill could not pass and break the utility monopoly held by his friends.[79]

That March fourth was one of the watersheds in the history of the United States. As if to symbolize his close relationship to the new President, Senator

Baker played a prominent role at the inauguration ceremonies.[80] For Trumbull, watching from the outer edge of the circle of dignitaries, the victorious inauguration of a Republican President left an ashen taste.[81]

Baker enjoyed many advantages in the race for Lincoln's confidence. He was an old friend and political comrade-in-arms of Lincoln's from his Whig Springfield days. Lincoln had esteemed Baker so highly that he had named one of his sons for him. Moving out of Illinois into the Far West, Baker helped to found the Republican party, first in California, and then in Oregon, from which he was elected senator.[82] Yet even in matters touching his own Pacific coast, Baker never had things completely his own way.[83]

Trumbull watched the appointments to the new administration with mounting dismay. After the inauguration, Trumbull found few occasions to consult with Lincoln. Therefore, by the middle of March, Trumbull wrote, "I see very little of Lincoln, & know little of his policy as to appointments or anything else."[84] Finally, in disgust, a scant two weeks after Lincoln's inauguration, Trumbull, according to William Jayne, sulkily announced "that he would not step inside the White House again during Mr. Lincoln's four years, unless he changed his course."[85]

Trumbull felt the pressure to "take care" of his friends, and each unsuccessful aspirant blamed Trumbull personally, even when the senator had done his best to obtain a place for him.[86] Trumbull felt each disappointment for jobs keenly, since it struck at his influence within the Republican party.[87] This struggle over appointments during the early weeks of the Lincoln administration seems to have completed the break in the friendship between Julia Trumbull and Mary Lincoln.[88] Each wife only saw her husband's side of the imbroglio. The part, however small, that Mary Lincoln played in keeping Judd from the cabinet post had further cooled the Trumbulls toward the first lady.

As evidence of the social "cold war" that had grown up between Julia and Mary, the "cousin Lizzie" case is apropos. Mary Lincoln's cousin, Mrs. Elizabeth J. Grimsley, known in the family as "cousin Lizzie," visited the White House for an extended period from March to August, 1861. During her visit, Julia Trumbull refused to call upon her. Instead, Julia sent word that she expected Lizzie to call first upon her, as that was merely "etiquette." Lizzie was unimpressed, since other senators' wives had called first upon her, and wrote to the Illinois home folks, "I conclude in the present state of affairs, . . . that Mrs. Trumbull might waive ceremony also if she wished to see me."[89]

Trumbull was unduly pessimistic in viewing the patronage squabble with Lincoln. His intra-party rivals were never entirely successful. For example, David Davis never could obtain for his friend Leonard Swett the post as American consul at Liverpool.[90] While Trumbull failed to influence heavily the composition of Lincoln's cabinet (Judd was an unsuccessful claimant, and Cameron, Seward, and Smith all won seats over Trumbull's protest), yet he had helped to secure the vital treasury position for Chase. Trumbull also succeeded in placing his friends in many lesser places. Judd found consolation when he was awarded the first appointment that Lincoln made to the diplomatic corps — minister to Prussia.[91] A regular Trumbull correspondent, German-American newspaperman Theodore Canisius, received a position as consul at Vienna.[92] Gustave Koerner was ultimately appointed minister to Spain.[93]

Nor were Trumbull's relatives overlooked. William Jayne, who had been elected to the Illinois Senate at the cost of so much treasure and effort, was then named governor of the Dakota Territory.[94] There was much criticism of this appointment, as thereby the Republicans lost control of the upper chamber.[95] Lyman's brother, Benjamin M. Trumbull, was given a post in the Omaha land office.[96] Despite Trumbull's explanations of these appointments, they created so much unfavorable comment that Lincoln, in refusing a place to one of his own relatives, wrote: "You see I have already appointed William Jayne a territorial governor and Judge Trumbull's brother to a land office — Will it do for me to go on and justify the declaration that Trumbull and I have divided out all the offices among our relatives?"[97]

In the special session of the Senate, called by Lincoln after March 4 so that his new appointees might be confirmed, Trumbull was sworn in for his second six-year term. Also, since the Southern senators largely had withdrawn, the Republicans, for the first time, found themselves in undisputed control of the Senate. Enjoying their new position, the Republicans met in caucus and selected a special subcommittee, consisting of William Fessenden of Maine, Preston King of New York, and Trumbull, to organize the Senate committees. The plums, the committee chairmanships, passed mainly to New England senators, but Trumbull received the chairmanship of the powerful judiciary committee and a more modest assignment on the committee of the post office.[98]

Late in the session, on March 28, disgruntled by the passive handling of the tense situation at Fort Sumter, where less than a hundred regular army troops were besieged in Charleston harbor by many times their number of Southern troops, Trumbull offered a resolution that the "true way to preserve the Union is to enforce the laws of the Union. . . ."[99] Jesse Bright of Indiana and John C. Breckinridge, now a senator from Kentucky, shouted their willingness to vote, but more moderate Republicans shunted aside Trumbull's incendiary resolution. A motion to go into executive session passed 25 to 11. The Southern Democrats still present, and Douglas, Trumbull, and Wade, a strange coalition, all opposed the move.[100] Trumbull already had met with Wade, Chandler, and other more "radical" Republican congressmen and warned Lincoln that reinforcements must be promptly sent to Fort Sumter.[101] Such public performances speedily earned for Trumbull the enmity of conservative Republicans.[102] As events unfolded, they had little reason to retract their judgment; Trumbull had veered under the stress of the secession crisis into an "ultra" position.

Despite the tense situation, the Senate, having completed its vote on the Lincoln appointments, adjourned until December. After a few days in which he tried to push the administration into positive action,[103] Trumbull, disgruntled, started his return trip to Illinois, where he received the shocking news[104] that, on April 12, the Confederates had shelled Fort Sumter. A great civil war had begun and with it a new phase of Trumbull's usefulness to the nation.

CHAPTER NINE

LYMAN VIEWS WAR AT FIRST HAND

THE CONFEDERATE CANNON firing upon Fort Sumter ushered in an era of profound change in the nation's life. Caught in the wild activity that then engulfed the North, Trumbull, upon his arrival at Springfield, at once conferred with Yates. Quickly, they agreed to furnish the Illinois militia requested by Lincoln.[1] Yates seemed overwhelmed by the crisis and welcomed Trumbull's help. In this crisis, Trumbull moved into the governor's private office. There, surrounded by a mountain of law books, Lyman hammered out the special legislation which the legislature, meeting in special session on April 23, would be asked to pass. The gas lamps burned in the governor's office until dawn for several days, but at last Trumbull and Yates completed the emergency legislation.[2]

The country wallowed in crisis. To the seven states of the original Southern Confederacy were added four others, Arkansas, North Carolina, Virginia, and Tennessee. Illinoisans felt as if the Confederacy would come to their doorsteps, as Kentucky and Missouri teetered between the Union and the Confederacy. From Alton just across the Mississippi River from St. Louis, few places seemed to Trumbull more tangled in problems than Missouri. The Governor, Claiborne F. Jackson, sympathized with the secessionists. He wanted Missouri to join the Confederacy, but his plans were blocked by a loyal convention. Then Jackson decided to capture the well-stocked St. Louis federal arsenal, he conspiring with General Daniel M. Frost, the commander of a small militia brigade, to do so. The plot's execution was delayed by an artillery shortage, and while waiting for heavy guns, Frost let his opportunity slip away.

The Missouri Union adherents were led by the Francis Blair family. When South Carolina seceded, the Blair supporters had organized "home guards." An aggressive regular officer, Nathaniel Lyon, then in charge at the St. Louis arsenal, made no pro-Union moves because of his hesitant superior, General William S. Harney. Unconditional Union men such as Lyman Trumbull considered Harney to be either a waxworks figure or a traitor. However, in response to an appeal sent him by Yates and Trumbull, Lyon, despite Harney, shipped arms to Illinois; others he distributed to the Blair home guards. Lyon also deployed his troops around the arsenal, preventing a Frost attack.

At this, Frost established Camp Jackson, on the city's western edge on the far side from the arsenal. Then, while General Harney was absent from St. Louis, Lyon struck at Camp Jackson and with about seven thousand men, swiftly captured it and its garrison of six hundred. As the Union troops were shepherding their prisoners through the St. Louis streets, a secessionist mob unsuccessfully attacked them. What new action Lyon would have taken can only be conjectured, since an outraged Harney returned to St. Louis, reassuming command.[3] This action drew Trumbull across the Mississippi to see events for himself. After a quick survey, Trumbull congratulated Lyon for his activities, and decided to have the hesitant Harney removed.[4] The latter, fearing further action, arranged a truce between the factions. At this, Trumbull became angry. He immediately boarded a train to report to Washington authorities about Harney's conduct. Although the Blair family is credited with having Harney removed, it is certain that Trumbull helped in his dismissal. On May 31, Union men hailed the news of Harney's removal and Lyon's elevation to the Missouri command.[5] By mid-June, Lyon forced Governor Jackson to flee Missouri. Ultimately, Lyon's impetuosity led him to attack a superior Confederate force at Wilson's Creek, bringing his defeat and death. Yet, he had saved Missouri for the Union.[6]

Trumbull became disgusted by the lack of enterprise in Washington. He demanded that a general offensive be launched to clear the Confederates out of the upper South and bring the rebellion to a speedy close. The legalist senator inadequately appreciated Lincoln's many problems.[7] Lincoln summoned Congress into special session eighty days after Sumter. There were reasons why it could not meet sooner; not the least compelling was that Lincoln wished to be unhampered by Congress during the war's crucial opening days.[8]

Arranging his personal affairs, Trumbull left for Washington for the unseasonal meeting of Congress. One worry had eased. His son Walter had returned with the *Vandalia* to the United States. Because of Julia's newsworthy letters to Walter which he had passed on to Captain S. P. Lee, in early March Lee turned the U. S. S. *Vandalia* around at Capetown, South Africa and returned to the United States. Walter had grown fond of the sea, and Lincoln appointed him a midshipman at the United States Naval Academy. Walter attended the academy for two years before dropping out.[9]

Leaving Julia and the smaller children in Illinois, Trumbull traveled alone to Washington.[10] He now had a new colleague from Illinois; Douglas had died. With the firing on Sumter, the Little Giant had rallied to the

Union's support. Then he became ill and died on June 3, 1861, leaving a void at the top of the Illinois Democratic organization and an unexpired Senate term of almost four years. Governor Yates appointed Orville H. Browning to the vacant Senate seat. Browning was an old-line Whig who grated upon Trumbull's nerves because of his "timid" policies.[11]

Yet Trumbull tried to work with Browning, and the day after his arrival in Washington, he called upon him at his lodgings. There, they discussed how to formally announce Douglas' death to the Senate. It was a stylized ritual, but Browning and Trumbull were both fussy about official etiquette. After consulting precedents, they decided that the surviving colleague had made the announcement, with his successor taking no part in the proceedings. Upon reflection Browning found this not to his taste and to Trumbull's irritation, announced that he would "say something," and he did.[12]

When Congress convened on July 4, Trumbull presented Browning's credentials so that the new senator could be sworn.[13] The next day Trumbull, as chairman of the important judiciary committee in the division of Senate patronage, secured the post of sergeant-at-arms and doorkeeper for George T. Brown, who needed employment. In early 1860, financial reverses had caused Brown to sell the Alton *Courier*, and after that his financial situation had further deteriorated. An unsuccessful race for Alton city attorney capped his misfortunes, and he had earned only a meager existence practicing law for the past year and a half.[14]

On July 9, Trumbull made the formal announcement of Douglas' death, and pronounced a eulogy of his dead colleague. He was careful, however, throughout his speech, while lauding Douglas the man, to say nothing approving the Little Giant's political career before Fort Sumter's fall.[15]

Trumbull joined other congressmen who demanded a vigorous prosecution of the war. Their "ultra" views caused them to be dubbed the "Radicals." Fifteen Republican senators, of whom Trumbull was the most vociferous, urged passage of an incendiary resolution in the Republican caucus. As worded by Trumbull, the resolution directed an immediate Union advance, so that Richmond could be occupied by July 20, the meeting date of the Confederate Congress.[16] Although conservative members of the Republican party viewed the resolution as "both absurd and dangerous,"[17] Trumbull battled for his proposal. It was adroitly shunted aside by the president's supporters.[18]

Worried by Confederate subversion behind the Union lines, Trumbull shepherded a bill through the Senate which strengthened the powers of the United States Attorney General. It provided that the United States marshals and district attorneys regularly report to the attorney general and that officers be made responsible for their supervision,[19] a move which led eventually to the establishment of the department of justice. Ironically,

Edward Bates, the attorney general, used this additional power to restrain rather than encourage prosecutions against Confederate sympathizers under the laws that Trumbull so desperately desired enforced rigorously.

Meanwhile, the Union armies began the forward movement for which Trumbull had so long clamored. Union General Irvin McDowell's raw levies advanced against the Confederate forces around Manassas Junction in northern Virginia, commanded by General P. G. T. Beauregard. In the Valley of Virginia, it was believed that the Union General, Robert Patterson, would prevent Joseph E. Johnston's Confederate army from joining Beauregard. Patterson failed in this holding operation, and part of Johnston's army reinforced Beauregard before the battle was joined; still more troops arrived at a crucial juncture to reinforce the hard-pressed Southerners. As Manassas lay about thirty miles from Washington, on Sunday morning, July 21, a ragtag crowd of civilians, clerks, hangers-on, and congressmen sallied forth from Washington to see the rebellion crushed at a single master stoke.[20]

In company with Benjamin Wade, Zachariah Chandler, George T. Brown, and James Grimes, Trumbull left Washington at nine on that hot July morning. The group drove in a carriage to Centreville, only a few miles from the battle. There the party split, as Grimes and Trumbull rode forward on horseback. They met a Union officer, who explained to them that although the Northern army had attacked the Confederate flank with some success, he feared a Southern counterattack. Upon the officer's advice, they reined about and visited a Union hospital. The sight of the wounded was a shattering experience to the two lawmakers, and as soon as they could gracefully leave they did. Then a fellow-senator from California, a former Illinoisan, James McDougall, overtook them. McDougall, a convivially noisy Westerner, soon restored the spirits of his senatorial colleagues. At mid-afternoon, McDougall, who had eaten no lunch, declared that he was returning to Centreville for food and drink. Grimes and Trumbull accompanied him.

At a farmhouse, the three senators persuaded the inhabitants to sell them a lunch. Eating it picnic-style in the farmyard, they commented that the battle's sounds were moving toward them. Just as the senators had finished eating, they were surprised to hear a great roar, and glancing down the road, they saw a disorganized horde that once had been an army streaming back toward Centreville. Mounting their horses, the three senators pressed out onto the road, now clogged with rushing, pushing troops. Trumbull was at a loss to discover what had happened, but from his questions which were answered in monosyllables and grunts by several officers, he learned what had occurred. The Union troops had fought bravely, but in a crucial moment of the battle, the timely arrival of Confederate reserves had overpowered them. In a twinkling, the Union army had melted away from the

Bull Run battlefield. Borne along with the mob, the senators rode back to Centreville. Becoming separated from McDougall, Grimes and Trumbull left about six o'clock for Washington, arriving about two-thirty on a dreary Monday morning. Grimes and Trumbull were disillusioned by what they had seen of war at first hand. They both vowed never to willingly visit a battlefield again — and they never did.[21]

Trumbull became convinced that the Union troops had been defeated because of faulty leadership. This defect was evident, he felt, not alone in the army, but was displayed in the cabinet itself. In Trumbull's view, Secretary of State Seward favored a rosewater prosecution of the war, and Cameron, the Secretary of War, was a venal incompetent.[22] While Trumbull blamed others, the New York *Herald* declared that he and the Radicals who had forced the administration into premature action must bear part of the guilt.[23]

After the rebellion's serious character had been revealed, Congress grimly returned to work. One congressional proposal was a bill, already introduced by Trumbull, calling for a limited confiscation of Southern property. The policy of confiscation emerged almost simultaneously from so many sources that its origin is impossible to trace.[24] The Confederates themselves had set a pattern when, in May 1861, the provisional Confederate government enacted a law requiring Southerners to pay all debts owed to Northern residents into the Confederate treasury in exchange for five-percent bonds. A later act of August 1861 provided for the sequestration of alien-held property in the South, i.e., the possessions of Union sympathizers.[25] With the first of these Confederate acts as both example and spur, Trumbull had on July 15 introduced a very limited confiscation measure into the Senate. His proposal was not to apply to all Confederate property but simply to that used for "insurrectionary purposes." At that time, the bill was referred to the friendly judiciary committee.[26]

On July 22, a sleepy-eyed Trumbull, still tired from his trip to the Bull Run battlefield of the previous day, attended the day's Senate session. He had heard that during the recent battle, some Southerners had hired or given their slaves for menial tasks, helping the Confederate army. The judiciary committee had previously refused to accept an amendment to his bill striking at this practice, but now as a result of the reports he could relay almost from the battlefield, Trumbull successfully added such an amendment to the bill upon the Senate floor. Trumbull's amendment, illustrating the early queasy days of the war, used various circumlocutions for slavery. It read:

> That whenever any person claiming to be entitled to the service or labor of another person, under the laws of any State, shall employ any such person in aiding or promoting any insurrection, . . . he shall for-

> feit all right to such service or labor, and the person whose labor . . . is thus claimed shall be thenceforth discharged therefrom any law to the contrary notwithstanding.

As was the senatorial custom, Trumbull painstakingly explained his amendment in great detail. Indolent senators did not read the printed versions on their desks, and the sponsors of legislation had to spell out orally the implications of their bills.[27] The day after Bull Run, the Senate was receptive to harsh measures. It therefore accepted Trumbull's amendment and passed the bill, 33 to 6. The sole opposition came from the border state senators.[28] Trumbull was deluged with mail from Radicals, applauding his stand.[29] Meanwhile, the confiscation bill was sent to the House for its approval. Sentiment there was generally opposed to the Senate's confiscation bill, and it was ultimately committed to the House judiciary committee.[30] There, Trumbull's amendment pertaining to the freeing of slaves was stricken, and a new fourth section written for the bill. This amendment was sponsored by John A. Bingham of Ohio, chairman of the committee. It read:

> That whenever hereafter, . . . any person claimed to be held to labor or service, under the law of any State, shall be required or permitted by his owner . . . to take up arms against the United States, or . . . work . . . in . . . any military or naval service whatsoever against the . . . United States, then in every such case, the person to whom such labor or service is claimed to be due shall forfeit his claim to such labor. . . . And whenever thereafter the person claiming such service or labor shall seek to enforce his claim, it shall be a full and sufficient answer . . ., that the person whose service or labor is claimed had been employed in hostile service against . . . the United States, . . . [31]

Trumbull's amended bill speedily passed the House by a vote of 60 to 48.[32]

Trumbull was not disgruntled by the House action. When the bill returned to the Senate for its concurrence, Trumbull said that he thought the House changes were not consequential.[33] Since Trumbull had endorsed the House changes, the Senate accepted it by a vote of 24 to 11.[34] President Lincoln signed the bill into law on August 6, 1861, the First Confiscation Act. It proved of little practical importance in freeing the slaves. The language of the bill freeing certain slaves was inexplicit; moreover, no provision was made actually to forfeit the slaves. Hence, this section proved a dead letter. The amount of Confederate property confiscated under this act was miniscule. The act's importance was as a precursor of further legislation.[35]

During the special session, Trumbull continued to candle all bills by two lights. First, were they constitutional? Secondly, would they preserve the Union? When no one introduced a bill to regularize the many arbitrary arrests of Southern sympathizers made by federal officers, Trumbull, with his usual abhorrence of a constitutional vacuum, proposed such a bill. After it was referred to the judiciary committee, he refashioned it for the widest Senate support. In its final form, his bill provided that military commanders in the districts in rebellion could issue proclamations effective within their commands. If the civil authorities declined to cooperate, the military could use force, suspending the writ of habeas corpus for military prisoners. Persons resisting federal authority could be tried for treason or before a court martial in accordance with the rules of war governing armed bands.[36]

When his bill reached the Senate floor, Trumbull quickly encountered opposition from two quarters. First, there were the President's apologists; they regarded the President's action as better than Trumbull's substitute. Two exponents of this line of reasoning were the mild Edgar Cowan of Pennsylvania and Trumbull's own colleague, Orville H. Browning. These two claimed the President already had ample constitutional basis for his actions, and a law such as Trumbull proposed would cast a shade of illegality over Lincoln's previous moves.[37] Second, there were the senators from the border states where most of the arbitrary arrests had occurred. The bland J. S. Carlile of Virginia, partisan-tongued Willard Saulsbury of Delaware, and the renowned James A. Bayard, Jr., of Delaware, all simmered under Lincoln's arbitrary actions, and did not wish to regularize them.[38] As a result, Trumbull's bill was opposed by both of these groups; he was unable to force a vote upon it at this special session.[39]

Andrew Johnson of Tennessee, the only loyal pre-war senator from the seceded states, proposed a resolution on the origin and object of the war which declared that the federal government was waging the war to preserve the Union and that the states' rights should emerge unimpaired from the war. A conservative view, it was supported for its popular appeal even by the Republican Radicals. It appeared that only several border state senators would quibble over its wording. Such a view reckoned without Trumbull. He disliked the resolution as guaranteeing the same South that had precipitated the war. Yet he could not oppose the resolution as a whole; instead, he carped about its ambiguous phrasing. All Trumbull's attempts at modification failed without a division. So, after stating that his dislike was one of phraseology, he joined four of the border state senators in voting against it, as it passed 33 to 5.[40] The Republican Senate leadership was disgusted by Trumbull's action, since it viewed his conduct as placing the Republican party in a bad light.[41]

Both Trumbull and William Pitt Fessenden were named as Senate Regents of the Smithsonian Institute, where they continued their periodic wrangling. Trumbull remained one of the Regents of the Institute so long as he served in the Senate.[42] Early in August, Congress adjourned until

December. Trumbull had learned much from this session. Until then, his Senate service had consisted mainly in obstructing the Democratic majority, but now the work of affirmative legislation was his. Trumbull, an "againer" by nature, found the tactical switch a difficult one. In this session, in which he exhibited only grumbling support of the administration, he presaged his role for the next four years.

Perhaps the awareness that he preceded Lincoln as a national figure prevented Trumbull from ever deferring to his fellow Illinoisan. Besides, Trumbull never appreciated Lincoln's ability to play the President's role by ear; to Trumbull, such flexibility smacked of the chameleon on plaid. More perceptive than many of his Republican fellows, Trumbull realized that Lincoln had the faculty of compelling almost every man within his reach to be his tool, the more cunning the man, the sharper the tool. Instead of as a figurehead, Lincoln emerged a fountainhead of power.

As a result, Trumbull displayed a tendency to stand with the Radicals on many issues. Yet he insisted upon both the letter and the spirit of the Constitution. He was unable to work closely for long with any senator; neither did he feel any lasting attachment to any subgrouping of the Republican party. As a result, how to characterize Trumbull has been a problem to historians. Leonard P. Curry has placed him in the "Moderate bloc" as a result of his Senate voting record between 1861-1863.[43] Hans L. Trefousse labels him a "Wartime Radical Leader" in the Senate, but drops Trumbull from the list of "Postwar Radical Leaders."[44] Glenn M. Linden calls him a member of the "Unaligned Senators," after viewing the entire period 1861-1873.[45] One of Trumbull's biographers entitled his book "Conservative Radical."[46] Nothing fits. Perhaps in the end, Trumbull is best described as *sui generis*.

After the adjournment of Congress in August 1861, Trumbull rejoined his family on vacation in northwestern Connecticut. He soon found that playing croquet with members of his family and boating on a nearby lake, diversions in which he once delighted, seemed childish in a country torn by war. He read the newspapers by the hour and the news greatly upset him. General Lyon had been killed and his troops beaten at Wilson's Creek, and a large part of Missouri passed into Confederate hands.

At this, Trumbull sat down and poured out his disgust in a letter to James Doolittle. He raged that after "four months . . . [of war] we are . . . on the defensive." The practice of having the army return all runaway slaves to their owners Trumbull felt was immoral. He harped on the theme that the trouble lay with the cabinet. As he phrased it, "The truth is, Judge, there is a lack of affirmative positive action & business talent in the Cabinet. Lincoln, though a most excellent and honest man, lacks these qualities." Trumbull hoped to replace Cameron as secretary of war with a more honest and dynamic individual such as Joseph Holt. He had decided that John C. Fremont in the West and George B. McClellan in the East were the generals who had the timber of heroes.[47]

Fremont, in command at St. Louis, proved to be a bone of contention between Conservatives and Radicals. Hardly had he settled in his command than rumors of his extravagance and malfeasance filtered back to Washington. Attention was soon distracted from these tales when on August 30, he issued a controversial and far-reaching proclamation — that all persons within his command resisting United States authority were to have their property confiscated and their slaves freed. A storm erupted. Radicals hailed the move; Conservatives bemoaned it. Lincoln was instantly involved. Step by step, Lincoln had picked his way among the great pressures, now forced right and now pushed left as he faced specific problems, always moving toward a goal, the salvation of the Union. In this instance, Lincoln decided that Fremont's proclamation was too harsh, revoking it. He did this as gently as possible, because of Fremont's powerful Radical support. He retained Fremont in his command. This half-loaf measure satisfied few.[48]

Trumbull joined in the affair. Leaving Connecticut for Alton, Illinois, he pushed on across the Mississippi River to St. Louis. For a while Trumbull seemed to be everywhere, interviewing Fremont as well as the Blair adherents who had now become Fremont's avowed enemies. Trumbull wrote a carefully balanced letter to Lincoln. Although he refused to take sides between the general and the powerful Blair family, his pro-Fremont sympathies were evident to the perceptive Lincoln. Nor could Lincoln have been insensitive to the ill-concealed jeers Trumbull planted in the letter concerning the administration's war policy.[49]

What influence Trumbull's letter had upon Lincoln is debatable, but in any event Lincoln was forced to remove Fremont at the beginning of November.[50] To Trumbull and many other Radicals, Fremont remained in essence a martyr to the backstairs influence in the cabinet.[51] Before October was out, Trumbull had returned to the capital. Julia was expecting their sixth child, Henry, who was born early in January, but she loyally accompanied her husband to the capital.[52]

Trumbull found that the military stalemate had continued. Major General George B. McClellan, called to the command of the troops around Washington after his victories in West Virginia, was busy drilling his raw levies. This military inaction did not appeal to Trumbull, who demanded results. Soon, he conferred with two kindred spirits, Benjamin Wade and Zachariah Chandler. ''Bluff Ben'' Trumbull had once approvingly called Wade in a letter to Lincoln.[53] Zachariah Chandler, a craggy man with a tongue like a skinning knife — once called a ''Xantippe in pants'' by a fellow-senator — appealed to Trumbull for his unblinking Republicanism.[54] Eventually, on October 25, the three called at Postmaster

General Montgomery Blair's residence, across the street from the White House. Blair had invited Wade and Chandler to his house, and when Trumbull joined the duo, they asked him to accompany them to Blair's home. It was already ten in the evening when the senators arrived and found that Blair had another guest, George B. McClellan. McClellan could be a persuasive talker, and as the five men discussed the war, McClellan declared that he would have moved decisively if he were in supreme command. Yet, hampered by his infirm superior, Winfield Scott, he could accomplish little. McClellan suggested that Scott be retired, and he himself elevated to supreme command. Skillfully, McClellan deflected the senators' wrath from himself to Scott. Chandler, Trumbull, and Wade left that night, vowing to press for Scott's retirement. Yet the three senators had not lost their suspicions of McClellan as part of the problem.[55] The next evening, they went together to Lincoln, demanding that he order the military into action. Lincoln refused to decree any precipitous action and defended "McClellan's deliberateness."[56] The next day, Sunday, October 27, the three senators urged swift military moves upon Seward and Cameron.[57]

Thus, the senators built the anti-Scott pressure which steadily mounted until the old man resigned on October 31.[58] Despite their misgivings, the Radicals had helped make McClellan; soon they would proceed to share in his unmaking.

CHAPTER TEN

A REPUBLICAN ACHILLES

IN DECEMBER 1861, the first regular Republican-controlled congressional session began. A young Chicago *Tribune* reporter, Horace White, soon became good friends with Lyman Trumbull. To describe the senator, White availed himself of his best nineteenth-century prose: "five feet ten and one half inches in height, straight as an arrow, weighing one hundred and sixty-seven pounds, of faultless physique, in perfect health, and in manners a cultivated gentleman."[1]

A fundamental issue gripped Trumbull's attention. In the North, a serious problem of disloyalty had developed. Thousands of Southern sympathizers were willing to obstruct the Northern war effort. When the military situation warranted, many arrests of Southern sympathizers were made under the authority of the secretary of state, William H. Seward. After the immediate danger had passed, the prisoners were released with no formal charges filed against them.[2]

The general public paid little attention to this procedure. To Trumbull's legal mind, the arrests loomed as dangerous practices, contrary to the American Constitution. He was challenged to act by one of such prisoners, F. K. Howard. Reading a newspaper account of a Senate speech in which Trumbull declared that only constitutional measures should be used to suppress the rebellion, Howard wrote, daring Trumbull to correct abuses such as his own arbitrary arrest.[3] Immediately, Trumbull proposed a resolution, asking the secretary of state to justify his arbitrary arrests.[4] A debate followed. The Republican conservative wing warmly attacked Trumbull's resolution. As a group, they tended to be less sensitive to human rights but more zealous of property rights than many like Trumbull, whom they labeled "Vindictives" or "Radicals." By contrast, Trumbull reacted as a latter-day Jacksonian to the problems of the Civil War period.

Dixon of Connecticut defended Seward's action on the hard ground of military necessity. Impatiently, Trumbull asked, "What are we coming to if arrests may be made at the whim or the caprice of a cabinet minister?" Trumbull emphasized that he sought additional legislation, if it were required, so that arrests might be legally made. Trumbull deplored a Dixon statement that deprecated constitutional scruples at such a time, replying, "... in just such times as these... the foundations of tyranny... are laid...." Wilson of Massachusetts replied, "I regret... that the Senator from Illinois has introduced the resolution, and I deplore the speech he has made in its support." Republican Hale of New Hampshire, an old Free Soiler, supported Trumbull. In describing his relations with the Chief Executive he really spoke for Trumbull as well as himself: "I have been so long in the minority, I have been so long in the habit of finding considerable fault with them [the Executive branch], that I may not be sufficiently schooled in the new position in which I stand as a political friend of the President, to treat with that deference which seems to be demanded for him by some of his friends everything that he does."[5]

Lyman's and Hale's arguments were unavailing; the resolution was referred to committee by a majority of 25 to 17. Trumbull's effort was not entirely in vain; in February 1862, the administration took steps to modify the practice of arbitrary arrests. There was a wholesale release of political prisoners and control of arrests was transferred from the state to the war department.[6] In the meantime, many pressing issues arose. Lincoln's secretary of war, Simon Cameron, had now become a center of controversy. From the beginning of his tenure in the war department, Cameron had demonstrated gross unfitness for his post. Cameron had become an albatross to Lincoln. Consequently, Cameron's resignation as secretary of war was accepted on January 11, 1862. He was too politically potent to be excluded from the government, so Lincoln nominated him minister to Russia.[7]

Cameron's name then came before the Senate for approval. Normally, his ratification would have been routine, since the foreign affairs committee had unanimously agreed to his commission. The committee reported its action on January 15, and the Senate stood ready to ratify it, when, under the Senate rules, Trumbull objected. This delayed the report until the next day, allowing time for the opposition to jell.[8] Then, the Senate went into executive session to consider Cameron's nomination. Leading the opposition, Trumbull mercilessly attacked Cameron.[9] Nevertheless, though the opposition ranks were now fattened by the addition of Trumbull and five other Republicans, Cameron's nomination sailed through, 28 to 14.[10] The Senate thus conferred a certain dignity upon Cameron, but Trumbull had the last word, releasing to the press the details of the opposition to the Pennsylvanian's new appointment.[11] The explosively energetic but politically amoral War Democrat, Edwin Stanton, replaced Cameron in the war department. Trumbull hailed the appointment, seeing only Stanton's prodigious virtues and not his monumental faults.[12]

From the session's beginning, Trumbull labored to legislate further about confiscation. On December 5, he introduced a bill, and explained his proposal.[13] In the South, property would be seized by the military; in the North, Confederate holdings would be confiscated by court action. Slaves of Confederates were to be freed, and the President could colonize them, if they chose to go, in "some tropical country." Trumbull argued that his bill conformed to the Constitution by providing that any person in reach of the federal courts convicted of treason would have his personal property confiscated forever, but his real property forfeited only for life.[14] His bill was referred to the judiciary committee.[15]

Trumbull's introduction of the confiscation bill drew wild applause from Radicals.[16] Petitions favoring confiscation flowed into the Senate. Many were sent directly to Trumbull. Skillfully, Trumbull used these petitions to bludgeon judiciary committee opposition to confiscation. Meanwhile, several other senators had introduced their own confiscation measures. All were referred to the judiciary committee where Trumbull, at the controls as chairman, sidetracked all others in favor of his own proposal.[17] On January 15, Trumbull reported his bill from the judiciary committee to the full Senate.[18] With severe competition for the Senate's time, Trumbull struggled for consideration of his proposal. In January and February, Trumbull fought for his proposal, only to meet delay and evasion.[19]

Finally, by deft political footwork, Trumbull obtained Senate consideration for his confiscation bill. Then he proposed minor amendments to perfect the measure, which were accepted by the Senate. After smashing several parliamentary moves by conservatives to strangle his bill, Trumbull made an elaborate speech defending it. He emphasized the necessity for it and its constitutionality.[20]

Under a hail of fire from those to the right of the measure, the confiscation bill was now attacked from the left by "Subsidy Sam" Pomeroy of Kansas, who grumbled that it did not free all slaves, and that he disapproved of the colonization of freed slaves abroad.[21] Senate sentiment had solidified. There were three groups. First, there were the Radical Republicans, passionately in favor of the hard-knuckled Trumbull measure. Although some of them desired a stronger bill than Trumbull proposed, they closed ranks behind it. Second, there were the moderate Republicans who desired the mildest possible bill. Lastly, there were the Democrats and Conservatives who adamantly opposed any such legislation. A quick nose-count revealed to Trumbull that the first group was a distinct minority. Thus if his bill were to pass he had to gain moderate support; he sought that by offering only minimum concessions.

After much effort, Trumbull obtained the floor for the consideration of his bill.[22] Browning attacked Trumbull's proposal as being flagrantly harsh toward the South. Like most Conservatives, Browning trusted Lincoln to perform confiscation on his own authority, since he had displayed a merciful course toward the South.[23] Behind the scenes, moderate Republicans campaigned to have the party caucus pick an ad hoc special committee to frame a compromise confiscation bill. Torn by conflicting opinions, the caucus met several times without action. At length, Browning, Collamer of Vermont, and Cowan of Pennsylvania, all ebullient evangelists of conservatism, forced a vote upon a special committee. The Radicals won a pyrrhic victory by the margin of 10 to 11. The caucus, despite protests, continued debate upon the special committee.[24] Also, the White House took a stand against a strong confiscation bill. Lincoln showed that he disapproved of the measure. He had adopted a cautious policy toward slavery because of conservative Northern opinion. Heartened confiscation opponents now wrapped themselves in the mantle of administration supporters.[25]

Trumbull permitted the confiscation bill to be put aside for several weeks while he labored in the cloakrooms to recruit fresh support for it. On April 7, he again called up the bill. Lyman proposed an amalgam of minor amendments to meet known objections. Then he defended his measure. He denied that his proposal called for "wholesale" confiscation in the South, since it would not reach "one in ten." His bill, he pleaded, was prospective; any Southerner could save his property by returning to his federal allegiance. Trumbull declared that leaving confiscation to the President's discretion without any limitation of law, as some Conservatives advocated, was more extreme than his solution.[26] By now, Trumbull had won over every Republican Radical to a wholehearted support of the bill, except for truculent Charles Sumner.[27] Still, it was not enough. Trumbull's confiscation bill remained stalled;[28] the principal device used to frustrate Trumbull's efforts was taking the Senate into executive session.[29]

At last, Trumbull forced the confiscation bill's consideration upon the Senate floor. It proved an empty victory, as John Sherman, who had proposed a softening amendment, spent the rest of the day's session declaiming his suggestion's merits.[30] The next day, the confiscation bill retained the floor only to find a tenacious opponent, Jacob Collamer. He expressed dislike of *in rem* proceedings, a key feature of the Trumbull bill, against Confederate property. Collamer proposed many softening clauses. His substitute won approval from Sherman, and the Ohioan withdrew all of his amendment, except for a clause limiting confiscation to five enumerated classes.[31]

Trumbull leaped into the fray. He demonstrated that Sherman's amendment both limited and broadened the bill. While the total number affected by the bill had diminished, a new class previously exempt from the bill — those personally in reach of the federal courts — had been added. Thereupon, Trumbull called Sherman's proposal unconstitutional.[32] But the Senate adopted Sherman's proposal, 26 to 4. Trumbull, undeterred, stubbornly voted *No*.[33] Emboldened, moderate Republicans demanded the appointment of a select committee to frame a compromise confiscation measure.[34] On April 30, a motion to refer the politically-fused confiscation bill to a select committee of seven narrowly failed. The shadows lengthened over the Trumbull bill.[35]

On May 2, Trumbull addressed the Senate, complaining that the bill's alleged friends were helping its foes to talk it to death. As an example, he cited Fessenden. The Maine senator asked how Trumbull knew he was an insincere friend of confiscation? Trumbull thereupon recited Fessenden's voting record, winning the argument, but not Fessenden's vote.[36] On May 6, the Conservative and moderate senators corralled sufficient strength to move that a select committee consider the Trumbull bill, together with eleven pending amendments.[37] Since several supporters of his bill now favored the select committee arrangement to write a compromise measure, Trumbull announced that he would fight the move no longer. He said, "I hope that we may be able, notwithstanding the reference of these measures to a committee, to pass a bill that will have some life . . . in it. . . . "[38] Yet, when Clark's motion passed 24 to 14, Trumbull and a hard core of Radicals voted against it.[39]

A select committee of nine, headed by Clark, was then appointed by the chair. Trumbull had been named to the committee, but he adamantly refused to serve.[40] A week later, the select committee reported a compromise measure, very much weaker than the original Trumbull proposal.[41] Twenty years later, Trumbull still regarded it as "a mere apology for a bill . . . never meant by anybody to be of practical effect."[42] Trumbull resolved to amend the proposal into something "better," by offering sweeping amendments. He claimed that the bill was unconstitutional, pointing out that it ran afoul of the constitutional provision that forfeiture of real property could not extend beyond a traitor's life. In his own bill, he pridefully observed, he had avoided this snare.

The first section of the committee bill provided that a traitor adjudged guilty could be hanged and have his slaves freed, or could instead receive at least five years imprisonment and a fine of not less than $10,000, having his slaves made free. Trumbull called this puzzling, since slaves were mentioned twice. Lyman said, "It would seem on the principle that seems advocated by some Senators, as property is more valuable than life, that he will probably elect to be hung and save his land."[43]

Trumbull proposed that the first section of the bill be stricken, since the second section already provided that all rebels could have their property confiscated.[44] He collected few votes for his proposal.[45] As a result of Trumbull's tireless probing of the weak spots in the committee bill, the irascible Fessenden contended that Trumbull really wished to force a fresh start. Trumbull sat silent, acknowledging the veracity of the Maine solon's charges.[46] When the next day Clark lashed him for his relentless scolding, Trumbull responded that for months it had been the foes of a strong confiscation bill who had pursued delaying tactics.[47] Clark claimed that every shade of opinion had yielded ground in the name of party unity; the result was the committee bill.[48]

Adherents of a stringent confiscation bill decided to stall the Senate bill until the House could send its harsher measure to the upper chamber. Trumbull, however, refused to endorse this strategy.[49] Vainly, Trumbull fought to keep the Senate bill from being lost in the tangled legislative underbrush.[50] Meanwhile, the House approved a far-reaching confiscation bill, 82 to 68.[51] The confiscation issue languished until late June, when the House measure was considered by the Senate. Clark suggested the Senate bill as a substitute.[52] However, the Senate tried to ignore the issue.[53] After vigorous behind-the-scenes maneuvering by senators as far apart as Trumbull and Clark, the House confiscation bill gained the Senate floor. Trumbull had become an ardent supporter of the latter measure; therefore, he opposed weakening amendments as a gateway to still others which could cripple the House bill.[54]

Discussing Clark's move to substitute the bland Senate confiscation measure for the more severe House bill, Trumbull charged that the maneuver could be accomplished only by a coalition of moderate Republicans, Democrats, and border state Conservatives. When this move was accomplished, the latter two groups would oppose the bill on final passage. In an analysis of the Senate bill, Trumbull demonstrated that the property of state officers of the Confederacy could be confiscated, but not that held by the Confederate government itself. Moreover, certain civil officers of the Confederacy were liable to have their property confiscated, whereas military officers would get off scot-free.

Defending the controversial proposal that blacks should be used as Union soldiers, Trumbull cried, "Sir, no traitor shall come and murder my child or my brother or any soldier of my State or my country, . . . with my consent. If there is a negro or anybody else in God's world that has got an arm to strike him down, I will say 'strike.' " Trumbull went on to attack moderates who opposed confiscation as unconstitutional, but would accept the notion that the President's war powers allowed him to appoint military governors for the South.[55] Dixon then declaimed, "The Senator from Illinois has, at last, unmasked himself as an opponent of this Administration." Hotly, Trumbull retorted that he was not a "sychophant" to praise every presidential move, but that he felt Lincoln fully realized his own fallibility. Trumbull added, "He [Lincoln] is a believer in the intelligence of the people, and knowing his own fallibility, is not above listening to their voice."

Several of Trumbull's friends became disturbed that he had allowed himself to utter anti-Lincoln statements. Therefore, to give Trumbull a chance to realize the enormity of the pit into which he had fallen, Hale of New Hampshire interrupted on a point of order to claim that Harlan of

Iowa, who sat rifling through a newspaper, was violating the Senate rules. After Harlan had put away his paper in response to the warning of the chair and the debate had resumed, Trumbull backed down from the awkward position he had assumed. The more he thought of his previous remarks, the more disconcerted he became. After an awkward silence, Trumbull uttered a final word, deploring that Lincoln's name had ever entered into the debate.[56] Trumbull had feared that the anti-Lincoln label fastened upon him by Dixon would seriously undercut his position within the Illinois Republican party. His fears proved groundless; the Republican press followed the lead of the party bellwether, the *Illinois State Journal*, which, in its report of the debate, studiously ignored Trumbull's intraparty joust with Dixon.[57]

On June 28, the Senate came to grips with the confiscation bill while sitting as a committee of the whole. At that time, the Senate substituted its own bill for the House version by the narrow margin of 21 to 18; Trumbull stubbornly voted *No*.[58]

Trumbull refused to accept this defeat as final, since the formality of a vote by the Senate as such remained. Fighting for a strong confiscation proposal, he turned both to the House confiscation measure and a separate House emancipation bill freeing the slaves of rebels. Trumbull thought the House emancipation bill of crucial importance, since it furnished machinery freeing the slaves which both the Senate and the House confiscation bills lacked. To obtain the best features of both House bills, Trumbull moved to strike out everything after the introductory wording of the Senate confiscation bill and substitute the House emancipation bill. Then, he proposed to graft the resulting measure upon the House confiscation bill.[59] His proposal drew so little support that he did not press a vote. Instead, with an air of reasonableness, he offered to settle for the House emancipation measure grafted upon the Senate confiscation bill.[60] But Trumbull found the climate in the Senate Chamber unrelievedly hostile, and he withdrew his entire scheme. Then, the Senate speedily ratified its actions as the committee of the whole; the vote was a close 19 to 17, with Trumbull doggedly voting *No*. On the final passage of the bill, he reluctantly supported it with his vote as better than no legislation at all. The measure glided through the Senate, 28 to 13.[61]

However, the House rejected the Senate action, and a deadlock ensued. The days of the session were growing short when the Senate considered a way out of the impasse. Clark suggested that the Senate repass its own version of the bill as a substitute for the House measure, and then ask for a conference committee. Trumbull vociferously argued to have the Senate pass the House measure. Then the Senate shouted through Clark's motion in a voice vote.[62]

A conference committee composed of moderates was chosen to represent the Senate in the crucial haggling with House members.[63] On July 12,

Clark reported an agreement which accepted the Senate bill with modifications. The traditionally greater influence of the Conservative Senate had beaten the Radically-controlled House. In the second section of the Senate bill, which dealt with the punishment for treason, Clark reported an amendment omitting the forfeiture of property and instead, as a penalty, a fine not to exceed ten thousand dollars. The fifth through ninth sections of the Senate bill dealing with confiscation of property and freedom of the slaves were stricken and reworded sections were submitted. Routinely, the Senate agreed to the report.[64] The final bill differed from Trumbull's original proposal in several vital ways. It provided new and lighter penalties for treason; it proposed confiscation for only limited classes of Confederate leaders instead of all disloyal Southerners; ordinary Confederates fell under the ban of confiscation only if they continued fighting sixty days beyond formal notice; it sanctioned the arming of freed blacks as Union soldiers; and it provided that the President could extend pardon and amnesty to rebels by proclamation.

The "perfected" bill did resemble Trumbull's proposal in several respects. Despite the congressional oratory concerning the brutality of *in rem* proceedings, the compromise bill provided for them. Another Trumbull suggestion that found its way into the final draft provided that cases of forfeiture should not begin as ordinary suits with an indictment, but with a libel of information as in revenue and admiralty cases. The sections of the compromise bill dealing with the freedom of slaves of rebel masters and their possible colonization in some "tropical country" were close to Trumbull's original phraseology. Yet, the final draft of the bill was a wheezy patchwork of legislation. It is true, that while Trumbull's bill had been clearer on the vital provision of freeing slaves of rebel masters, his original wording in other respects was only a slight improvement over the final version. The congressmen, Trumbull included, envisioned the freeing of Southern slaves by the advancing federal army and were hazy as to the part federal courts were to play. In the last analysis, the lack of success which the bill as law enjoyed was due not so much to its muddy phraseology (it was finally drafted by congressmen interested in only nominal legislation on the confiscation question), but to the hostile attitude displayed toward it by the officers of the executive branch from Attorney General Edward Bates down.[65]

Yet, the supporters of even watered-down confiscation found no clear sailing. Lincoln had viewed the confiscation progress through Congress with grave misgivings. Discussing confiscation, he once wrote, "The severest justice may not always be the best policy."[66] Also, Lincoln had constitutional scruples about the bill which violated the constitutional prohibition against forfeiture beyond the life of a traitor. A presidential veto now hung over the confiscation bill. The leaders of Congress were concerned. To override the President on this issue would mean grievous scars on the body of the Republican party. At this juncture, William P. Fessenden was sent out by several congressional leaders to spy out the presidential mood. Calling upon Lincoln, he ascertained that the President would not veto the bill if two changes were made in it: First, that the penalty of confiscation of slaves be completely prospective; second, that there be no forfeiture of real property beyond the life of an offender.[67]

Lincoln's minimum demands posed grave problems. There was no time to rework the bill. What saved the confiscation bill was a rare deal between the President and congressional leaders. To prevent a presidential veto, a resolution had already passed the House of Representative stating that the confiscation act should not be construed to be retroactive nor to extend to state officers who did not take an oath of loyalty to the Confederate constitution. When the resolution was considered in the Senate, Clark moved to bring the House resolution into complete conformity with Lincoln's conditions by adding that the act was not to be construed as forfeiting real property beyond the life of an offender.[68]

Trumbull objected to Clark's amendment, citing the case of former Senator John Slidell of Louisiana who was reported to hold 40,000 acres of Illinois land. If this holding were confiscated under the act as interpreted by the amended resolution, a life estate would bring the government nothing.[69] Fessenden's mission had been a secret from the Radicals. In the debate, the question was raised as to which senator had consulted the President in regard to this bill. At length, Fessenden admitted that it was he. Reacting to Fessenden's statement, Trumbull blurted out that the President was not part of the legislative process except in his possession of the veto power, and hence, his opinions should not guide legislation through Congress.[70]

But, Trumbull soon found that the rebellion against Lincoln's dicta had more lung power than vote power, and that Clark's amendment would pass. Therefore, he proposed an amendment to Clark's amendment which provided: When any persons were tried for treason personally, any forfeitures of real property would be for life estate only; in the case of *in rem* proceedings, the court could decide whether or not to accept this limitation. Clark objected; Trumbull's amendment was shouted down. Clark's amendment then sailed through by a vote of 25 to 15, Trumbull voting *No*.[71]

When the House had concurred in Clark's amendment, the resolution was rushed to the President. After grave soul-searching, Lincoln signed the measure, with the explanation that he regarded the bill and the explanatory resolution as "substantially one."[72] Disturbed by the measure, Lincoln sent his intended veto message to Congress. In it, Lincoln declared that parts of the confiscation bill inconsistent with the explanatory resolution had no validity.[73]

Despite the party-splintering ordeal of passing the confiscation bill, because of badly drafted phrasing and executive indifference, it gathered more dust than dollars for the Union cause. Best estimates place the total amount realized at $300,000. The emancipation features of the act were futile, as no machinery for the freeing of slaves by the courts had been provided.[74] Its service to emancipation was confined to placing Congress on record in its favor and preparing Northern public opinion to accept later emancipation moves.

Trumbull fretted that spring as McClellan finally led his hosts of blue-clad troops against Richmond in the Peninsular campaign. This maneuver, so promising in its conception, was brought to a frustrating stalemate by summer because of the brilliant tactics of Lee and Jackson, the timidity of the high administration's officials in Washington who withheld promised reinforcements, and McClellan's own dilatory moves. As a result, in the sticky July heat, Trumbull attacked the military appropriation bill. He argued that there should be a ceiling of 750,000 men in the Union army, because more men could not be profitably employed and would be only a burden upon the treasury.[75]

Nor was this all. Trumbull and Chandler often discussed the inglorious end of the Peninsular campaign, and they finally decided that it required some public airing. Chandler introduced a resolution asking for the campaign's official papers.[76] To drum up support for Chandler's resolution, Trumbull spoke at length. He marvelled at McClellan's inactivity in the winter of 1861 and spring of 1862. With the advantage of hindsight, Trumbull blistered the general's inept handling of his troops.[77] As a result, Chandler and he rammed through the resolution, 34 to 6, since even Lincoln's staunchest defenders could not defend this Northern military fiasco.[78]

At this time Trumbull favored a number of bills striking at black slavery. He supported a bill abolishing slavery in the District of Columbia, with nominal compensation to the owners.[79] Later in the session, he backed a supplemental bill freeing slaves of District of Columbia residents, regardless of where the slaves worked. He favored a Sumner-backed amendment allowing blacks to testify in any federal court. The amended bill passed.[80] Trumbull also fought for a House bill which enacted an article of war forbidding use of the Union army to return runaway slaves.[81]

Trumbull joined Senate Republicans in pushing through a proposal abolishing slavery in the territories.[82] This measure, once the crowning ambition of the Republican party, became law on June 19. It was significant in that slavery was abolished there without compensation to the owners. Trumbull ardently backed a bill implementing a treaty with Great Britain for the effective suppression of the foreign slave trade. Hitherto-fore, Southern opposition had blocked American cooperation in an effective patrol of the African slave trade.[83] Also, Trumbull successfully supported several bills to translate the Republican platform into actuality. Among these were the homestead bill,[84] a proposal to set up land grant agricultural colleges,[85] and the Pacific railroad bill.[86]

In the last days of the session, Trumbull tried anew to regularize the state prisoners' arrests. When the House passed a bill for the orderly discharge of state prisoners, and authorizing federal judges to accept bail, Trumbull secured favorable consideration for it in the Senate judiciary committee. The House bill met a cool response in the Senate. Many senators favored some legislation on the subject, but they disliked seeming to correct the previous practice of the Lincoln administration. So a small group of senators, led by Henry Wilson, staved off a vote on the measure by one indirection after another.[87]

Not for a moment during the session had Trumbull forgotten the necessity of winning the support of the Illinois Republican party to his stand as opposed to that of the conservative Browning. Trumbull franked a torrent of printed speeches to his constituents, explaining and defending his stands upon confiscation and a vigorous war policy.[88] His supporters were numerous and active on the grass-roots level.[89] Men who had been receiving favors from Trumbull for years sprang into action, as Trumbull cashed his checks of political support. Most Republican newspaper editors, the recipients of free documents for years, unhesitatingly lined up behind Trumbull. By mid-summer of 1862, the mass of the Illinois Republican party marched behind Trumbull's standard.[90]

The Illinois Radical Republicans planned, should they retain control of the legislature, to drop Browning as their senatorial candidate and to replace him with Governor Yates. Since Browning was an interim appointment, his successor for the remainder of Douglas' term would be chosen by the legislature.[91]

In most Northern states, the political map showed enough roadblocks for the Republicans that the party's congressmen met in a secret caucus in the last week of the session to plan campaign strategy. Then the deep fissures within the party on the issues of the war and slavery were starkly revealed: an address already prepared by a select committee was rejected as too specific in its wording; in its stead, only a general resolution was adopted, calling upon all citizens to sustain the Union and support a vigorous prosecution of the war.[92]

Upon the adjournment of Congress, Trumbull served this warning upon Lincoln and his cabinet: "Give the country proof that you are in earnest and you can raise one hundred thousand soldiers in Illinois alone; adhere to the present peace policy and you get none at all." Lincoln and the cabinet were conciliatory to the irate senator, and Horace White reported that "the result of the conference was such as to give Mr. Trumbull considerable encouragement."[93]

Still, Trumbull did not rush back to Illinois, but spent five weeks with his family at his Connecticut summer retreat. Finally, in response to urgent messages from the Illinois Republican leaders, he returned to Springfield. He immediately went into an all-day conference with Governor Yates. Republican prospects in Illinois had further deteriorated since early in summer when the party had barely defeated a Democratic-written state constitution. McClellan's replacement by John Pope as the principal commander in the East had brought no victories to the Union standard. War weariness had set in, and the Republicans feared a grim harvest of voter resentment. The Democrats were energetically in the field, led by colorful William Richardson, formerly Douglas' first lieutenant, now campaigning hard, with his eyes fixed upon Browning's place in the Senate.[94]

The dismal outlook and party divisions paralyzed the top Illinois Republican leadership. The state committee had made no arrangements for a convention, fearing the diverse elements of the party might publicly fly apart. Even the Chicago *Tribune* displayed signs of confusion and uncertainty. Editor Joseph Medill, whom legend would claim had once told Abraham Lincoln in his pre-presidential days, "Take your goddam feet off my desk, Abe!" could only complain that "old fogies" had taken over the party.[95] Trumbull avoided stumping Illinois in behalf of the Republican cause, since he refused to defend administration policies. Events cheered Trumbull in September. McClellan, restored to command after General Pope's debacle at the Second Battle of Bull Run, won a small victory after the mighty battle at Antietam. Lincoln felt sufficiently encouraged to issue his Preliminary Emancipation Proclamation on September 22, 1862. In a prediction that was to haunt him for months, Trumbull optimistically hailed it as harbinger of a future tough war policy.[96]

On the heels of Lincoln's Proclamation, the belated Illinois Republican state convention met at Springfield on September 24-25. The Radicals were heartened by Lincoln's action, while the Conservatives felt correspondingly downcast. Control of the convention was only listlessly contested by the Browning faction, and the Trumbull men won.[97] The convention tried to restore party unity; Yates was praised as governor, but the convention discreetly avoided commending either senator.[98] The Browning faction refused all peace overtures, sulking angrily. Indeed, Browning refused to campaign for the party after the issuance of the Emancipation Proclamation.[99] With the fued between the Illinois Radicals and Conservatives, Trumbull realized that victory there seemed remote. Consequently, he campaigned in Michigan to ensure the return of Zachariah Chandler to the Senate.[100] With both Browning and Trumbull absent from the stump, the candidates themselves carried the burden of the campaigning in Illinois.[101]

Trumbull did feed "public documents" to the Illinois Republican press,[102] avoiding any personal appearances until after his foray into Michigan. Only in late October, after the campaign had turned into the homestretch, did Trumbull yield to the entreaty of his old Belleville friends and address a party rally there. Never since his return to active politics in 1854 had he appeared so little before the Illinois voters. At Belleville, he ripped the Democrats as the party of the faint-hearted and called for the election of Republican candidates. The local Republicans felt rekindled enthusiasm, and they effusively thanked Trumbull for his effort.[103] When the hum of politicking had faded, the people cast their ballots; the result: a near disaster for the Republicans. In the House of Representatives, the number of Democrats almost doubled. Although New England stood firmly in the Republican camp, and the party recorded some gains in California, it was in the border states where federal bayonets supplied an unsubtle pressure that the Republicans gained their thin margin of control — about eighteen House seats. New York, Pennsylvania, Ohio, Indiana and Illinois — all Lincoln states in 1860 — sent Democratically-dominated congressional delegations to Washington. Leonard Swett, running in Lincoln's home congressional district, was beaten by a Democrat. Although the Senate's composition was not greatly altered by the Republican debacle, the general result of the election was an undisguised rebuke to Republicans and the Lincoln administration.[104]

Trumbull had his own view of the root cause of the Republican defeat. He wrote Chandler, who had been re-elected in Michigan despite a heavy Democratic tide, "In this state [Illinois] we are used up horse, foot & dragoons. Hundreds of Republicans who believed that their sons & relatives were being sacrificed to the incompetency, indisposition or treason of pro-slavery Democratic generals were unwilling to sustain an Administration which allowed this." Trumbull added, "I felt myself when in Mich. and all during the canvass, that [it] was an uphill business to attempt to sustain the Administration, & nothing but the belief that to suffer the government to go into the hands of the Democracy would be worse enabled me to do it at all."

Of the loss of the Illinois legislature to the Democrats, Trumbull inquired, "Do you think it will be any loss to exchange Browning for a Respectable Democrat?" In his opinion "a political revolution" had occurred in the North, and the country's future looked dark and forbidding.[105]

CHAPTER ELEVEN

CONSTITUTIONAL ISSUES

FOLLOWING THE FALL ELECTIONS, Lyman, accompanied by Julia, her younger sister, Ellen, and the young Trumbulls, returned to Washington.[1] Anxiously, he searched for a change in administration policy because of the 1862 congressional vote. He saw none. While Lincoln had shortly after the election dropped McClellan as a commander of the Army of the Potomac, he replaced him with the unstable Ambrose E. Burnside. Watching Burnside's uneven bursts of energy, Trumbull felt the bright promise of victory quickly tarnish.

Trumbull, wanting to see how Lincoln was taking the electoral reverses, spent an hour with the busy President. Aides came and went; secretaries poked their heads into Lincoln's study with news, and callers burst in unannounced. As a result, Trumbull could not wring a commitment from Lincoln for more drastic action. Lincoln, an adroit manipulator of men, skillfully used his office's confusion to put off Trumbull. Trumbull reported to a correspondent, saying, "Mr. Lincoln's intentions . . . have always been right, he has lacked the *will* to carry them out — I think he means to act with more vigor hereafter, but whether he will be able to do so as at present surrounded is perhaps doubtful —"[2]

"At present surrounded" meant Conservative Postmaster General Montgomery Blair, opinionated Edward Bates, the Attorney General, but most of all, bland Secretary of State William Seward. Trumbull long had disliked Seward's claims to party leadership.[3] The New Yorker's course during the winter of 1860-1861 caused Trumbull to regard him as a "milk and water Republican."[4] Finally, Seward's opposition to a confiscation bill had destroyed whatever respect he still had in Trumbull's eyes.[5] To Trumbull, Seward and his fellow cabinet Conservatives were a brake against effective action by Lincoln. The Union defeat at Fredericksburg, in December 1862, fired Trumbull and the Radical senators to action against Seward. Seward had carelessly included a private letter in a published volume of official correspondence which he had written to C. F. Adams, the American minister to Great Britain. In this letter, Seward indiscreetly had likened abolitionists and pro-slavery zealots as both possessing a desire to overthrow the republic to attain their ends.[6]

Chase and Stanton skillfully fed Radical discontent by their well-timed comments upon Lincoln's cabinet meetings. Consequently a murmur arose in Congress that the cabinet Radical element must be strengthened. Three days after the disaster at Fredericksburg, Trumbull spoke first at a senatorial caucus he had engineered. He told the senators that they must heed the public clamor for results, and he "assail[ed] the administration very bitterly." Grimes offered a resolution, declaring a "want of confidence" in Seward. Trumbull urged an immediate vote upon the resolution, but a motion to adjourn cut him short.[7]

The next day, the senatorial caucus reconvened. Several violent Radicals voiced support for a resolution demanding Lincoln's resignation.[8] Sumner then "moved that a Committee . . . be appointed to call on the President and represent to him the necessity of a change in men and measures." The resolution drew unanimous support, except for Preston King of New York, Seward's close friend. A committee of nine was speedily selected. The chairman, Jacob Collamer of Vermont, and Harris of New York, were Conservatives; but the other seven were then Radicals — Wade, Sumner, Grimes, Fessenden, Pomeroy, Howard, and Trumbull.[9] Meanwhile, Preston King rushed out of the capitol, hurrying to Seward. After hearing the breathless King, Seward concluded that the pressure was too great to be resisted; he and his son, Frederick, the Assistant Secretary of State, both penned resignation letters and placed them in Lincoln's hands that very evening.[10] The senatorial committee and Lincoln met at seven the next evening at the White House. Collamer summarized the senatorial charges against Seward in a lengthy document. It declared that only supporters of the war's vigorous prosecution should be allowed in the cabinet. Fessenden concurred, making specific mention of Seward. Other senators muttered their assent. Lincoln was too astute to argue with the committee; instead, he listened to their wordy three-hour lecture. Then Lincoln dismissed them, saying that they would meet the next evening.[11]

When the senatorial committee called again at the White House, they found Lincoln, with all the cabinet except Seward. The surprised senators were thus confronted with the cabinet. The squirming Chase would have to make the same statements about Seward publicly that he had leaked privately to the committee. Adroitly, Lincoln read Collamer's memorandum of the previous meeting. He then claimed that there was unity in the cabinet, and that decisions, once made, were loyally executed. Then, Lincoln turned to his cabinet members for concurrence, calling first upon Chase. Chase became confused, irritated, and angry in quick turn. After his lion-like complaints, he now uttered only lamb-like utterances, not substantiating senatorial charges.

With Chase backing water, the senatorial committee grew uncertain. Only Grimes, Sumner and Trumbull stuck grimly to their guns, arraigning Seward "sharply."[12] After four hours of discussion, the "meeting broke up in a milder spirit."[13] Lincoln's superb handling had thrown the senators off balance. As they were leaving, Trumbull, who appreciated keenly the sorry figure the committee had cut, returned for a private word with Lincoln. He told the President "with great vehemence" that Chase had sung "a very different tune" previously.[14] Chase never again stood so high with Trumbull. The meeting redounded to Lincoln's advantage. Badgered by his conscience, Chase also tendered his resignation; this placed the last card in Lincoln's hands. With both Seward's and Chase's resignations in his possession, he gracefully declined both.[15]

Then, in mid-session, Browning was replaced by William A. Richardson. Richardson, Douglas' former lieutenant, was the choice of the Democratically-controlled Illinois legislature to finish the Little Giant's term.[16] Trumbull and his new Democratic colleague were soon at swords' points. Richardson, in the Douglas tradition, never minced words. His favorite taunt was the charge that while the Illinois Democrats were out fighting the war, the Republicans of that state were fighting among themselves. Trumbull threw a counter-jab, claiming that four-fifths of the Illinois troops were Republicans.[17]

In this session, Trumbull interested himself in reconstruction. He favored a bill to establish provisional governments in the captured states of the Confederacy. Nevertheless, he never could push the bill to a vote.[18] Then Trumbull tried to pass a more modest measure providing for the election of congressional representatives from Tennessee and Louisiana, where Lincoln governments had been established. Despite the rush of last-minute bills, Trumbull maneuvered to bring the measure to the floor, but the obstructionist tactics of Garrett Davis of Kentucky, acting for the border state senators, prevented a vote before final adjournment.[19] In view of the general censure which Radical efforts to obstruct Lincoln's reconstruction plans have incurred by historians, it is interesting that at this time his policy's more bitter opposition came from the border state Conservatives, who found Lincoln's bland reconstruction recipe still too harsh for their political palates.

Early in the session Willard Saulsbury, once dubbed by a reporter as the "most handsome Senator when sober," had questioned the legality of the arrests of state prisoners. Saulsbury mercilessly criticized the Republicans as faithless guardians of civil rights. Trumbull replied that the remedy for Saulsbury's complaints could be found in House bill No. 591, which regularized the suspension of the privilege of habeas corpus.[20] The House had passed this bill at the last session, and Trumbull decided to use it for the necessary reforms. Trumbull, in the judiciary committee, had rewritten the measure, striking the second provision of the bill which allowed the

President alone to suspend the writ of habeas corpus. Also, he had provided that civil suits involving such federal officers should be tried in federal not state courts.[21] This was as far as Trumbull wished to go, although Harris of New York wanted to extend the immunity to criminal suits as well. Trumbull labeled this move unconstitutional, but the Senate agreed with Harris and approved its addition to the bill.[22]

The Senate continued the debate. Sherman proposed an amendment that no civilian could be imprisoned longer than two days without formal charges placed against him. This amendment seemed to have passed the Senate by the tight margin of 21 to 19 when Trumbull bobbed up to say, "Although I sympathize with the object of this amendment, I think it will embarrass the passage of this bill. I will therefore change my vote and vote 'nay.' " The amendment then failed on a tie vote.[23] Because the amendment had been defeated in the committee of the whole, it was raised anew in the formal Senate. After it had been amended by Wilson to allow a maximum of thirty days imprisonment, it was accepted over Trumbull's violent objections. The bill passed the Senate, 33 to 7, Trumbull voting *Yes*.[24] This bill, as passed by the Senate and sent back to the House for its concurrence, had *not* provided for a discharge of current state prisoners; therefore, the House approved a new bill providing for their immediate release.

In the Senate, this bill became extremely controversial. Trumbull penned a substitute to replace this measure and also the bill previously passed by the Senate concerning state prisoners. Trumbull felt that the latter bill would never be accepted by the House with the Senate changes. His proposals included: first, that Congress extend to the President the power to suspend habeas corpus during the rebellion; second, a procedure whereby federal officers could resist the discharge of their prisoners under habeas corpus; third, a provision that the secretaries of state and war, under whose direction the arrests would be made, must furnish federal judges with a list of state prisoners, and, if these prisoners were not indicted by the next grand jury session held in their district, they could be freed by the judge upon taking an oath of allegiance and furnishing bond for good behavior. In the event that cabinet officers had failed to include the name of a prisoner on the list, this fact could be called to the judge's attention by any petitioner, and the judge could immediately discharge that prisoner.[25]

Trumbull skillfully guided his substitute bill past those senators who did not wish Lincoln hampered in his practice of state arrests and other senators who opposed arbitrary arrests of any duration.[26] The bill was adopted in place of the House measure, 25 to 12, and passed, 24 to 13.[27] Meanwhile, the lower house had rejected the Senate changes in the previous immunity bill. Since the session was coming to an end, the Senate appointed a conference committee headed by Trumbull to bridge its differences with the House.[28] In the conference committee, it was suggested — just who made the suggestion was later hotly disputed — that the group not only reconcile differences in the immunity bill, but also include in the package Trumbull's substitute bill suspending the writ of habeas corpus, which was then dangling precariously between the two Houses. A wholly new bill emerged, blending features of both the immunity and habeas corpus bills. The result was new legislation by the conference committee, a procedure Trumbull had long attacked. Yet, the opportunity to obtain this legislation overshadowed in Trumbull's mind the chance to indulge himself in total rightmindedness.[29]

Ironically, Trumbull himself, on March 2, made the conference report to the Senate. That body noted approvingly that the first section of the bill closely followed the ambiguous wording which Trumbull had written into his substitute habeas corpus bill, previously approved by the Senate. This artful wording allowed supporters of the President to argue that his power to suspend habeas corpus had been recognized by Congress; conversely, supporters of the legislature's right to suspend could claim a grant to the President of that power.[30]

Trumbull clamored for action, but the Senate studied the bill. Importuned by both sides for delay, Trumbull reluctantly agreed to postpone the measure until seven that evening.[31] When that hour arrived, the Senate was passing private bills and only reluctantly abandoned this politically profitable pastime.[32] Lazarus Powell of Kentucky led the opposition in debate. It soon appeared that while the stalling tactics of the opposition might not be dubbed a filibuster, they had the same effect. The drowsy hours of talk droned on past midnight. The opponents of the bill, in attempts to consume time and hoping to catch Trumbull napping, moved again and again for adjournment. Each time Trumbull rallied his weary supporters, defeating the maneuver.[33] Finally, at about five in the morning, there was a period of confusion, and, for just an instant, no one claimed the floor. ''Subsidy Sam'' Pomeroy of Kansas, who was presiding in the chair, quickly chanted, ''The question is on concurring in the report of the committee of conference. Those in favor of concurring in this report will say 'aye'; and those opposed 'no.' The ayes have it, . . . the report is concurred in.''[34]

Immediately upon the completion of Pomeroy's singsong chant passing the bill, Trumbull leaped to his feet and, clutching at a random paper on his desk, asked to discuss a bill dealing with the ''deeds of public squares and lots in the city of Washington.''[35] Only then did the opposition realize the trick. Pink with rage, Powell demanded to know what had happened to the immunity bill. With a patient smile Grimes told him that the bill had just passed. Spluttering, Powell loudly called for the ayes and nays, only to be told that Trumbull had the floor on another matter. Then the Senate adjourned.[36]

The best the opposition could manage the next day was to win an agreement that a vote should be allowed upon a motion to reconsider, so that opponents of the bill might record their names. Predictably, the motion to reconsider failed, 13 to 25.[37] The House overcame a filibuster to pass the bill, 99 to 44,[38] and Lincoln promptly signed the measure into law.

The section of the bill providing for the discharge by the judiciary of prisoners held without charges proved in practice a dismal failure. Federal officers seldom furnished the necessary lists, and when arrested persons were released, it was not by the action of judges, but by war department officials.[39] The immunity sections of the bill were also unsuccessful. The bill's fifth section, permitting a case involving federal officers decided in a state court to be retried in federal courts, was declared unconstitutional in 1869.[40]

The resulting patchwork was commonly called the Trumbull bill,[41] despite the contributions of others. In reconstruction days, the bill proved embarrassing to Trumbull, since it was used by the Supreme Court to free a Conferedate sympathizer, Lambdin P. Milligan.[42]

In 1863, Trumbull moved from Alton to Chicago.[43] There were several reasons for his action. Alton had not lived up to its early promise. With the coming of the railroad, Chicago had become one of the foremost cities in the nation. Alton's legal business had become much smaller than that of burgeoning Chicago. Overshadowing other considerations was a political motive. Since the death of Douglas, no Chicago resident had represented Illinois in the Senate. If the Republicans were successful, Richardson's seat would pass in 1865 to Governor Richard Yates, also a downstater. As a result, in 1867 there might emerge a clamor that Trumbull be supplanted by a Chicagoan.[44] But now Trumbull could at the time of his re-election be considered a Chicagoan.[45]

After his permanent move to Chicago had been delayed by the illness of his younger sons,[46] Trumbull left for Chicago, where he had overdue legal business. While Trumbull was still there, in early June, a storm erupted over the military suppression of the Chicago *Times*. For a long time, the *Times* had been a leading Democratic party mouthpiece. Wilbur Fiske Story, its publisher, a tough political marksman, had been sniping away at the Lincoln administration, particularly since the issuance of the Emancipation Proclamation. In June 1863, General Ambrose E. Burnside, then commanding the midwestern department and still smarting after his debacle at Fredericksburg, took action against disloyal elements. The general arrested a vociferous Peace Democrat, Clement L. Vallandigham and tried him before a military tribunal. When the New York *World* and the Chicago *Times* heavy-handedly condemned his action, Burnside banished the circulation of the New York paper from his department. In the case of the *Times,* Chicago being within his command, he directed Brigadier General Jacob

Ammen to suppress the newspaper for its "disloyal and incendiary sentiments. . . ."

The army authorities warned Story, on the evening of June 2, not to publish the next day. Story never considered obeying the order. Instead he hastily obtained a temporary writ from Judge Thomas Drummond of the federal circuit court, which enjoined Captain Putnam from action until after a hearing. The Union army ignored the court injunction. In the early morning of June 3, Story's lookouts could see the blueclad columns moving out of Camp Douglas down the road toward town to suppress the *Times*. Receiving warning, Story speeded the printing of the *Times* to publish an edition. Some papers were already on sale in the Chicago streets when the soldiers seized the newspaper building. Story fled the plant to petition the federal court to restrain the military. Although sympathetic to Story's plight, Judge Drummond refused to proceed, as the army's legal representative was absent. The judge issued a statement from the bench, pleading for a government of law not force.

Then Trumbull entered the controversy. He realized that his action could be politically explosive, but he would not countenance military interference with the country's legal process. By noon, many leading Chicago citizens held an indignation meeting in the federal circuit court room. At that time, a petition was signed, asking that Lincoln set aside the suppression order.[47] Lyman Trumbull and Isaac N. Arnold, the Chicago Republican congressman, who had been present for the meeting, sent a telegraphic post-script to the petition in which they said, "We respectfully ask for the above serious and prompt consideration of the President."[48] Arnold later recanted his action, after Republicans rebuked him for defending a copperhead sheet.[49] Trumbull refused to equivocate.[50]

Feelings ran too high to end the affair with the afternoon meeting. That night, June 3, twenty thousand people, roughly half of them Republicans, pushed into a mass meeting at Court House Square. At the edges of the crowd, the extreme anti-war Democrats agitated the mob to burn down the Republican *Tribune*'s offices in retaliation for the *Times*' seizure.[51] The presence of several militia companies had a sobering effect, and the mob, settling down, listened to the speeches. Although there were many Democratic orators, the Republican speakers were only two. One, Wirt Dexter, was a star of only the third magnitude; the other was Trumbull. On this occasion, Trumbull stated that military seizure was the wrong remedy, and, if the *Times* were guilty of wrong-doing, legal avenues were open to the government.[52]

Lincoln regretted the suppression of the *Times,* and if Burnside had cleared his order with Washington, his action never would have been permitted. Yet, the President hated to override a military order in the critical days of June 1863, a month which saw Lee's second invasion of the North. When the telegram from Arnold and Trumbull arrived, however, Lincoln was convinced he must set aside the *Times'* suppression.[53] Upon instructions from Washington, Burnside returned Story's property.[54]

Illinois Republican leaders, fearing a further blow to their weakened party morale, held a counter-demonstration. They hastily commandeered their heaviest political artillery, including Trumbull himself. In his case, his friends upon the committee on arrangements gave him this opportunity to "explain" his action in the *Times* suppression, since some Republicans grumbled that Trumbull was a renegade. Trumbull grasped the chance to appear. Speaking to the Republican crowd, he passed lightly over his part in lifting the *Times* suppression and spent most of his time making a "patriotic speech,"[55] but that was unacceptable to many rabid Republicans, who were in no mood to listen to his defense. Loud cries of "Dry up and leave," exploded from the angry crowd. Trumbull refused to become upset and continued reading his prepared address at a normal voice and speed. Thereupon, the crowd set up a chant for the next speaker. Doggedly, Trumbull finished his speech.[56]

Nor was that all. The Illinois Republican press generally pelted Trumbull with abuse. The typical comment, that of the Peoria *Daily Transcript,* claimed that Trumbull was motivated by pure jealousy of Lincoln.[57] Yet admirers sent bouquets of praise. From St. Louis one Republican wrote, "It took a good deal of courage to make the speech you did on Thursday night [to the Republican rally]." He added, "To go with the current is easy."[58] A Maine Republican wrote, "Unless some stand is made against the errors (doubtless well meant) of the men at Washington, we may . . . restore the Union, but at the expense of all the rights of personal liberty . . . inherited from our English ancestory."[59] An Illinois paymaster in Grant's army at Vicksburg wrote that when he first heard of Trumbull's stand, he was "anoyed [sic]" but that, upon second thought, he realized, "This last act of yours will in a few months give you higher and stronger hold on the people than any other of your life."[60]

As the weeks went by, disapproval of Trumbull passed. He was again invited to speak at Republican rallies throughout Illinois.[61] In neighboring Wisconsin, the state central committee urged him to campaign there.[62] And he did speak that summer at a giant "Union" party (as the Republican party then chose to style itself) rally in Springfield.[63] Trumbull decided to emphasize his party regularity by vigorously stumping Illinois in the campaign of 1863. In September, he toured the party's strongholds in northern Illinois, lauding the Union coalition of War Democrats and Republicans and supporting his stand on civil liberties in wartime.[64]

In October, he capped his tour with an address to the Chicago Union Club. The Union Club, a rabid Republican organization, by inviting Lyman, symbolized the new harmony between the senator and the Radical wing of his party. In his address, Trumbull fulsomely praised the Union

Club and was rewarded with a resounding ovation at his speech's conclusion.[65] With harmony restored, the Illinois Union party, as was generally true in the North, swept to electoral success in the fall of 1863.[66]

In December, Trumbull made the first of what became an annual pilgrimage from Chicago to Washington. For him, the first session of the Thirty-Eighth Congress would differ from most in that Trumbull made the trip alone. The confusion of changing households from Alton to Chicago and the illness of their two youngest sons kept Julia at home. In Washington, Trumbull stayed at the Avenue House, a second-rate hotel on the corner of 7th West and C Street North. Wartime inflation and a general shortage of hotel rooms in Washington had combined to send Trumbull into less comfortable quarters.[67] In this Congress, he continued as chairman of the important judiciary committee. In addition, he served on the unimportant public buildings and grounds committee, but he had a major assignment on the select committee to set terms for the building of the Pacific railroad.[68]

In mid-February, Trumbull was called home, when Arthur, then only three and a half years old, suffered a severe relapse; the boy passed away on February 21, the third Trumbull son to die in childhood. Trumbull, prostrate with grief, was absent from the Senate Chamber until March 15, although there were many important measures pending in which he felt a vital interest.[69] He returned a shaken man to the Senate Chamber in mid-March, and with his customary reaction to personal grief buried himself in his work.

Trumbull's position in 1864 regarding black rights lagged behind the most advanced Radical thinking. He felt that bills granting the suffrage and civil rights to blacks went too far, too fast. Undoubtedly, the depth of feeling in Illinois against extending equal rights to blacks influenced his thinking. Accordingly, Trumbull voted with the majority against a Sumner-sponsored amendment to the Washington city charter permitting literate tax-paying blacks to vote.[70] Trumbull and Sumner also differed over a bill repealing the fugitive slave law. The fugitive slave law of 1850 long had been bothersome to the Radicals, but it was not until this session that a serious effort to repeal it was made. Although the Thirteenth Amendment abolishing slavery was then being pushed by Trumbull, Sumner considered it as inchworm progress and concentrated upon his own program of anti-slavery legislation. Trumbull helped brush Sumner's fugitive slave law repeal aside until the Thirteenth Amendment had been passed by the Senate.[71]

As a result, it was not until mid-April that Sumner gained the floor for his bill. At that time, he was joined in its support by Trumbull, and together they beat off the assaults of the border state senators.[72] After further delay, in late June, the fugitive slave law repeal came to the Senate floor for final passage. Reverdy Johnson of Maryland moved a compromise amendment which drove a wedge into Republican ranks. It amended the wording of the bill so that it only repealed the fugitive slave law of 1850, passed as part of the compromise legislation of that year, but left untouched the milder fugitive slave law of 1793. Trumbull and a number of Republicans bolted the party ranks to vote for the amendment; it failed, 17 to 22. At this, Trumbull rejoined the Republican phalanx to push through Sumner's measure, 27 to 12.[73]

On other matters touching the future of the blacks, Trumbull veered left and worked closely with Sumner. They collaborated to shove through a House-passed freedmen's bureau bill. This measure established an agency to care for the newly-freed black slaves who were then being haphazardly helped by the Union army. But this bill was caught in the congressional log-jam and stalled for the session. Sumner, supported by Trumbull, battled to keep the bill alive.[74] In late June, the congressmen itched to leave Washington for the hustings; the freedmen's bureau bill remained unpassed, a tribute as much to the indifference of many Republican senators as to the hostility of border state solons. At that time, Trumbull created a furor when he proposed an amendment repealing the last clause of the joint explanatory resolution of the second confiscation act. This clause had declared that the confiscation of real estate held by Confederates was not to extend beyond the offender's life. Senators shouted that this introduced an extraneous element into the bill. Trumbull coolly responded that his amendment was germane in that the bill proposed to give confiscated lands to freedmen, and they would have nothing to receive if the explanatory resolution stood.

Sumner, however, with hard-eyed realism, was horrified at the Illinois senator's amendment. It raised the spectre of a presidential veto, since Lincoln would view the repeal darkly.[75] McDougall of California and Carlisle of Virginia protested that Trumbull's amendment was unconstitutional and contrary to his stand in 1862. The Illinoisan replied, "I always maintained that the clause in the Constitution limiting the effect of a conviction for treason had nothing in the world to do with the waging of war in a district . . . governed by the military power, and where there were no civil tribunals."[76] In the debate which followed, Trumbull, made irascible by his personal problems, conceded that not all Southerners who obeyed the Confederate authorities were rebels; those who acted out of fear were simply victims of coercion. In referring to the second confiscation act, Trumbull contemptuously spoke of it as not amounting "to much; it has never been enforced."

As the law stood, Trumbull complained, a plantation owner killed fighting against the Union would have his confiscated land returned to his heirs, and any blacks given the use of the land then would have it taken from them. He cried, "I would have divided out the plantations long ago. I would not have allowed rebel generals who have been fighting us for the last three years to hold estates in the North from which they derived large incomes with which . . . to contend against us." He concluded, with dry severity: "In my judgment, war means desolation; it means death; it means destruction; and if I could have my way, these rebels would have all three, death, desolation, destruction, and I almost said damnation."[77]

In the voting the next day, Trumbull's amendment was adopted, 23 to 15,[78] and all efforts to strike it out later failed.[79] The bill, as amended by Trumbull, passed with ease, 21 to 9.[80] But it proved unacceptable to the House. The chasm between the two chambers was too wide for bridging, and the bill hung over in a legislative limbo until the next session.[81]

Yet another Sumner legislative proposal concerning the social position of blacks split the Illinois and Massachusetts senators apart. Sumner wished to amend a bill altering the Washington and Georgetown Railroad Company's charter so that no discrimination against black passengers would be licit.[82] Trumbull thought the bill unnecessary, as blacks already rode street-cars. He said that the Republicans ought to avoid the mistakes of the Democrats in the 1850's by not overplaying their hands.[83] Sumner refused to be swayed and pushed his amendment through the Senate by the close margin of 17 to 16, only to see it die in the House.[84] On the same principle, Trumbull fought unsuccessfully against two Sumner amendments to the civil appropriation bills, which allowed blacks to testify in federal courts, and banned the coastal slave trade.[85]

That Sumner and Trumbull should collaborate at times, only to break poles apart, was not surprising. Sumner viewed the slavery question through moral spectacles. Trumbull saw slavery as more a legal and political question than a moral issue. This difference in outlook, added to the pride of the two senators, made each a poor lieutenant. The relationship of Trumbull to Sumner was analogous to the leaders of two absolutely independent guerrilla bands; they fought a common enemy, but each in his own way.[86]

Reconstruction again surfaced in Congress that session. Lincoln already had rebuilt the civil government in several Union-held Confederate states. There, the President experimented with reconstruction on mild terms under his authority. In Arkansas, presidential reconstruction had progressed to the point where claimants for senatorial seats appeared.[87] In June 1864, James Lane of Kansas offered a resolution recognizing Arkansas as restored to the Union.[88] Although some Radicals, led by Wade, tried to table the resolution, it was referred to the judiciary committee along with the cases of the two senatorial claimants.[89]

Lincoln was asked formally by Trumbull for any supporting data the President could supply for the Arkansas claimants.[90] Lincoln replied in a curiously non-committal fashion. He referred Trumbull to the House appropriation committee for the evidence requested. Almost casually, Lincoln offered to have copies made for Trumbull if the senator thought that "more satisfactory."[91] The judiciary committee was unimpressed, and, on June 27, Trumbull reported Lane's amendment adversely, denying seats to the claimants.[92] Two days later, Democratic Senator Nesmith of Oregon asked Trumbull if the committee had decided whether Arkansas was in or out of the Union. Trumbull answered that the committee had evaded this thorny question, confining itself to an investigation of whether the two senators had been elected "in a constitutional sense."[93] In the end, Trumbull insisted upon and obtained a favorable vote, 27 to 6, accepting his committee's report.[94]

Trumbull voted for the Wade-Davis bill which would have substituted for Lincoln's plan a more harsh mode of reconstruction for the seceded states.[95] The President successfully pocket-vetoed it, leaving reconstruction an unresolved question.[96]

A monument to Trumbull's entire career was his successful sponsorship of the Thirteenth Amendment. Despite Lincoln's Emancipation Proclamation, freedom for the slaves remained starkly unfinished.[97] The loyal slave states had not been included within Lincoln's manifesto. In addition, the President had exempted all of Tennessee and parts of Virginia and Louisiana from the document. Thus, even if the President's proclamation was entirely legal, a moot point, his solution was incomplete. A constitutional amendment to abolish slavery was not new. Early in the war, an abolitionist drive to garner a million signatures had fallen short but did attract very many signatures for a petition which asked for an end to slavery by constitutional amendment. Many other petitions on the same subject were sent to Congress.[98]

The Thirteenth Amendment began with the introduction by Senator John B. Henderson of Missouri, on January 11, 1864, of a joint resolution calling for the abolition of slavery. The proposal was referred to the judiciary committee.[99] Nearly a month later, Sumner introduced a resolution calling for the abolition of slavery, saying that all persons were equal before the law. Sumner hoped to steer this resolution to the committee he headed on slavery, where he could control its destiny. Trumbull, alert to this possibility, objected so violently that the chair referred Sumner's resolution to the Illinois senator's committee instead.[100]

On February 10, Trumbull reported out from the judiciary committee a substitute for Henderson's original resolution. Trumbull, as chairman, had rewritten the resolution so that, as he explained it, it would "amend the Constitution of the United States so that neither slavery nor involuntary servitude, except as punishment for crime, whereof a party shall have been duly convicted, shall exist within the United States or any place subject to their jurisdiction; and also that Congress shall have power to enforce this article by proper legislation."[101] The wording of the substitute resolution followed the phrasing of the Northwest Ordinance of 1787.[102] With this resolution, Trumbull began fighting for Senate consideration of the amendment.[103] When in mid-February he was called away by Arthur's death, the amendment languished. No progress was recorded until his return. Then, Trumbull recovered the ground lost during his absence.[104]

Trumbull was under fire from both the left and the right. On his left stood Sumner, a host in himself, who regarded the constitutional amendment process as too slow; moreover, he was smitten with his own resolution as the best way to accomplish the task.[105] He fought Trumbull with one parliamentary device after another. The two senators' maneuvering for position seemed more like a minuet than a legislative exercise.

On Trumbull's right were the senators from the border states, where slavery was important, who opposed Trumbull's amendment, since it abruptly ended the institution without compensation to the owners.[106] Then there was the great mass of Republican senators who were indifferent to the wording of Trumbull's constitutional amendment and held various degrees of friendly feeling toward ending slavery. They believed that it would take a minor miracle to pass the amendment through the lower House where the Republican party did not have the necessary two-thirds control. Therefore, since the action by the Senate seemed to them little more than a gesture, they felt unwilling to allocate large blocks of Senate time to a lost cause, when vital pieces of legislation might be passed.[107] Trumbull realized that, with this Senate attitude, he must press the admendment early in the session or not at all. Trumbull dodged neatly through every parliamentary loophole to get the constitutional amendment to the Senate floor. On March 28, he argued that the prime cause of the rebellion had been slavery; he pointed out that predictions that slavery would wither away in the course of time had proved false; he emphasized that previous congressional laws against slavery and the Emancipation Proclamation as well had been ineffective measures; Lincoln's Emancipation Proclamation might be overturned in the courts. He pleaded for the enactment of the constitutional amendment as the only effective sanction against slavery.[108]

Trumbull's cause received an enormous boost when Reverdy Johnson, a Conservative senator from Maryland, made a long, well-polished speech in which he admitted that slavery was mortally ill and that the amendment offered the best chance for a decent interment of the corpse.[109] Although the border state senators tried to change the constitutional amendment so as to make it less distasteful to them, all their attempts failed.[110]

After this advance, the drive for the passage of the constitutional amendment again bogged down.[111] On April 7, the debate was resumed when Democratic Senator Thomas A. Hendricks of Indiana, in a long, rambling speech, pleaded against passage of the amendment, reiterating many racial myths.[112] The resolution inched closer to passage when Henderson, who had been absent for some time, announced his support of Trumbull's wording of the amendment.[113] But having beaten down the opposition from the right, Trumbull now found Sumner again sniping from the left. Sumner delayed consideration of the constitutional amendment, until he could polish an elaborate phillipic against it.[114] At a later date, Sumner called for the adoption of his resolution as a constitutional amendment.[115] Speaking for the judiciary committee, Trumbull argued that the existing form of the amendment accomplished its purpose and that the inexorable congressional calendar would not allow the acceptance of Sumner's substitute.[116] When Sumner realized that he had obtained no converts for his cause, he reluctantly withdrew his constitutional amendment.[117] After the usual last-minute flurry of crippling amendments had been defeated, and the border state senators had predicted the early end of constitutional liberties if the constitutional revision passed, the Senate passed the Thirteenth Amendment, 36 to 6.[118] Trumbull had won.

Lincoln had remained on the sidelines while the constitutional amendment was before the Senate. He was indifferent to its wording and felt confident that an amendment would be passed by the staunchly-Republican upper chamber. After the Senate approved the amendment, Lincoln vigorously backed it in the struggle in the House of Representatives. Also, he tugged the necessary strings to make its passage and ratification part of the Union (Republican) national platform at the Baltimore national convention.[119] In the House, where the Republicans fell far short of a two-thirds majority, the amendment's future remained clouded. Finally, the Republican leaders there pressed it to a vote, on June 15. Predictably, the amendment only garnered 93 affirmative votes to 65 cast in opposition, far below the constitutional majority required. The defeat was not final; a reconsideration was possible at the next session.[120]

There matters rested until Lincoln had been re-elected and the Republicans had won a resounding congressional victory in the fall elections of 1864. This meant that the new Thirty-Ninth Congress would have the Republican strength to pass the Thirteenth Amendment if the Thirty-Eighth continued its refusal. Waiting was not necessary. When the second session of the Thirty-Eighth Congress convened in the winter of 1864-1865, enough House Democrats, either rationalizing that the passage of the amendment was inevitable or falling willing victims to Lincoln's patronage blandishments, shifted their votes. As a result, on January 31, 1865, the House adopted the constitutional amendment, 119 to 56 and sent it to the states for ultimate ratification.[121]

As the years went by, Trumbull became prouder of his part in making the Thirteenth Amendment a reality. As a grizzled law professor lecturing to a class of hopeful legal students at the Union Law College, he would climax his lectures on constitutional law by raising his right hand and proclaiming, "Gentlemen, this good right hand wrote this Amendment to the Constitution."[122]

CHAPTER TWELVE

A WINTER OF DISCONTENT

IN THE EARLY MONTHS of 1864, Trumbull's relationship with Lincoln reached its nadir. Many authors have characterized Trumbull as "Lincoln's friend," but this description is incorrect for most of Trumbull's career and is most inappropriate for this period. As Lincoln's presidential term wore on, Trumbull became more and more disillusioned and unhappy with his place at the President's elbow rather than his ear. Moreover, Trumbull believed that he had not obtained sufficient patronage; actually, Lincoln had been generous with the senator's friends and relatives. Trumbull's demands seemed insatiable to Lincoln. In the Robert Todd Lincoln Papers, there is an envelope from Trumbull which contained patronage requests and upon which Lincoln had scrawled one word, "impossible."[1]

Yet patronage and personal squabbles alone do not explain Trumbull's thorough disillusionment with Lincoln by the winter of 1863-1864. Despite his failings, Trumbull was a sincere patriot. If he could have believed that Lincoln was not frozen in conservative positions, he would have supported him. Part of the explanation for Trumbull's disapproval of Lincoln lay within the senator himself. One of his many anomalies was an attitude more characteristic of Whig than a Jacksonian Democrat — he distrusted the executive branch of the federal government. He weighed Lincoln on the same scales he used for others; all Presidents from Pierce to Cleveland seriously failed in his critical eyes, and none won his continuous support.

During the winter of 1863-1864, while Julia remained in Illinois, lonely Lyman received invitations to the small dinner parties given by Kate Chase Sprague, Salmon P. Chase's ambitious daughter. Even solemn Lyman Trumbull could not wholly withstand Kate's arguments on behalf of her father. Kate was then using her husband's wealth to launch a Chase-for-President boom.[2] While Trumbull had become disillusioned with Chase during the cabinet crisis of 1862,[3] he admired Chase's firm anti-slavery stand and his able administration of the treasury department.[4] Yet in the end, Kate did not greatly influence Trumbull's choice for President.[5]

Trumbull did not stand alone in the Union (Republican) party in his disgust for Lincoln's weak war policy. Many congressional leaders agitated for a change in the Union presidential ticket.[6] The drive to block Lincoln's renomination profited from the argument that there was a one-term tradition: no President since Jackson had gained a second term. Trumbull was so openly anti-Lincoln that his friends became alarmed. Norman Judd, minister to Prussia, returned in 1863 for a visit to the United States. Trumbull complained about the Lincoln administration to him. When Judd remonstrated with him that he was endangering his political future, Trumbull blurted out that he did not care, as he was thinking of political retirement. Judd remonstrated that Trumbull might change his mind by his term's end in 1867.[7] Bluff Governor Yates tendered Trumbull the same advice.

By February 1864, Trumbull had almost decided that Lincoln would be renominated. He reported to a correspondent: "The surface current is running in favor of Mr. Lincoln's renomination, but I find with many that the feeling for Lincoln is only apparent."[9] A factor encouraging Trumbull's anti-Lincoln hopes was the role his political confidant, Joseph Medill, of the Chicago *Tribune*, was playing. Medill, in alliance with Chicago attorney, John Wilson, had formed a pro-Chase organization in 1863 called the Strong Band Association which claimed seventy-five thousand hard-core members.[10] Trumbull did remain aloof from two Chase trial balloons in February 1864. The first, a document entitled *The Next Presidential Election* branded Lincoln's re-election chances infinitesimal and called for a new presidential candidate. The minimal reaction to this effort caused the Chase supporters to launch a new document, the "Pomeroy Circular." It was named for Kansas Senator Pomeroy, a leading Radical. The circular branded Lincoln a losing candidate and suggested Chase as his substitute. But this maneuver also failed.[11]

With Chase floundering, the opposition to Lincoln fragmented. Lincoln weathered the discontent of the chiefs, since they had insufficient warriors. Quickly, he arranged a counter-stroke. Many state legislatures endorsed his candidacy, and an early convention date, June 7, was named, which was favorable to his chances;[12] this, together with Lincoln's shrewd neutralization of Sumner,[13] assured his renomination. Although Trumbull remained aloof from the clumsy maneuvers to unseat Lincoln, he could not refrain in the spring of 1864 from venting his spleen upon the administration in several Senate speeches.[14] Despite his grumbling, he remained politically inactive as Lincoln was renominated by the Union convention with a War Democrat from Tennessee, Andrew Johnson, as his running-mate. Yet during the summer months of 1864 Trumbull did not campaign actively for the President. Invitations to speak rained upon him,[15] but until very late in the canvass, he refused all of them. His excuse was invariably that he was too busy superintending extensive renovations in the house he had bought south of Chicago to engage in politics.[16]

Late in September, after much soulsearching, Trumbull began active campaigning. His reasons for taking the stump were similar to those animating his political friend, George Allen. After surveying the political landscape, Allen wrote Trumbull: "I have felt . . . that he lacks much of the firmness with which God so usefully blessed Andrew Jackson. But I made up my mind . . . that we could not risk a change of President. . . ."[17] Trumbull spoke at Ottawa[18] and at great rallies at Springfield[19] and Chicago.[20] In his typical speech, Trumbull flayed the Democrats and praised the Union party's platform. Comparing Lincoln for President versus the Democrat's candidate, George B. McClellan, the best that Trumbull could manage was to say, "Two candidates are presented for your suffrages. I shall not appeal to you for men; the country is everything."[21]

The military tide having shifted in favor of the Union by the fall of 1864, the Democratic platform plank that termed the war a failure became an incongruity; Lincoln was triumphantly re-elected, carrying every Union state except Kentucky, Delaware, and New Jersey. The House and Senate were also firmly in Republican (Union) hands.[22]

After a short visit with the Jayneses at Springfield in November, the Trumbulls left for the capital. Julia, but not the children, accompanied her husband to Washington, where they rented rooms at 424 15th Street, near the Riggs Bank. Walter still attended the naval academy. Although Lyman thought him "pretty contented" at the beginning of 1865, he soon resigned. Walter did not mix socially with the other midshipmen. This, plus his academic difficulties with mathematics and seamanship, caused his resignation. Meanwhile, Perry attended the University of Chicago (a predecessor institution to the present university of the same name), while Henry remained with his grandparents in Springfield.[23]

The status of the Lincoln-reconstructed governments in Louisiana, Tennessee, and Arkansas that session weighed heavily upon Congress. The Louisiana governor forwarded the credentials of two senators-elect to the Senate.[24] These papers concerning Louisiana were quickly sent to the judiciary committee.[25] Since Trumbull and his committee had denied seats to the Arkansas senators elected from a Lincoln-restored government at the last session, many Radicals believed that their attitude agreed with their own. Trumbull quickly revealed that he was flexible on the question of reconstruction. Lincoln, who had made no special effort at the previous session to influence Trumbull on the Arkansas question, now won the Illinois senator's support for his reconstruction governments. To win Trumbull over to accept presidential reconstruction was a formidable task. Trumbull never easily changed political course and, more than most of his colleagues, he fully realized Lincoln's ability to bend men to his design.[26]

Yet, Trumbull was vulnerable to Lincoln's arguments on two scores. First, Lincoln had never retaliated for Trumbull's negative attitude toward his re-election. Trumbull was amazed "how little Mr. Lincoln allowed personal feeling to influence him in public matters." Second, Lincoln's prestige from his smashing re-election triumph made it imperative that Trumbull work with him. In interviews with Trumbull over a period of weeks, Lincoln persuasively argued with him that regular constitutional relationships between the federal government and the Southern states could be effectively established most quickly by the presidential plan. While not completely convinced, Trumbull framed a resolution to recognize Louisiana's restored government.[27]

Lincoln's tolerant attitude toward Trumbull has a further explanation. As Robert Todd Lincoln remembered it years later, Trumbull, full of complaints, called at the White House. Lincoln listened patiently, accepted some of the criticism, but softly rejected some of the senator's arguments. After Trumbull had departed, young Robert Lincoln asked his father why, since their goals were similar, they could not agree. The President quietly replied, "We agree perfectly, but we see things from a different point of view. I am in the White House looking down the [Pennsylvania] Avenue, and Trumbull's in the Senate looking up."[28]

On the Louisiana question, Trumbull's support of Lincoln's reconstructed government was fortified by that politician-in-army-dress, N. P. Banks. Banks, an old political acquaintance, enjoyed the senator's respect as a staunch Republican congressman of the pre-war days. When Banks, who had engineered the restored government in Louisiana, appeared in Washington and testified before Trumbull's committee, the senator accepted the necessity for accepting the Louisiana government.[29] In the judiciary committee, Trumbull obtained majority approval for his resolution, declaring that the two Louisiana senatorial claimants should be seated. A companion resolution recognized the Lincoln Louisiana state government. On February 18, Trumbull reported the committee actions, causing a buzz of excitement, since senators recognized that these resolutions would be test measures for reconstruction. The report and resolutions at that time were placed upon the crowded Senate legislative calendar.[30] On February 23, Trumbull moved for consideration of the judiciary committee report upon Louisiana. In response, Sumner and Chandler revealed their opposition to that state's recognition.[31] Trumbull continued to press the resolution, but yielded to a new senator, who made a long maiden speech.[32] Not wishing to alienate any senator, Trumbull temporarily postponed the Louisiana discussion as a matter of courtesy.

After the new senator's maiden speech, Trumbull proposed taking up the Louisiana issue as a privileged question, since it concerned the Senate's proper composition.[33] Hendricks of Indiana next took the floor, announcing that the Democratic minority opposed consideration of so important a matter in the ''heel'' of the session.[34] Despite the Democratic objections and the protests from Howard of Michigan and Sumner of the Radicals, opposed to the measure as too lenient, Trumbull persuaded a Senate majority to take up the proposal.[35] Lane of Kansas asked about the consideration of Arkansas' status. Trumbull answered that while the facts of the two cases were different, if Louisiana were approved, he would move ''immediately'' to consider Arkansas.

When Sumner, Howard and conservative Lazarus Powell of Kentucky all asked for an extended debate on Louisiana, Trumbull agreed to wait until the next day.[36] Then, on February 24, when Trumbull called for Louisiana's consideration as the special order of the day, Chandler informed him that, as Lyman habitually disregarded special orders when he was pressing his own bills, he could not expect those courtesies from others. Vice-President Hannibal Hamlin ruled Trumbull out of order; the floor was then seized by John Sherman for another question. Trumbull complained, but had to wait until Sherman had finished.[37] Chandler and Sumner worked together well upon this occasion, by one parliamentary device after another frustrating all Trumbull's efforts to press the Louisiana issue to a vote.[38] At a night session, by sheer persistence, Trumbull obtained the floor for Louisiana recognition. He soon found that he had won a round but not the fight. In a long, rambling speech, Lazarus Powell opposed recognizing Louisiana.[39] Trumbull could not dissuade Missouri's Henderson from speaking on the Louisiana question, and the session continued far into the night, when a tired Senate shouted for adjournment.[40]

On February 25, Trumbull fought successfully for Senate consideration of Louisiana, only to discover Howard and Sumner stubbornly opposing his resolution in lengthy, vituperative speeches.[41] Next, Sumner loosed a blizzard of maiming amendments, whose consideration convulsed the Senate until the dinner recess.[42] When the Senate reconvened, Trumbull forced a continuance of the debate. He chided Sumner for banding together with the Democrats and pro-slavery border senators to defeat senatorial recognition of this reconstucted state. Sumner did not deny the allegation, retorting that the Louisiana resolution of acknowledgment was so pernicious as to justify any parliamentary maneuver to defeat it. After a flood of talk, the Senate adjourned, with Louisiana recognition unresolved.[43] Holding many finance bills, Sherman grew restive at the delay forced by Louisiana. At the next Senate meeting, therefore, he proposed that Louisiana be delayed in favor of a pending tax bill. Trumbull immediately protested the Ohioan's move. He declared that if the Senate showed the anti-Louisiana's filibustering solons that they could not succeed, then they would back down. But, he added, if Louisiana were once shunted aside, the obstructionists would have won.[44]

At this, Wade shouted at Trumbull, ''You have pondered over it all winter, and your mind was made up entirely adverse to what it is now. How do you know but that your first view of the subject was the true one?'' Abruptly switching to a new tack, Wade charged Trumbull with inconsistency, since the Illinoisan had voted to bar the counting of Louisiana's electoral ballots. In reply, Trumbull declared that Louisiana had then been unrecognized by Congress, a condition that he sought to remedy.[45] As quickly as Wade subsided, Howard lashed out at Trumbull, crying, ''There has not been, and is not now, upon this floor a single Senator whose sarcasm has been so unscrupulous, vociferous, and sweeping, as that of the Senator from Illinois in reference to these same acts of military usurpation, as he called them, and which acts he now undertakes to set up as a . . . government of a State.''[46] The Radicals attacked Trumbull mercilessly, one after another in rapid succession. At last, the ever-practical Sherman moved that the Louisiana consideration be put aside until his tax measure could pass. Trumbull quickly called for the ayes and the nays on Sherman's proposal, which all senators recognized as a test vote.[47]

Trumbull realized that his Senate majority was dissolving. A recent development had hurt Trumbull's cause for Louisiana recognition. It was a fracas started by one of Louisiana's congressional claimants, A. P. Field, with a Republican wheelhorse, Pennsylvania congressman William P. ''Pig Iron'' Kelley. This brawl, in a crowded Washington restaurant, had ended only when Field had slashed Kelley seriously with a knife. The Radicals used this incident to argue with Republican senators that the Southerners did not possess the restraint necessary for self-government.[48] Therefore, with many moderate Republicans unwilling to fight for Louisiana any longer, Sherman's motion to postpone the Louisiana question until ''tomorrow'' carried, 34 to 12. Among the stubborn twelve were Republicans such as Trumbull, Harris, and Doolittle, as well as Western Democrats like McDougal and Nesmith.[49] In the end, ''tomorrow'' never came for the postponed Louisiana measure. The Lincolnian plan of reconstruction never received congressional sanction. While Senate action would not have assured House approval, senatorial assent might yet have altered reconstruction's course.

In assessing the Senate's failure to approve Louisiana's reconstruction, the slow progress of Trumbull's conversion from hostility to support of the measure while it was yet before the committee played a major role. Reporting the resolution out late in the session afforded the Radicals and border state Conservatives the opportunity to scuttle it. The Radicals seized the ''glory'' of the defeat of Louisiana recognition. At least until recently, historians have overlooked the important role the border state Conservatives played in the demise of the Louisiana resolution.[50]

The freedmen's bureau bill remained as unfinished business from the previous session. To Trumbull, the bill's heart was his proposal to repeal the explanatory resolution of the second confiscation act. That provision would allow the government to confiscate the abandoned plantation lands and give them to the freed slaves. Trumbull believed that the freed slaves could not be fitted into American society until adequate economic provision was made for them.[51] Over his vehement opposition, a conference committee deleted his provision in reconciling the differences between the two houses,[52] and the Senate accepted the result.[53] Undeterred, Trumbull unsuccessfully attempted upon two separate occasions, by independent resolutions, to have the necessary portion of the second confiscation bill's explanatory resolution repealed.[54]

The Senate session of March 3 lasted all night. The next morning, Trumbull, waspish in his frustration that session, retaliated against two of his most persistent gadflies, Chandler and Sumner. These two senators favored a bill to shatter a New Jersey monopoly, the Camden and Amboy Railroad, which had aroused violent complaints that it was hampering the war effort. Sumner and Chandler were motivated by more than pure patriotism; New Jersey was a solidly Democratic state, and a blow at the monopoly would embarrass the Democratic party.[55] In the last hours of the session, Zachariah Chandler desperately begged the Senate to pass the bill. Trumbull, however, had a tight grip upon the Senate time.[56] Chandler scowled and growled to no avail. Finally, Trumbull had all business suspended that did not deal with the inauguration,[57] in which he played a major role. He served on the House Senate joint committee, which officially notified Lincoln and Johnson of their election. It was Trumbull who made the official report of the two men's acceptance to the Senate.[58]

Thus it was that Lyman, Julia, and Walter Trumbull, together with George T. Brown, gathered in the Vice-President's office off the Senate floor to greet the weak Vice-President-elect, Andrew Johnson, shortly before the inauguration ceremonies. There, Johnson, who had just recovered from an attack of typhoid fever, and who was usually a mild drinker, had fortified himself for the inauguration ceremonies with brandy, followed by whisky. When he stood up to take the oath of office, weaving slightly, he made an unscheduled, fiery speech. Notables tugged at his coattails, but Johnson paid no heed. The Vice-President was quite drunk.[59] By contrast, Lincoln took the oath of office with simple dignity, and with his flair for crisp yet vivid imagery, touched new heights with his Second Inaugural address.[60]

Trumbull did not leave Washington immediately after the inauguration, since the usual special session of the new Senate was held. In addition to the routine appointments to be confirmed, the credentials of senators-elect from the Lincoln-reconstructed governments were referred to the judiciary committee. The committee, through Trumbull, agreed to wait until the Senate's regular December meeting. The upper chamber agreed.[61]

Late March and early April witnessed the accelerating collapse of the ginia surrendered to Grant. Although other Confederate armies were still in the field, peace was at hand. Lincoln's steady hand was not to guide the ship of state during reconstruction. He was shot by John Wilkes Booth on April 14, and died the next day. Opinionated and tactless Andrew Johnson would complete the legal restoration of the Union. Reconstruction, always a considerable problem, became more formidable in the wake of the horror and indignation which rocked the North on the heels of Lincoln's assassination.

Trumbull took a conspicuous part in the sad ceremonies through which the nation expressed its grief at the loss of its leader. Spontaneous meetings were held across the nation. In Chicago, on the evening of April 15, Trumbull and two prominent Chicago clergymen addressed a sorrowing, subdued crowd at Bryan Hall. Trumbull prophetically remarked that "Abraham Lincoln would go down to posterity as the great apostle of human liberty, and that the South had slain its best friend."[62] When Lincoln's funeral train reached Chicago, Trumbull served as a pallbearer, as Lincoln's body was drawn through streets lined with sorrowing thousands.[63] As chairman of a special committee of ten, Trumbull represented the Chicago bar at Lincoln's grave-side rites at Springfield.[64] Lincoln was in his grave; the nation looked to his successor with mingled hope and misgivings.

CHAPTER THIRTEEN

A TALE OF A TENNESSEE TAILOR

WITH THE END of the Civil War, a new era had dawned. Yet the results of wartime problems remained. The conflict's emotions, intensified by Lincoln's murder, were not easily quieted. The Republican party had fulfilled its original purpose with slavery's abolition and faced breaking apart. But fitting the freed black into society and simultaneously punishing the South for its rebellion provided the necessary cement to hold the party together. Although purely economic issues became increasingly important, the Republican party preferred to emphasize the less divisive (in the North) reconstruction issue.

Andrew Johnson, a hill-country politician, was cut from a bolt of plain, rough cloth. As President, he vacillated when prompt action was called for; when compromise was needed, he displayed the stubbornness of the weak. In April 1865, Trumbull knew him as a loyal Southerner who had continued to serve as United States Senator after Tennessee's secession. In 1862, Johnson left the Senate Chamber, serving as Tennessee's Union military governor. As a result, Trumbull considered him dependable. In his speech eulogizing Lincoln, Trumbull had expressed confidence in Johnson.[1] Within a week of Johnson's ascension to the presidency, Trumbull pledged his support. Trumbull pointed to his own Louisiana stand as evidence of his desire for "harmony" with the Southern people, but he emphasized that the "leaders of the rebellion" must be punished, and men untainted by treason elevated to power in the South.[2]

Although during the war, Johnson had declared that he would make treason odious, upon reflection, he was uninterested in a reworking of Southern society so that whites would be subjected to black control. A poor white (no one ever reached the White House from humbler origins), he viewed the poor white as the person who would suffer most if the blacks were allowed political and social equality. Therefore, under his direction, a mild political reconstruction of the South was quickly accomplished in the summer and fall of 1865.

While building along the lines that Lincoln had indicated, Johnson added innovations of his own. Whereas Lincoln had urged a limited black suffrage upon the South, Johnson was content to see the South reconstructed with no black participation in political affairs. He accepted the Southern "black codes" with their rigid strait-jacket for black economic and social rights. Trumbull anxiously followed Johnson's actions during the first months of his presidency. Much of what he saw chilled his admiration for Johnson. Still, he felt that every effort must be made to get along with Johnson. Despite a nagging dispute with the Illinois Central which wanted to put a cattle spur line diagonally across his Chicago property,[3] Trumbull took his family East for their summer vacation and stopped off at Washington to sample the political climate there. After a survey, he concluded that Johnson had not committed any irreparable error; Secretary of the Navy Welles noted in his diary that he believed Trumbull generally approved of Johnson's course.[4]

Leaving Washington, Trumbull spent a quiet summer in northwest Connecticut and Venango County, Pennsylvania.[5] While playing croquet and boating, he kept in touch with the political situation. A clash between the Radicals and Johnson loomed. Trumbull felt neither faction was right. What position ought he to take? He realized that hungry rivals within the party eyed his Senate seat. Trumbull had forgotten his earlier misgivings and ardently desired another term. Still mulling over the situation, he returned to the capital.

From Washington, Trumbull wrote his brother-in-law, William Jayne, saying he had no clear answer as to whether Johnson and the congressional Republicans would irretrievably split. He knew that his opposition to Lincoln had hurt his re-election chances, and he wished no jousts with the new President.[6] Then on a visit home, Trumbull spent several weeks conferring with his lieutenants in Illinois before returning for Congress' winter session. Julia accompanied Lyman, bringing young Henry with her. They had rented their Chicago home. Perry withdrew from the University of Chicago and returned to Washington to join the family. That session, Walter served as his father's secretary. The Trumbulls rented a large house at 430 D Street, an excellent location. Washington rents had fallen after the war, until they had sunk below those in Chicago. Julia had sold some inherited property, and so the Trumbulls had four hundred dollars with which to rent their new Washington quarters. Yet thrifty Lyman cut expenses by sharing his home with his long-time supporter, Illinois Representative Burton C. Cook, his wife, and their sixteen-year-old daughter. Trumbull thereby had capital enough to speculate in both gold and oil, with minimal success.[7] In May 1866, Julia returned to Illinois, taking Henry with her. Trumbull gave up his house on D Street and rented rooms at 402 G Street, which he shared with Walter and Burton Cook.[8]

Most congressmen spurned the lenient Johnsonian reconstruction terms. They felt the political necessity of keeping the South from the control of the secessionist leaders and they wished to show the President that Congress would share in reconstruction. Moderate Republicans' hopes for cooperation rose when Johnson's first annual message to Congress took a middle ground. He quietly reported upon Southern reconstruction, and seemed to ask for a cooperative effort with Congress to protect the blacks' rights.[9] Since "ultras" like Sumner were planning to legislate in the same area, Trumbull quickly announced that he would frame a bill safeguarding the freedmen's civil rights.[10] Trumbull divided his proposal into two measures, the freedmen's bureau bill, and the civil rights bill.

On January 5, Trumbull introduced his first measure into the Senate. The bill increased the scope of the freedmen's bureau, giving it jurisdiction over freed blacks anywhere in the country. It also granted blacks title to abandoned lands given them by the military authorities. In unreconstructed states, the bill provided that the bureau agents could try cases of discrimination against blacks' rights, unhampered by the usual judicial guarantees — trial by jury and the right of appeal. Trumbull introduced his second bill guaranteeing to blacks their civil rights in defiance of the Southern black codes. Both bills were referred to the judiciary committee where Trumbull could guide them to ultimate passage.[11]

Both measures were unusual for Trumbull, who feared "big" government. Only the unprecedented problem of the freed slaves justified this action. Acting first on the freedmen's bureau bill, Trumbull won in two days of committee hearings and discussion a favorable recommendation to the full Senate.[12] He made a convincing case for his bill, since he had consulted closely with O. O. Howard, the head of the freedmen's bureau, during its drafting.[13] Trumbull believed that the measure's heart lay in the provision that the abandoned lands given to the blacks by the military authorities be confirmed. Johnson had pardoned so many former Confederates that under the existing legislation the real estate would revert to its original owners, dispossessing the former slaves. One of Johnson's actions that Trumbull thought extremely unwise was his wholesale pardons.[14] On the floor of the Senate, Trumbull argued: "I believe that a homestead is worth more to these people than almost anything else; that so long as the relation of employer and employee exists between the blacks and the whites, you will necessarily have a dependent population."[15]

Trumbull defended his bill against Conservatives and Democrats, who charged the bill created a large bureaucracy and interfered with states' rights,[16] and some Radicals, who felt that it might hinder black suffrage. To the Radicals, he argued that the bill reached problems more elemental than the suffrage. To the Conservatives, he argued that the trial procedure for persons accused of transgressing black rights had been copied from the fugitive slave law of 1850, which many of them had supported. Trumbull believed that the bill must apply nationally, since freedmen had fled all over the Union. Answering arguments against the bill's unconstitutionality, he pointed to the Thirteenth Amendment whereby Congress could pass legislation necessary to ensure a final end to slavery.[17] Trumbull and the Republicans beat down all crippling amendments of the Conservative opposition, pushing the bill through, 37 to 10, on January 25.[18]

There were enough conservative-minded House Republicans so that the measure there was amended to apply only to the former Confederate states;[19] the measure was then referred anew to the Senate judiciary committee; there, Trumbull had no difficulty deleting the limitation.[20] On the Senate floor, the bill was attacked from the Radical left. The Radicals reluctantly had supported the original passage of the bill. Now, upon reflection, they became convinced that the bill would impede black suffrage. Trumbull, believing that the country was unready to force black suffrage upon the South, and that it was more important to guarantee the Negroes' economic well-being, answered them: "It [Negro suffrage] is the most sovereign remedy since the days of Townsend's Sarsaparilla.[21] The Senate then shouted through the bill as amended by the judiciary committee.[22] The House reluctantly accepted the Senate action, and the bill was forwarded to President Johnson's desk.

With the fate of his freedmen's bureau bill uncertain, Trumbull sent his civil rights proposal to the Senate floor after the judiciary committee approval of the measure.[23] In a speech, he defined its principal objectives: it guaranteed to all persons, regardless of color, their civil rights, including the right to sue, give evidence in court, hold, inherit, or sell property, and to enjoy the equal protection of the law against state officials' actions. He stressed that federal courts had jurisdiction over suits arising out of this measure to prevent state interference with its operation.[24] Trumbull had omitted any reference to political rights — voting or officeholding. He felt that the granting of these rights would not be sustained by Northern public opinion.[25]

Later, Trumbull amended his bill, declaring that all native-born blacks were American citizens. When opposition senators objected, he cited precedents to show that Congress, by statute, had conferred citizenship upon entire Indian tribes.[26] The next day, upon reflection, Trumbull broadened his grant of citizenship to include Indians who paid taxes, and also the Chinese.[27] The opposition tried to weaken the bill, but all crippling amendments were defeated; the Republicans then passed the bill, 33 to 12.[28]

In the lower House, a Republican, John A. Bingham, spearheaded the opposition. Bingham claimed the bill, although desirable, was unconstitutional. Burton C. Cook, Trumbull's co-tenant in the house on D Street, rallied support there for the measure.[29] Bingham displayed a jealous heart, since he had under consideration a constitutional amendment to accomplish the same purpose — the Fourteenth.[30] After House passage, this bill was also sent to President Johnson for his signature. Trumbull believed until the last moment that Johnson would sign both bills.[31]

Meanwhile, Johnson fidgeted about accepting the freedmen's bureau bill. He turned to advisors on the right edge of the political spectrum. Predictably, these counsellors urged a veto. No consideration was given to accepting the bill lest worse (from the Conservative viewpoint) follow.[32] Finally, Johnson vetoed the freedmen's bureau bill; his veto message called it unconstitutional, unwise, and unnecessary.[33] In the Senate, Garrett Davis made a rambling speech echoing the President's arguments. Trumbull, stung by the unconstitutional label pinned on his bill by Johnson and Davis, made a spontaneous answer, a torrent of words which covered several pages of the *Congressional Globe* and which compared favorably with any prepared speech on the same subject.[34] He sought repeatedly to refute the charges that his bill was unconstitutional.

Trumbull denied that he had sought a quarrel with the President; rather he said that he had accepted Johnson's state of the union message at face value. Hence, he thought that he was carrying out the Chief Executive's wishes. Then, to find his bill rejected by the President as unconstitutional caused Trumbull to "vindicate" his position. Analyzing the bill section by section, Trumbull made a speech which made many veteran senators, who had heard his sharp arraignments of Lincoln, wonder if this were the same man. Trumbull was considerate in references to the President. He peppered his address with sentiments such as, "I desire to speak respectfully of the Executive."

First, Trumbull said that the life of an essential agency such as the freedmen's bureau must continue in an orderly manner. Second, the bill did not, as opponents had claimed, establish a military jurisdiction over the entire country. Rather, Trumbull said, the bill made freedmen's bureau agents subject to the articles of war. This was a departure from usual procedure, as Trumbull admitted, but he said that these were unusual times. The war was not yet officially over, and the writ of habeas corpus was still suspended by executive order in the Southern states. Third, the federal government had fed indigent people before — Indians and Africans captured from slavetraders. Fourth, as to the criticism leveled at the sections giving the blacks title to certain abandoned lands which they were currently working, Trumbull stated that the bill's provisions were actually limited. They merely regularized the title given to the Negroes a year earlier by General W. T. Sherman. The title conferred by the act was for less than three years' time, until January 1868, and the original owners could reclaim their lands. With a smile and a shrug, Trumbull said the owners could have their lands returned sooner if they made provisions for the black tenants.

As to the charge that the bill was unconstitutional, Trumbull reiterated that Congress had been granted the power to legislate for the freed Negroes from the second section of the Thirteenth Amendment. He lashed at Johnson's argument that Congress should wait to legislate until the Southern states were again represented in Congress. If action taken without the Southerners were of doubtful constitutionality, then all the wartime legislation was included in that category. He closed, saying: "Now sir, with these remarks, made without any unkind feeling toward the Executive, with whom I should be glad to agree, but in justification of my own position, I submit the bill, so far as I am concerned to the decision of the Senate."[35] The *Nation* crowed that it was the "calmest, most logical, and most statesmanlike speech of the session. . . ."[36]

Most of the Illinois Republican organization ranged itself behind Trumbull upon this issue, although there were many who hoped to avoid a final break with Johnson.[37] The Senate served as the principal battleground, since it was conceded that the House would override the President's veto. In the Senate, the President's friends constructed a jerry-built coalition of Democrats, Conservative Unionists from the border, and tepid Republicans to sustain Johnson's veto.[38] To uphold the veto, six senators reversed their earlier positions; the vote was 30 to 18. It was a pyrrhic victory for Johnson, as he depleted his stock of political good will with several important moderate Republicans.[39]

This did not end the freedmen's bureau bill. A new measure was framed as a result of collaboration between Howard and Trumbull, and House leaders Stevens, Colfax, and T. D. Eliot of Massachusetts.[40] Eliot introduced the new bill in mid-May; by that time, Trumbull's attention had been distracted to other matters. His active support of the freedmen's bureau bill was no longer required, since Congress by then possessed a sufficient Radical majority to override the President. Johnson vetoed the bill following its final passage in July 1866, but Congress almost immediately overrode him.[41] This law differed from Trumbull's original proposal; its most important omission was land for the freed blacks' use.[42]

Despite the first freedmen's bureau veto, Johnson was still able to claim a tenuous perch within the party, but the President soon proceeded to jump off. In an ill-advised speech, he slashed at Stevens, Sumner, and Wendell Phillips, calling them as much at war with constitutional government as any Confederate had ever been.[43] Trumbull feared that in the coming Illinois senatorial election, he might be crushed between Radicalism (the Radicals he feared would never consider him one of their own) and Johnsonism. Therefore, he tried to keep his lines of communication open with Johnson. Also, he made no personal attacks upon the President and hoped he could convince other Republican congressmen to take the same moderate course.[44] Trumbull's conciliatory hope received a jolt when, on March 27, 1866, Johnson, with a stinging message, vetoed the civil rights bill.[45] For a time, Johnson had been in an agony of indecision over what to do, but in the end he rejected this far-reaching bill for the sake of political expediency.[46]

In his veto message, Johnson called the bill unconstitutional. In an appeal to prejudice, the President charged that the measure made citizens out of the gypsies and the Chinese as well as the blacks. He pointed out that foreigners, no matter how intelligent, had to undergo a naturalization process, whereas this bill granted citizenship to every black. Johnson repeated a theme he had used earlier with the freedmen's bureau bill, namely, that far-reaching legislation should be postponed until the Southern states had been readmitted to Congress.[47] In answer to the President this time, Trumbull did not make an impromptu speech, but carefully prepared an oration replying in detail to Johnson's veto message. Now Trumbull openly attacked the President, expressing his regret that Johnson had rejected the bill.

Trumbull declared the clauses conferring citizenship upon the blacks had been added merely for clarity, as even Edward Bates, Lincoln's attorney general, had admitted that blacks were citizens since the Thirteenth Amendment. Many times in American history, he stated, Congress had by statue conferred citizenship upon entire Indian tribes: As to Johnson's claim that no extraordinary legislation should be passed until the South was again represented in Congress, Trumbull declared that the excuse could be used to veto all legislation. Trumbull also asked whose fault it was that the South was unrepresented because of its attempted rebellion. To Johnson's offering as a compelling reason for vetoing the bill that Chinese and gypsies would gain citizenship, Trumbull turned back the pages of the *Globe* to the pre-war years. Then, Senator Andrew Johnson had attacked President Buchanan's veto of the homestead bill on the ground that Chinese and gypsies would be given homesteads. Trumbull declared that upon that occasion Senator Johnson had answered the objection years later of President Johnson: he had labeled this mention of Chinese and gypsies as pure prejudice. The law was not, Trumbull averred, aimed at states that protected the black equally with other citizens, but only at those who discriminated upon the basis of color.

Trumbull underscored Johnson's unreasonableness, declaring that he had held "numerous interviews" with the President while framing the bill and that he believed that it met Johnson's reservations. While the bill was before Congress, Trumbull stated, Johnson had numerous opportunities to indicate objections to it, but he had preferred silence. Then the President had precipitated a crisis with his veto. Concluding his speech, Trumbull asked that the bill be made law by overriding Johnson's veto.[48] Comment upon Trumbull's oratorical effort, which had covered six pages of the *Congressional Globe*, varied with the political views of observers. The New York *Times*, then supporting Johnson, sneered, "Upon one point, and that the starting point . . . Trumbull may be said to beg the question."[49] The Illinois Democratic press echoed the *Times* view.[50] The Radicals wildly applauded Trumbull.[51] Reverdy Johnson of Maryland, who was the Conservatives' most impressive orator and who had sat attentively throughout Trumbull's address taking copious notes so that he could reply, did so. The burden of Reverdy Johnson's harangue was that the power of Congress could not extend to the definition of citizenship, since that was a state function.[52] The vote in the Senate was again crucial. Both sides saw to it that every senator who would vote "right" was summoned or, if necessary, dragged to the Senate Chamber.[53] The Senate voted to override the veto by a count of 33 to 15.[54]

The House vote to override three days later was anticlimactic. The civil rights bill became law. If the Senate's refusal to override Johnson in the case of the original freedmen's bureau bill had been sobering to the Radicals,[55] their spectacular victory now was intoxicating.[56] The civil rights bill offered another instance where Johnson might have beaten a strategic withdrawal; instead, he preferred to charge at Congress head down. The effects were enormous. The chasm between the Radicals in Congress and Johnson had widened, never to be bridged, although for nearly a month after the civil rights veto, Trumbull continued to hope for an accommodation with the President. Personally, the effect upon Trumbull was far-reaching as well. The mantle of Senate Radical leadership was thrust upon him. He had not planned it, but the confrontation with Johnson proved a shot of adrenalin to his flagging career. It was painful to break with old associates, like James Doolittle of Wisconsin, who stubbornly stood by Johnson. On the other hand, Fessenden and Grimes, forced to choose like Trumbull himself, also went over to the Radicals. Old senatorial opponents, like Chandler and Sumner were now again allies.[57] By July, Trumbull realized that it was unconditional war with Johnson. He wrote William Jayne, "We have got to fight Johnson, because he *will* fight us."[58]

Now, even the blindest party hack could see the schism was irreparable. Moderates had to take sides at one extreme or the other of the political spectrum. The Radicals had captured the Republican party in Congress. The Johnson Republicans and the border state Conservatives, who had been elected under a variety of labels, gradually faded into the Democratic ranks. A wide gap opened between the two arrayed political armies on the question of reconstruction and its related issues.[59]

The classic picture of the Radicals that has emerged from the brushes and palettes of revisionist historians of the first half of the twentieth century, depicts a group of politicians favoring punitive action against the South for political reasons, men who uniformly favored lavish favors to business, and who were unwavering supporters of a protective tariff. Although the idea that the Radicals were so monolithic a group has recently itself been revised, Trumbull never fitted that classic picture of a Radical. His tariff position in the post-Civil War years was anti-protection. During the war, he had often supported the tariff measures proposed because the extra revenue which they generated was vital to the war effort. With the war over, he desired a thorough tariff revision. He was not a free trader, although as the years went by he had a tendency to consort with this doctrinaire group.[60] He favored a low tariff generating sufficient revenue to pay the national expenses, since he hoped for rigid government economy.

At this session of Congress, Trumbull presented many petitions from his constituents asking for tariff reductions.[61] Despite the sentiment for tariff reduction in the agricultural areas, congressmen from the northeastern section of the country pressed a bill providing further tariff hikes. This bill passed the House and came before the Senate. Even protectionist circles in the Illinois Republican party realized that this bill, if passed, would ruin that party's chances to carry that state in the crucial fall election. Trumbull's mail overwhelmingly asked him to defeat the new tariff measure.[62] Trumbull helped to postpone the bill for that session, although he proved unable to kill it outright. Even the Democratic press joined in the chorus of praise for his opposition to the hated tariff measure.[63]

Trumbull disapproved of the internal revenue system which had been created during the war. He thought it inequitable, grinding hardest upon ordinary farmers. When a new tax was proposed upon agricultural machinery, Trumbull helped defeat it.[64] Lashing out at internal taxes, he argued unsuccessfully against a levy of two dollars a gallon on "distilled spirits" which had been imposed in 1865. The existing tax had thereby been raised ten-fold. Trumbull argued that the tax was prohibitive and had badly injured the domestic industry. Moreover, it had caused tax evasions which the internal revenue service could not eradicate.[65]

Trumbull generally opposed favors to business or any measure to foster monopoly. He fought a bill to allow the Montana Iron Mining Company to purchase public land not on the open market. He opposed granting to one company the exclusive right to build bridges across the Mississippi River.[66] Yet he also opposed government favors to farmers, declaring upon one occasion that he did not see how the government would "ever get rich by appropriating money to enable farmers to cultivate larger crops and then collecting a tax from farmers."[67]

Trumbull's important role in drafting the civil rights bill became confused with authorship of the Fourteenth Amendment, which burned portions of the bill into the Constitution. Newspapers in the 1880's and 1890's often gave him credit for this amendment, but in truth his role in passing it was small. The Fourteenth Amendment was written in the joint committee on reconstruction; Trumbull's judiciary committee refused to act on the amendment, waiting until the reconstruction committee had framed a proposal.[68] The first section of the amendment did embody features of Trumbull's civil rights bill, but they appeared there through the efforts of Representative John A. Bingham, who had contended that the civil rights bill was unconstitutional.[69] The remaining sections of the amendment were all the invention of others.[70]

Trumbull played only a minor role in the amendment's Senate debates, saying that if Congress wished to chisel into the stone of the Constitution features of his civil rights bill, he had no objection.[71] He supported the amendment with his vote in the preliminary skirmishes and again upon final passage.[72] He never foresaw the use of the Fourteenth Amendment in the last quarter of the nineteenth century to protect corporations from state regulation. To him, it was purely an attempt to protect the black and resolve other troublesome issues raised by the recent rebellion.[73]

The reconstruction remained unsettled. Although the Johnson governments in the South continued to function as de facto governments, Congress had barred them from representation in that body. The question on everybody's lips was, "What now?" As early as March 1, when Trumbull spoke in Baltimore, he spent much of his address assuring his auditors that Congress speedily would evolve a reconstruction plan.[74] The Radicals finally devised their reconstruction program, although it was an improvisation. The Fourteenth Amendment, having passed Congress, had been sent to the states for ratification. On the advice of the President, all of the Southern states except Tennessee, which was firmly in the Radical camp, spurned it. This action gave the Radicals an opening which they exploited. Tennessee would be readmitted to the Union, and the claim was made that if other Southern states had acted similarly, they would also have been readmitted.

The House promptly passed Resolution No. 83, which stated that Tennessee, having ratified the Fourteenth Amendment, was declared restored "to her former practical relations to the Union. . . ."[75] Feeling the grain of public opinion, Trumbull had already introduced a Senate resolution recognizing the Tennessee government.[76] When the House resolution reached the Senate, Trumbull decided to use it as a basis for action, but proposed amendments to quiet his constitutional scruples. The judiciary committee agreed.[77] The same day the judiciary committee considered the House resolution, Trumbull reported his amended version to the Senate. His principal innovation was a preamble asserting congressional power to reconstruct a state, and recounting the Tennessee government's loyal manifestations, including the ratification of both the Thirteenth and Fourteenth Amendments. He had reworked the resolution's body to read that Tennessee was recognized as "entitled to all the rights of a state government under the Constitution. . . ."[78]

In the ninety-degree temperature of the Senate Chamber, the oratory boiled. Sherman led several senators who questioned the preamble's wisdom, holding that it needlessly antagonized Johnson and invited a veto.[79] Trumbull replied that the preamble was a constitutional necessity, and that Andrew Johnson would never veto a resolution readmitting his home state.[80] When Sherman persisted in his opposition, pedagogue Trumbull lectured him that Tennessee had done more than ratify the Fourteenth Amendment and that the preamble justifiably emphasized this fact.[81] In the end, the Senate accepted the judiciary committee amendments,[82] and approved the amended resolution.[83] The House rejected the Senate amendments, but a conference committee bridged the differences between the chambers so that Trumbull substantially won his points. The measure was then sent to the President. Finally, he signed the resolution, but came out swinging at his favorite target, Congress, announcing his refusal to recognize the preamble as legislation.[84]

A great political battle now developed over Trumbull's re-election. Since he had broken with the President, his patronage had been given to a Johnsonite, his former colleague, Orville H. Browning.[85] Some of his staunchest supporters holding federal appointive offices were removed by the President.[86] So keenly did Trumbull feel the patronage squeeze that he authored an amendment to the post office appropriation bill protecting the remaining loyal employees from presidential removal after Congress had adjourned for the summer. Trumbull's amendment touched off a three-weeks' debate which ended in a vote of 23 to 16 against it. Trumbull was bitter, since some Radicals broke ranks to vote with the Democrats and Conservatives. Several historians have dubbed Trumbull's measure the progenitor of the tenure of office act.[87] Not only were the Johnsonites drawing a bead upon him, but Trumbull faced a violent battle for renomination within his own party. The returned Civil War veterans were noisy in their claims for political recognition of their sacrifices.

The most eager soldier-politician who thirsted for Trumbull's place was Governor Richard J. Oglesby. Oglesby had a built-in advantage; he had been severely wounded in action while winning a major generalcy. Although he had succeeded Yates as Illinois governor in 1865, his political ambition was not slaked. He had one unsurmountable obstacle: his successor under the Illinois constitution was a universally unpopular lieutenant governor.[88] Oglesby hoped for a deadlock, so that he could win as a compromise candidate. Therefore, he nurtured the hopes of other soldier-aspirants, such as John A. Logan and John M. Palmer. At the same time, he wrote Trumbull, advising him on political matters — as though he were Trumbull's best friend.[89]

The strongest emerging candidate was John Alexander "Black Jack" Logan, an innate opportunist who could not support his family out of office. A native-born Illinoisan, with jet-black hair and mustaches, he had a flair for spread-eagle oratory. With a pretty, intelligent wife to manage him and a war record that gleamed, he seemed invincible. Logan already had enjoyed a considerable political career. He had been elected twice to Congress as a Douglas Democrat. His campaigning always had been hard-hitting; "Dirty Work" Logan irate Republicans had dubbed him. During the war, he compiled a creditable combat record. Becoming a War Democrat, he supported the Lincoln administration, returning frequently to Illinois to campaign.[90]

At the end of the war, Logan, now a Republican, eyed Trumbull's senatorial toga.[91] In late 1865 and early 1866, Logan agonized over supporting Johnson against Congress. The President wooed him strenuously. Logan, however, with a talent for political survival, had deftly refused Johnson's blandishments, leaping nimbly aboard the tailgate of the Radical bandwagon. He soon elbowed his way to the front, where he hoped to drive the horses.[92] Keeping in the public eye, he made a lecture tour early in 1866 to raise money for a soldiers' orphans' home.[93] Oglesby and Logan, working in double harness, supported B. F. Stephenson, a former surgeon of the Fourteenth Illinois Infantry, in his scheme to build a veterans' organization — the future Grand Army of the Republic (GAR). While it was a fraternal group, the political implications for soldier-candidates were obvious. By spring 1866, Dr. Stephenson, aided by Oglesby's well-oiled statehouse machine, had successfully organized the society.

Trumbull quickly learned of the Oglesby-Logan challenge to him. His alarmed political friends relayed rumors of the soldier-candidates' activities.[94] Then he received intelligence that his opponents were using against him the fact that he had not supported bounty equalization.[95] The veterans' cry for bounty equalization meant that the federal government should equalize the varying amounts paid by counties and states as bounties to stimulate Civil War enlistment. Organized veterans also proposed that the federal government pass its own bounty measure. The House heeded the veterans' shout and passed a generous bill. The more conservative Senate stalled the bill while it warily eyed it. A proposal was made that those veterans receiving generous state and local bonuses should not share in the federal grant. Several senators vowed that if their states were to be discriminated against, there would be no bounty legislation.[96]

Under the spur of the many excited letters from his supporters, Trumbull charged into the fray, Senators Henry Wilson and Benjamin Wade previously had guided the measure, but now they were joined by an eager Trumbull. He spelled out his attitude with clarity for the homefolks, saying, "I have steadily voted [for] . . . equalizing these bounties."[97] In the end, the Senate cut the scope of the bounty bill. A conference committee labored manfully to harmonize differences in a bill that could be passed. A unique crazy-quilt of legislation emerged. Moderate benefits were included for veterans. Coupled with this was a two-thousand-dollar-a-year raise for congressmen! With something for everyone, the bill rolled through Congress.[98]

Trumbull fought back against the Oglesby-Logan machinations. Many minor Illinois politicians had been the recipients through the years of Trumbull favors and so were committed to him. After a little pressure, these politicians announced their solid support of Trumbull.[99] In addition Trumbull won the endorsement of many alarmed civilian-politicians; these included Gustave Koerner; Senator Richard Yates; Trumbull's protégé,

Springfield district Congressman Shelby M. Cullom; and his close friend, Representative Burton C. Cook.[100] Even before the adjournment of Congress, Trumbull's friends whispered that he would accept another election as a personal rebuke to the perfidious President Johnson.[101] "Spontaneously," pieces appeared throughout the Illinois party press, arguing that Trumbull's re-election would be the greatest reproach which the state could give Johnson.[102]

Trumbull had support from local leaders to whom he represented the image of what a senator should be. One of Trumbull's supporters wrote him, "I am for you for reelection against the field not only for the sake of 'auld lang syne,' but for the best interests of the state. We have too many partizans, drunkards, and stump speakers now in office."[103] Also, Logan unexpectedly had stubbed his toe in the first state GAR convention, held while Congress was still in session. Logan's followers had expected to control the organization machinery and use it to carry him to the senatorship. But in the secret session of the convention, Logan was defeated for state commander in favor of John M. Palmer. The Trumbull partisans in the GAR had used Logan's brief flirtation with the President against him. Also, Logan's obvious ambition had aroused misgivings among some delegates.

Trumbull adherents cheered the result. Yet Palmer's election proved a mixed blessing. Palmer himself nursed political ambitions, and he now was hailed by soldier-politicians as appropriate senatorial timber.[104] Trumbull became sufficiently alarmed to cancel his Connecticut summer vacation and head directly home to fight for his political life.

CHAPTER FOURTEEN

THE CAUCUS, AND REPERCUSSIONS

TRUMBULL'S RE-ELECTION CAMPAIGN began immediately upon his return to Chicago. Trumbull had two goals: first, to insure that favorable Republican legislators were nominated; second to elect them in a successful fall campaign in which he assisted so prominently as to hold their loyalty.

C. M. Hawley, then George Trumbull's law partner, and Horace White arranged a ''spontaneous'' celebration to signal Lyman's return to Chicago.[1] According to schedule, an arrangement committee called upon Trumbull at his home on Lake Avenue — then just outside the city limits. The property contained a spacious lawn and garden, and it was in the garden that the committee found Lyman hard at work. After they had explained their mission, Trumbull, feigning surprise, announced that he would change clothes and accompany them to the theatre for a report to his constituents. Trumbull and the committee then boarded an Illinois Central train to downtown Chicago. It was seven-thirty on a warm August evening as Trumbull arrived at the downtown station. An enthusiastic crowd greeted him, and a ''grand procession'' escorted Trumbull to the Opera House.

Inside the Opera House, every seat was filled. When Trumbull appeared bouquets of flowers were thrown down from the balcony, while applause shook the building. J. Y. Scammon, a veteran political journeyman, introduced Trumbull. Few stump speeches make acceptable reading, and Trumbull's proved no exception. Trumbull felt more comfortable in the realm of ideas than on the hustings, yet his speech accurately indicated his thinking. It would serve as his campaign speech for 1866. He told Chicagoans that Johnson had blustered about making treason odious and then had allowed the same Southern traitorous group to continue in power. Still, Congress had been willing to cooperate with the President. But Johnson had vetoed vital legislation, forcing a break with the national legislature. The President had then tried to form a rival Republican organization with federal officeholders as a nucleus. When this attempt collapsed, he had turned to the Democrats. In the finale, Trumbull declared ''the issue in the November election . . . [is] whether this country is to be governed by loyal or disloyal men.''[2]

Trumbull ignored a new movement stirring Illinoisans that had its basis in the state's long frontier aversion to monopoly. In late 1865 and early 1866, there was an antimonopoly rebellion against the high charges of grain warehouses and railroads. The rebellious farmers wanted to control these monopolies with the state's police power.[3] Trumbull did not realize this movement's importance and ignored it in his campaign. Perhaps he feared it would split the Republican party if made an issue. Besides, he was distant from the average prairie farmer's feelings, having spent most of the last twelve years outside Illinois.

The underground struggle between Trumbull and the Oglesby-Logan faction surfaced at the Republican state convention. Artfully, Trumbull's lieutenants split the Logan and Oglesby forces, thus capturing control of the convention machinery. To neutralize Logan, he was nominated for congressman-at-large; Logan protested that he did not want the nomination. However the Trumbull men, with straight faces, told him that, as a young man, he would thus achieve a state-wide reputation. While Logan was still arguing that he already possessed a state-wide reputation, he was nominated.[4]

As usual, Trumbull did not attend the convention, relying instead upon Norman Judd and George T. Brown to represent him. When he heard the news of Logan's nomination, he felt that it was a mistake, and so wrote Brown. No, replied Brown, Logan would find it impossible to run simultaneously for the House and the Senate.[5] Trumbull's cohorts could not yet quit. During August, the legislative nominating conventions were held at the county level. Koerner, Brown, Judd, and a dozen other Trumbull lieutenants generally manipulated these conventions to pick pro-Trumbull candidates. Trumbull himself made discreet appearances at Belleville, Alton, and Edwardsville. Nor was this all. Using Trumbull's dramatic rupture with Johnson, they usually obtained ironclad convention instructions to the candidates requiring them to support Trumbull's re-election.[6] Only in southern Illinois, where Logan as a native son had an irresistible appeal, were the Trumbullites unsuccessful.[7]

Trumbull kindled the party's fire by his relentless campaigning. In quick succession, he took the stump at Evanston, Fairfield, Flora, and Morrison, lashing the ''copper-Johnsonites.''[8] He campaigned at Ottawa, Pekin, Rockford, Woodstock, Monmouth, Macomb, Quincy, Bloomington, and Lincoln, where the gist of his text was that the electorate should choose a Congress that would dance to the Radical pipes.[9] Late in the canvass, at Havana, addressing an assemblage of ''Irish Radicals,'' he cried that the rebels had ''forfeited all claims and all rights except the right to be hanged and the right to be damned.''[10] The same theme was repeated by Logan, who also ducked the antimonopoly issues in his speeches. He and Trumbull ignored each other during their campaigning.[11] The Democratic tickets, despite support from the Johnson Republicans, proved grossly overmatched against the Radical Republicans throughout the North and West. Illinois chalked up impressive gains for the Radical faction.[12]

With the legislature Republican, Trumbull's campaign for re-election entered a new phase. Trumbull wrote many of his party's legislators, asking them for support. All except two of the legislators addressed, well over a majority of the Republican members, replied favoring his re-election.[13] Yet Logan and Oglesby refused to despair. Through their control of the state central committee, they had nominated several friends for the legislature. From this base, they still hoped to win. To confuse the situation, Palmer announced as the "soldiers' favorite," becoming an active senatorial candidate. Thus a four-cornered fight for the Senate developed. Trumbull's three opponents were hampered because they drew their support from common sources. Until they could unite their support upon one of themselves, they individually fell below Trumbull in strength.[14]

Logan's pen also scratched busily as he importuned doubtful Republican legislators. His replies fell into several categories. Four legislators declared in response to Logan that they had pledged their word to support Trumbull. They added that they had accepted Logan's candidacy for the House, thinking that he had forsworn his senatorial ambitions.[15] One legislator wrote Logan flatly telling him that he favored Trumbull as the best available man for the place.[16] Fifteen legislators responded in praise of Logan's statesmanlike qualities, but claiming to be irretrievably bound by district nominating conventions' instructions to support Trumbull.[17] Only two legislators who replied were favorable to Logan.[18] Despite this response, after conferring with national leaders in Washington, Logan wrote his wife, "I do not intend to be beat for Senator."[19]

Palmer wrote fifteen letters to selected legislators, but drew a near-blank in response. His replies indicated that a few legislators were backing Oglesby, a slightly larger group leaned to Logan, but the largest group was firmly instructed for Trumbull.[20] One of the latter group wrote Palmer: "Many are now instructed and committed who would not have been, if you and Oglesby and Logan had worked a tenth as hard as Trumbull did."[21]

In the midst of this feverish maneuvering, the second session of the Thirty-Ninth Congress convened. Returning to Washington, Trumbull entrusted his campaign to William Jayne and Norman Judd. In Illinois, Logan and Oglesby had persuaded Palmer to join in a coalition with them. Palmer found the chance irresistible. The three soldier-candidates tried to add veteran Congressman Elihu B. Washburne to their alliance, but Washburne refused, announcing his support for Trumbull.

The soldier triumvirate evolved a new scheme. They would ask by secret ballot to the Republican caucus, "Should Trumbull succeed himself?" The negative could be taken by friends of the three and by any secretly disgruntled Trumbull supporters. If Trumbull were eliminated, the three rivals could joust for his seat. Unfortunately for the conspirators, their plan was prematurely revealed in the *Illinois State Journal*. Trumbull immediately wrote Jayne, warning him of the plot and instructing him to press for a voice vote.[22] Trumbull's managers had been enlarged to include Colonel A. C. Babcock, a returned army veteran then on the state central committee. Trumbull also successfully begged the long-time political luminaries W. C. Flagg and Jesse W. Fell to assist his campaign. Blowzy U. S. Senator Richard Yates, a convivial man at home in Springfield's bars, lent his weight to the Trumbull team.[23]

One factor in Trumbull's favor was the wide press support he commanded in Illinois. The Chicago *Tribune*, edited by Trumbull's protégé, Horace White, served as his personal mouthpiece throughout the campaign.[24] The *Illinois State Journal* vacillated between neutrality toward Trumbull and open hostility.[25] Still, the only important Illinois newspaper which was unwaveringly hostile to him was the Chicago *Republican*, founded by men who hated the Chicago *Tribune*'s publishers.[26] Early in January 1867, the opposition resurrected *ex parte* Milligan. This case seemed a dead ash, since the suit had been decided the previous April, but the opposition managed to exploit it. Lambdin P. Milligan, an Indiana copperhead, had been freed by the United States Supreme Court because that tribunal stated that the habeas corpus act of March 3, 1863, had taken from military commissions the right to try civilians behind the Union lines.[27] Trumbull, as the supposed sponsor of this act, was blamed for the decision.[28] In the pages of the Chicago *Republican*, the Illinois senator was pictured, because of the 1863 act, as an inept bumbler. His opposition declared that Trumbull inadvertently had destroyed his two greatest post-war accomplishments, the freedmen's bureau bill and the civil rights bill, by his earlier sponsorship of the habeas corpus act. Also, his opponents implied, Trumbull agreed with the Supreme Court decision as nullifying his own reconstruction measures.[29]

In reply, Trumbull issued a forceful denial.[30] In it, he argued that he was not the chief author of the habeas corpus bill. In addition, he declared, the Milligan decision had not invalidated all trials by military commission and so his reconstruction measures were valid.[31] Trumbull had painted a better face upon both his responsibility for the habeas corpus bill and the effect of the Milligan decision than the facts warranted, but his letter of denial was effectively used by Jayne in the pre-caucus maneuvering.

After a hard look at the political situation, Logan abruptly withdrew from the senatorial contest. He wrote his wife: "I got out of the race as I am determined not to be beaten and injure my future prospects."[32] Oglesby also withdrew from the contest in response to the popular feeling that the governor should complete his term before seeking a new office.[33] Logan and Oglesby supported Palmer, who continued the fight with Trumbull. Logan fought with gusto, chuckling as he wrote his wife that for Palmer to defeat Trumbull "would be a great triumph after all the instruction he obtained in favor of himself."[34]

On January 7, Palmer's hopes plummeted. Republican members of the legislature's lower house voted 37 to 2 for Trumbull's re-election. Nevertheless, Palmer staved off a general Republican legislature caucus, pleading that he needed time to present his case. On January 8, a letter appeared in the Republican press, dated December 1865, from Palmer to Trumbull suggesting legislation to protect Southern blacks. The plain implication was that Palmer deserved the credit for the civil rights bill.[35] With this development, Trumbull remained away from Springfield no longer. He had been portrayed as skulking in Washington, unable to face Palmer. As soon as Trumbull left for Springfield, word was telegraphed to Palmer by his adherents. Quickly, a circular was printed attacking Trumbull alternatively for leading too much or too little, too timidly or too arrogantly. Copies of the circular were reprinted in several Springfield newspapers.[36]

Palmer's campaign seemed to have burst into flame, but only briefly, Trumbull ignored the other charges and concentrated upon the story that Palmer really authored the civil rights bill. Fortunately, he had kept Palmer's letter in its original envelope. While the letter had been dated in December with the heading of Louisville, Kentucky, it had been postmarked January 14, 1866, and had been mailed from Palmer's hometown, Carlinville, Illinois. As Palmer admitted much later, he had written the letter in December, but had not mailed it then. By the time he did, Trumbull had already introduced the civil rights bill.

Upon Trumbull's arrival in Springfield, he confronted Palmer. There, in front of gaping onlookers, he told Palmer that while many people had suggested a civil rights bill, that legislation's provisions had been drawn up by himself, and that Palmer had no more to do with its final form than "a child unborn."[37] On the night of January 12, the Palmer faction held a rally in Springfield. Palmer stoutly claimed that he and not Trumbull had authored the civil rights bill. Oglesby and Logan also addressed the throng, but spoke only concerning Palmer's superior qualifications.

What crushed Palmer's last hope was the announcement of the result of a poll taken by the Illinois Grand Army of the Republic posts. This poll had been made when Logan and Oglesby were still in the race. The result showed more posts endorsing Trumbull than any one of the soldier candidates.[38] On the evening of January 14, the Republican legislative caucus met. The Palmer men wanted a secret ballot. This proposal might allow disgruntled Trumbull supporters to violate their instructions. But the scheme failed; the vote was 47 to 29. The Palmer adherents capitulated; by a voice vote, Trumbull was nominated by acclamation.[39] With the Republicans united behind Trumbull, the vote in the joint legislative convention was a formality. Trumbull easily defeated the nominal Democratic contender, T. Lyle Dickey.[40] The rift between Palmer and Trumbull gradually closed. At the time of the Liberal Republican revolt in 1872, Palmer befriended Trumbull. In 1875, Trumbull's nephew married one of Palmer's daughters, with the consent of the two families.[41]

Trumbull did not play the commanding role in the second session that he had in the first session of the Thirty-Ninth Congress, yet he remained active. In December 1866, while his re-election remained in doubt, he still kept his Radical posture. Trumbull believed that Johnson's gravest mistake had been his indiscriminate use of the pardoning power. Therefore, on December 10, 1866, he introduced a bill which sailed through Congress to repeal section thirteen of the second confiscation act of July 17, 1862.[42] Trumbull's attempt to hobble Johnson failed, since the President maintained that his pardoning power was derived directly from the Constitution.[43]

In December, Trumbull demanded that the Johnson governments in the ten unreconstructed Southern states be dismantled as rebel-infested. He was in constant communication with the Louisiana Radical faction. He presented a petition from that group, asking that the Johnson government there be abolished by congressional act.[44]

After his re-election, Trumbull continued in the Radical orbit. He voted for the first reconstruction act which overturned the existing Johnson governments in all the former Confederate states except Tennessee. The ten Southern states were divided into five military districts, each subject to a major general commandant. A fresh start upon political reconstruction was to be assayed under military control. A new voters' list would be established including blacks, but excluding former Confederates ineligible for officeholding under the proposed Fourteenth Amendment. These voters would elect constitutional convention delegates to draft an organic document for each state. After the constitution, which allowed black suffrage, was accepted by the voters and the state had ratified the Fourteenth Amendment, it then could be readmitted to the Union.[45] Congress proved unable to compel the law's enforcement in the face of the executive's hostility. Unsympathetic to the reconstruction act, Johnson used every ambiguity to defeat its purpose. Therefore, Congress had to pass additional statutes to define the original act.

By special legislation, the Congress elected in November 1866, met in session early in March 1867. When it convened, the House passed a second reconstruction act, clarifying the first. The bill then was referred to the Senate judiciary committee. Trumbull proposed many changes to the House bill. One change provided that the constitutional convention must submit their product to a popular ratifying vote.[46]

In his insistence upon popular ratification, Trumbull became embarrassingly successful. The committee, after hearing his arguments about the

Democratic process in constitution-making, voted over his protest that a majority of the registered voters must approve new constitutions. As Trumbull explained, this was an impractical suggestion. He pointed out that opponents of reconstruction need only to register as voters and then shun the polls. Helped by absentees, prevalent in any election, they could defeat any new constitution.[47] The Senate spurned his appeal. But he was prophetic; Alabama Conservatives defeated the new constitution, using this tactic. Despite this deficiency, Trumbull reluctantly supported the second reconstruction bill in the Senate.[48] Johnson vetoed the bill, and Congress overrode him and recessed.

By construing the law narrowly, Johnson succeeded in hampering congressional reconstruction. In July 1867, Congress angrily passed a third reconstruction act, defining anew the congressional intention. A bill for this purpose was introduced into the House by Thaddeus Stevens, passed, and sent to the Senate.[49] Notwithstanding this fact, Trumbull framed his own bill. Trumbull's bill readily passed the Senate as a substitute for the Stevens measure. A conference committee adjusted the differences between the two houses, the final bill being closely modeled upon Trumbull's Senate proposal. In the end, the measure became law over the President's veto.[50]

This law declared that Congress intended to declare the Johnson governments to be illegal. It confirmed military commanders' right to remove any civil officer and temporarily to fill the vacancy. Concerning the new voting lists compiled in each state, the generals must investigate the loyalty of voters taking the ironclad oath. No voter could be barred because of race. Lastly, the measure provided that the reconstruction acts be construed "liberally."[51] Weighing the evidence, Trumbull had not favored black suffrage as a condition for the Southern states' readmittance. He believed that only a state could define the conditions of suffrage. While reconstruction was before Congress, Republican senators caucused to decide this vital issue, Trumbull arguing against forcing black suffrage on the South. But the more Radical wing of the party won this crucial vote by two votes.[52] Unconvinced, Trumbull contributed an essay to the inaugural issue of the Chicago *Advance* in August 1867. In it, he argued that Congress, under the Constitution, could not constitutionally set voting qualifications for the states.[53]

Toward the Southern people, Trumbull felt little malice. When an impoverished former student from Georgia needed money to pay debts that threatened his son with jail, Trumbull obliged him with the necessary sum. Trumbull did not offer the Georgian the money as a gift, probably because he knew the Southerner's pride would not permit it; instead, he loaned the man the money with the understanding that the Georgian would repay it at his convenience.[54] Although Trumbull had been characterized "as pure as the driven snow and nearly as cold,"[55] he was capable of many quiet charities. Frequently, both during and after the war, Illinoisans who were stranded without funds in the national capital turned to him for help. A friend who knew him estimated that Trumbull, who was never wealthy, thus spent hundreds of dollars.[56]

Despite his earnest efforts, Trumbull's financial status had not greatly improved. Although he switched out of oil investment and gold speculation,[57] he then bought heavily in the stock of the Rock Island Railroad, which promptly fell in value.[58] When it rose to nearly what he had paid for it, he sold.[59] Speaking of Lyman's investments, Julia candidly declared, "I think it will be your lot to loose [sic] whatever you do. . . . I dont [sic] think you were born for a speculator."[60] At this time, however, more of Trumbull's real estate holdings appreciated in value and their sale helped his financial situation.[61]

Although usually hostile to new federal functions, Trumbull advocated a small number of "vital" projects. Although many senators ridiculed the authorization of a department of education, Trumbull rebuked them, saying its establishment was "of great importance to the country."[62] And much in advance of his time, Trumbull opposed any discrimination in pay between men and women clerks performing comparable assignments.[63]

In the fall of 1867, Trumbull and his family moved into rented quarters in one of a row of red brick houses which enterprising George T. Brown had remodeled from the wartime Capitol Prison.[64] Walter took a job his father had obtained for him as clerk of the Senate patent office committee and settled down in Washington. Independent, Walter lived at a boarding-house on G Street.[65] Still, he acted as his father's confidential lieutenant, running many political errands for him.

When Congress convened in December 1867, an embarrassing situation confronted the Radicals. The new Alabama constitution had been rejected by the voters under the existing rules. Although the constitution had garnered a majority of the votes cast at the election, it had not received a majority of the total registered voters. Absenteeism, plus the Conservatives' calculated avoidance of the polls, had turned the trick.[66]

In answer, the House Radicals passed the fourth reconstruction bill, changing the rules for ratifying elections. This bill was bottled up in the Senate judiciary committee by Trumbull. He objected to a Radical amendment which allowed a majority of the votes cast at an election to ratify a new constitution and thus to validate retroactively Alabama's new organic law. Trumbull's sense of constitutional fitness was violated by this procedure. Finally, one of the new post-war Radical leaders, the wartime Governor of Indiana, O. P. Morton, leaked the report that he publicly would denounce Trumbull as a traitor to the Radical cause. Although Trumbull denied that it had forced his hand, in February 1868 he reported out the controversial bill. To answer critics of his deliberateness, Trumbull noted that at the previous session, he had favored the very amendment which the Republican majority now so hotly demanded. Then the Radicals had castigated him for being undemocratic. Nevertheless, bowing to party pressure, he now reported the bill as amended by the judiciary committee.[67] With Trumbull's vote, it easily cleared the Senate, 28 to 6.[68]

Early in 1868, Trumbull became involved in the McCardle case. It began with publication by a Mississippi editor, W. H. McCardle, of scathing attacks upon the army occupation authorities. He was promptly arrested on charges ranging from disturbing the peace to inciting a rebellion. Scheduled for trial before a military commission, McCardle applied to the United States circuit court for a writ of habeas corpus. Although the writ was granted by the court, the army refused to surrender its prisoner. Ultimately, the court sustained the army by ruling that the prisoner should remain in military custody. Through his attorneys, McCardle appealed to the Supreme Court. The case struck at the constitutional roots of reconstruction

At about the same time, Johnson rid himself of Secretary of War Edwin M. Stanton, who had been playing a double game. While sitting in the President's cabinet, he often seemed to be Johnson's loyal advisor; however, he secretly leaked cabinet secrets to the Radicals. Johnson replaced him with the military commander-in-chief, U. S. Grant, as secretary of war *ad interim*. One of the first problems Grant faced was to defend the army against McCardle, since the Attorney General, Henry Stanbery, refused to appear for it.[69] The alarmed Grant sought legal counsel, and settled upon Trumbull. To Grant, Trumbull seemed the logical man, an experienced constitutional lawyer and a prominent Radical who had framed the very laws which were then questioned. When Grant offered Trumbull the thorny case,[70] Trumbull immediately accepted.[71]

Then the situation took another twist. Under the tenure of office act, the Senate refused to concur in Johnson's dismissal of Stanton, and Grant quickly surrendered the place as secretary of war back to Stanton. This action did not affect Trumbull's employment, since Stanton was impressed with Trumbull's legal talents.[72] Reviewing the case, Trumbull decided to move that the Supreme Court dismiss it for lack of jurisdiction.[73] The Radicals became alarmed that the Supreme Court, using the Milligan decision as a precedent, would rule the trying of a civilian by a military tribunal to be unconstitutional, thus undermining reconstruction.[74]

Trumbull's attitude was revealed in January 1868, when he warned the Supreme Court to leave reconstruction alone. Trumbull argued, in a speech consistent with his attitude toward judicial review, that the courts were ill-equipped to handle a political question such as reconstruction.[75]

The McCardle case on the one point of the court's jurisdiction was argued before the supreme tribunal on January 31 and February 7. On the latter date, Trumbull, assisted by James Hughes and Matthew Hale Carpenter, argued the case for the army. Trumbull brought Hughes and Carpenter into the case, as he was impressed by their courtroom experience. Carpenter was a brilliant but unscrupulous lawyer. At first a Democrat, Carpenter had switched during the Civil War to being a War Democrat, and then during reconstruction openly to the Republican cause. However, Carpenter never allowed his current political opinions to stand in the way of his legal career.[76] In his argument, Trumbull emphasized that the act of February 5, 1867, did not apply. Trumbull waved it away, since it had been intended to protect Federal authorities from state interference — not to serve as an avenue of appeal for military prisoners.[77]

On February 17, the Court decided to hear the merits of the case under the act of February 5, 1867 in March.[78] The Conservatives, realizing the significance of the McCardle case, provided the imprisoned editor with the best legal artillery available, Buchanan's former Attorney General and Secretary of State, Jeremiah Sullivan Black of Pennsylvania. Black had a florid courtroom manner. For two days, he spoke on McCardle's behalf.[79] With his cold and dry manner, Trumbull was Black's antithesis. Ably assisted by Carpenter, Trumbull contended that the circuit court could not hear McCardle's appeal for a writ of habeas corpus. Further, Trumbull defended the reconstruction act against Black's attacks of unconstitutionality.[80]

As the Supreme Court made glacial progress toward a decision in the McCardle case, the Radicals in Congress acted. As early as January, a bill had passed the House requiring a two-thirds vote of the Supreme Court to reach a decision.[81] Fearing the House measure was too severe for Senate approval, Trumbull prepared his own bill. On February 17, 1868, he introduced a measure defining the federal courts' jurisdiction to exclude cases such as McCardle's. The measure declared reconstruction to be a political question not subject to judicial review.[82]

Although Trumbull pushed his bill through the Senate judiciary committee in less than two weeks,[83] it then dropped from sight. Faced by the Conservative senators' determination to filibuster the bill until the Supreme Court had decided the McCardle case, the Radicals searched for a more ready weapon. Oregon Senator George H. Williams, unconnected with previous anti-court legislation, sponsored a brief measure which innocuously changed the legal procedure in revenue cases. Listlessly, the Senate passed the bill. The proposal went to the House of Representatives, where the Radicals quietly tacked on an amendment repealing the section of the act of February 5, 1867, permitting appeals to the Supreme Court on a writ of habeas corpus. The amended measure passed the Senate, where the Conservatives never bothered to read the fine print.[84]

Old Thomas Ewing, Sr., grasped its significance. Ewing wrote a member of Johnson's cabinet, pointing to the proposal as one calling for a presidential veto.[85] Johnson obliged; in his veto message, he ripped the mask from the measure.[86] The House overrode the veto easily. The Senate, with Trumbull voting *Yes*, repassed the bill, 33 to 9.[87] Although the Supreme

Court could have decided the McCardle case before the bill became law, it avoided a head-on clash with Congress. When two justices pushed for a decision, they were overruled.[88]

In the spring of 1869, the Supreme Court allowed rehearings upon its jurisdiction. At that time, Trumbull and Carpenter nimbly argued that Congress had withdrawn the Supreme Court's jurisdiction and asked that the case be dismissed.[89] On April 12, 1869, speaking for the Court, Chief Justice Salmon P. Chase accepted this reasoning, dropping the suit.[90] Trumbull was well rewarded for the McCardle case, receiving initially $3,000, and later, $7,000 more from the war department.[91] Trumbull split the fee with Hughes and Carpenter.

Political opponents later mercilessly attacked the fee as excessive, although it was set by the war department and not by Trumbull. Later after Trumbull's conduct in the voting at Johnson's impeachment trial, the charge was raised that the President had bribed Trumbull by employing him as attorney in the case. This accusation Trumbull usually answered by pointing out that the war department at that time had been in the hands of Johnson's enemies. Another charge declared that it was improper for Trumbull as a senator to take money from the government for legal services; this, too, Trumbull could refute. There was no statute forbidding it, and it had been common practice for congressmen to represent the government in court. One charge which Trumbull could not dismiss was that he had used his position as a senator to aid his case as a lawyer. The many charges concerning the McCardle case caused Trumbull to spend so much time on the defensive that it probably would have been better had he never accepted Grant's offer.[92]

Historians have traditionally characterized Trumbull as a Radical from the spring of 1865 to the spring of 1868. He was always a Radical with a difference. His generally careful attitude toward the law foreshadowed his vote in Johnson's impeachment trial, a paramount issue in the spring of 1868.

CHAPTER FIFTEEN

A FUNDAMENTAL DECISION

AS EARLY AS DECEMBER 1865, some Illinois German-Americans had sent Trumbull a petition for Johnson's impeachment because of his handling of reconstruction.[1] In the popular parlance, ''impeachment'' covers the entire process of removing an official from office. Technically, it means only the first step, the preferring of charges by the House of Representatives. Since impeachment is a rarely-used process, there has been much confusion concerning impeachment grounds. At this time, some authorities believed that impeachment grounds were broad and included more than criminal offenses; others felt than an official to be impeached must commit a crime. The latter group had won a wider audience than the former, and this fact predetermined the Johnson trial outcome.[2]

In January 1867, three sets of impeachment resolutions were introduced into the House. One eventually passed, directing the House Judiciary Committee to investigate Johnson.[3] Although an investigation of criminal charges against Johnson turned up nothing, nonetheless, the House Judiciary Committee declared Johnson's political actions impeachable.[4] Months later, in December 1867, when Congress reconvened, the House voted down this report, 57 to 108, moderate Republicans rejecting impeachment.[5]

The Johnson impeachment drive stalled for several weeks, when a new opportunity appeared. A tenure of office act shielded Radical officeholders from Johnson's power of removal. Also applying to cabinet officers, it read that these officials held their places for the presidential term, plus one month. During this term, they could be replaced only with the Senate's consent.[6] Trumbull voted for this measure over Johnson's veto.[7] As we have seen, Johnson lost patience with Stanton and in August 1867 suspended him under the act, replacing him with U. S. Grant.[8] Since this action occurred during a congressional recess, Grant acted as secretary of war on an interim basis. When Congress reconvened, the Senate rejected Johnson's action.[9] Hastily, Grant surrendered his office to Stanton, incensing Johnson, who wished to test the law.[10]

Then, when Johnson appointed Adjutant General Lorenzo Thomas to Stanton's post, a Republican senatorial caucus denounced the new appointment.[11] In formal session, the Senate declared that the President alone could not remove a cabinet officer.[12] Trumbull voted his disapproval of Johnson's action. Stanton barricaded himself in his office, refusing to surrender his position. This led to an impasse, as Lorenzo Thomas sat in cabinet meetings.[13] Claiming violation of the tenure of office act, the House Radicals tried anew for an impeachment. This time, they did not frame charges, but requested an impeachment.[14] After a spirited debate,[15] on February 24, 1868, the House, by a party vote, impeached the President, 126 to 47.[16]

A select committee formulated impeachment articles, reporting to the House. On May 23, the House accepted eleven impeachment articles.[17] The first three dealt with Johnson's attempted removal of Stanton and his replacement by Lorenzo Thomas. Articles four through seven accused Johnson of a conspiracy to prevent Stanton from performing his duties. In the eighth article, the President was accused of violating the Constitution, the tenure of office act, and misdirecting public funds. The ninth declared Johnson guilty of attempting to persuade the Washington commandant of troops to violate the control of the army act. Johnson's scurrilous language against Congress during the campaign of 1866 formed the basis of the tenth article. The eleventh was an all-things-to-all-men article; it repeated the Stanton removal accusation, mentioned the presidential insults to Congress, and added that Johnson had obstructed execution of the reconstruction acts.[18]

The House chose seven managers to present its case to the Senate. Among them were Benjamin F. Butler, John A. Logan, and Thaddeus Stevens.[19] These managers pressed for an immediate trial, but the Senate refused to be hurried.[20] Still, even under the more generous Senate proposal, Johnson had only ten days to reply, and the trial began immediately thereafter.[21] As provided in the Constitution, Chief Justice Chase presided, and in the final voting, a two-thirds majority of the senators present was required for conviction. Chase gave the trial the tone of a judicial proceeding, and thereby suffered heavy Radical criticism.[22]

The President's attorneys were more distinguished than the House managers. The President could afford these legal specialists since his wealthy supporters raised a hefty defense fund. His counsel included Henry Stanbery, the attorney general who had resigned his post to defend Johnson. Another was Benjamin Curtis, a former Supreme Court Justice, who earned several hundred thousand dollars in legal fees between 1857 and 1874. In addition, there was William Evarts, an ornament of the New York bar.[23] Meanwhile, both the Radical press and the Conservative journals attempted to influence public opnion regarding Johnson's guilt.[24] Illinois party leaders held rallies, at which the crowds shouted, "Remove Johnson."[25] Trumbull was unimpressed; his Radicalism always had its legalistic boundaries. Johnson's trial required, as Trumbull believed, that he act as a judge.[26]

Opening the case for the House, Butler took the view echoed by the other managers and probably necessary to gain a conviction, that the senators did not sit as a court, but that they were gathered for a political purpose.[27] In the votes on the admission of evidence and the Chief Justice's role in conducting the trial, Trumbull's record, although not perfectly consistent, favored the President's side of the controversy.[28] And, as the weak House case unfolded (if narrow grounds for impeachment were considered), Trumbull seriously pondered acquittal.[29] When the House rested its case, a shadow of doubt that Johnson could be convicted was felt by even the stoutest Radical.[30]

To raise Radical hopes, the Chicago *Tribune*, which had no inkling of Trumbull's acquittal predilections, thundered that no Republican senator would vote for acquittal. Neither editor Horace White nor proprietor Joseph Medill realized Trumbull's low opinion of the case for Johnson's conviction.[31] Nor were Medill and White alone in misreading the signs. Representative Norman Judd guaranteed Trumbull's vote to the House Radical leaders, for in 1866, on the stump, Trumbull had favored Johnson's removal. Also, Representatives Burton C. Cook and Shelby M. Cullom thought Trumbull certain for conviction.[32]

All Radical senators whose actions seemed suspicious received mountains of mail urging, threatening, or pleading for conviction. Trumbull merely scanned his mail, throwing away abusive letters at once.[33] Since Trumbull might, if he voted for acquittal, start a stampede of senators in that direction, Radicals sent physical threats against Trumbull should he break party ranks.[34] Unperturbed, he sat calmly at his desk, waiting to see if Johnson's defense would justify his voting for acquittal.[35] Johnson's attorneys put two generals on the witness stand — General William Emory, commanding the Washington garrison, and General William T. Sherman, who demolished the charges that Johnson had planned a coup d'etat using the army.[36] In the defense of the President, William M. Evarts made a speech, light and flashing, which punctured the impeachers' main arguments. He pointed out that the charges against the President were not any treasonous act, but consisted of speaking ill of Congress and attempting to remove a cabinet officer.[37]

While opposing counsel clashed, the senators sat in their places. Some, their minds made up for conviction as Republicans or for acquittal as Democrats, gave the trial cursory attention. A few senators paid strict attention to the trial; Trumbull was one of these. He sat in his place, following the legal arguments from the stacks of law books with which his desk was heaped.[38] Such behavior branded Trumbull as a dangerous man in Radical eyes. The Radicals were painfully aware that their case was more political than legal, and if Trumbull studied legal precedents, he could be a backslider. Rumors lumped twelve Radical senators as possible defectors from party ranks. This intelligence infuriated the New York *Tribune* editorial writers, who read senatorial flinchers out of the Republican party.[39]

Sensing their opportunity, Johnson and his friends sought to defeat impeachment. They realized that some senators who were leaning toward acquittal considered boastful Lorenzo Thomas an impossible choice as secretary of war. To win wavering senators to acquittal, Johnson jettisoned Thomas. Tactful William Evarts sounded out Fessenden and his ally James Grimes about an acceptable successor to Thomas. The senators suggested General John M. Schofield, then commanding the military district of Virginia. Schofield agreed to serve. Johnson then officially sent Schofield's nomination to the Senate, where it was postponed until Johnson's fate could be determined.[40] Johnson also gave assurance through Grimes that if he were acquitted, he would make no more dramatic moves such as the Stanton ouster. The lawyer-politicians Grimes and Fessenden preferred the compromise of securing these Johnsonian pledges of future good conduct to the drastic step of ejecting the President from office. Trumbull was influenced by their arguments.[41]

Early in May, the Johnson trial ended, and the Senate pondered its verdict. Because of the intense pressure, it soon became clear that no more Republican senators than necessary for an acquittal would break party ranks: Seven Republicans must join the twelve Democrats and Johnsonites for the President's vindication. After wrestling with the pros and cons, Trumbull decided to vote for acquittal. To begin with, Trumbull considered the legal case against Johnson to be thin. Moreover, Trumbull considered Johnson's conviction an unwise precedent, not commensurate with the danger, since Johnson had only ten months to serve while being well-hedged by restrictive laws.[42]

In addition, Trumbull considered Wade, who would succeed to the presidency, no improvement. Once close to Wade politically, Trumbull had drifted away. Moreover, Wade, happily anticipating Johnson's removal, had selected a cabinet headed by Benjamin Butler and staffed by men Trumbull considered incompetent or venal. Rumor added that Wade would use his temporary post as President to seize a place on the Republican national ticket from a pliant Republican nominating convention. Trumbull was also troubled by reports that the iron lobbyists controlled Wade and would use him to hike the tariff. Too, Trumbull enjoyed displaying his independence from party discipline.[43] He thought that the impeachment movement had been initiated by a small, noisy clique headed by Butler and Stevens, a faction that had only temporarily seized power within the Republican party. If impeachment failed, a strong reaction would set in, and the Butler-Stevens faction would be ousted from control.[44]

The first concrete indication of senators' votes came at a closed Senate session. A senator could read his opinion; this action was analogous to a jury deliberation. Several senators read their opinions, with no surprises until Trumbull's turn. He talked for nearly half an hour, and although he covered only the first eight articles of impeachment, his attitude was starkly revealed. He declared the House case unworthy of sustaining a charge before a justice of the peace. As he began reading, a gasp broke out over the Senate. Several Republican House members visiting the Senate jumped to their feet. They bolted from the chamber, racing to spread the news. The House hastily adjourned so that its members might behold the Senate spectacle. As the impeachers rushed from the House Chamber, they heard the fresh news that Fessenden had joined Trumbull in his apostasy.[45]

In all, four Republican senators, Trumbull, Fessenden, Grimes, and John B. Henderson of Missouri, that day read statements flaying impeachment as unfounded upon legal grounds.[46] A wisp of hope remained for the impeachers if they could prevent three additional Republican senators from joining the known recusants. While the Radicals tried to prevent any further defection, as a warning to other waverers they heavily raked the four known apostates.[47] Soon, Trumbull felt a shower of abuse. His former friends Judd and Cook blazed away at him, calling his stand unreasonable.[48] In Illinois, word of his defection reached Chicago late in the evening of May 11. Despite the hour, an indignation meeting was arranged for the following night. The local Republican organizations turned out thousands of supporters to shout their approval of resolutions denouncing Trumbull. The local Republican chieftains feared impeachment's failure would seriously wound the party's chances in the fall elections, and they lashed at Trumbull.[49]

The impeachment fever spread over Illinois and, indeed, over the rest of the North. New indignation meetings blossomed everywhere. On May 13, in the midst of the hurlyburly, Senator Grimes suffered a paralytic stroke. The Washington correspondent of the Chicago *Republican* telegraphed that his affliction was a divine punishment.[50] The surprised Chicago *Tribune* collected its wits and asked for toleration for Trumbull and the other acquitting Republicans.[51] The Radicals turned their fury on the *Tribune*. Bending before the hurricane of disapproval from subscribers and advertisers, the *Tribune* reiterated its desire for Johnson's removal, stressing that it only asked for toleration not approval of Trumbull's course.[52] The Chicago *Post*, edited by Trumbull's long-time friend, C. H. Ray, expressed sympathy for the senator's position, only to face Radical disapproval. The *Post* then equivocated in its support of Trumbull.[53]

In other Northern cities, many influential Republican newspapers supported independent voting by Republican senators. Yet in almost every case, to withstand the Radical pressure, the newspapers voiced a preference for Johnson's removal.[54] The Democratic press, elated by this Republican split, had soft words for the acquitters.[55]

In an effort to determine their strength, the acquitting Republican senators caucused. Three senators who had shown interest in voting for acquittal on at least one article, had buckled under pressure. They were William Sprague of Rhode Island, Edwin Morgan of New York, and Waitman T. Willey of West Virginia.[56] To replace them, others were needed. Possible substitutes were Edmund G. Ross of Kansas, Joseph Fowler of Tennessee, and Peter Van Winkle of West Virginia. Trumbull spoke to all three of these senators, seeking to stiffen their resolve. His dry, logical arguments were most eagerly received by Peter Van Winkle, who had often broken ranks with the Republican party on reconstruction issues. Radical correspondents wryly noted that Trumbull bounced about the Senate floor, joining every group of doubtful senators, where he was soon the center of attraction, arguing, expostulating, and expounding.[57]

The Senate set May 12 for the initial vote, but the illness of Radical Howard of Michigan forced a delay. During this time, pressure was renewed on all waverers.[58] Refusing to disappear in a clap of political thunder, Trumbull wrote to his brother-in-law on May 15: "These people seem to forget that Andrew Johnson is not on trial before the people, but before a Senate sworn to do impartial justice. . . ."[59] At last, the day of decision arrived — Saturday, May 16. The forces favoring conviction used a trick. Since Johnson would be removed as President if a two-thirds vote for conviction were registered upon any one article, they decided to play their best card first; this meant voting on the eleventh article, a catch-all. Therefore, the Radicals moved up the eleventh article from its place to vote upon it first.

The voting procedure called for the clerk to call the roster of senators alphabetically. As his name was called, each senator responded "Guilty" or "Not Guilty." Groans and cheers burst from the packed gallery at each response. The roll call continued with no party deviation, until William Fessenden's name was called. His voice rang out defiantly, "Not Guilty"; Fowler, Grimes, and Henderson joined him in turn. The clerk called out the name of Edmund G. Ross of Kansas. It was believed that if any of the potential Republican acquitters cracked, it would be he. Ross, however, voted for acquittal, defying the pressure.[60]

Then, the clerk intoned Trumbull's name. While Trumbull had been marked down in the political books for acquittal, rumor whispered that he had weakened. All attempts to reach him had failed and he exclaimed, "Not Guilty," with more emphasis than any other senator had given the words.[61] Peter Van Winkle followed Trumbull into the acquitters' camp, and the deed was done — the vote: 35 Guilty, 19 Not Guilty, one short of the constitutional two-thirds majority. From the gallery, Radicals burst into a shrill chorus of rage.[62]

Trumbull believed that the number of acquittal-minded senators was greater than nineteen, and that thirty-five votes had resulted only from the strenuous efforts of the Radicals.[63] Indeed, if an additional vote or two had been required to acquit Johnson, it could have come from the many Republicans voting for conviction.[64] The Senate, in acquitting Johnson by a single vote, had severely rebuked the President, while additional Radical senators did not have to brave the party's wrath. Before any additional votes could be taken, the Radicals tried to change a defector's vote. Virtually ignoring Fessenden, Grimes, and Trumbull, the Radicals concentrated their fire on the four lesser-known acquitters. Ross was subjected to the cruelest taunts and the hardest tests.[65]

Since the Radicals had spread rumors that his acquittal vote had been bribed in some fashion, Trumbull took his case to the people. Trumbull got the Johnson-supporting New York *Times* and the everfaithful Chicago *Tribune* to print a categorical denial of the widely circulated rumors that in some manner he had been bribed.[66] During the recess of the impeachment court, the Republican national convention met in Chicago. The Radical press, led by the New York *Tribune*, clamored that the seven acquitting Republicans be read out of the party.[67]

Trumbull's loyal supporter, the Chicago *Tribune*, strenuously defended him and the other recusant senators. It argued that to split the party on the eve of a national campaign invited defeat.[68] Joseph Medill, one of the *Tribune*'s proprietors, who personally favored Johnson's removal, tirelessly made the rounds of Chicago hotels, arguing with delegates that the seven acquitters must be retained within the party. Horace White controlled the vital resolutions committee and saw to it that no action against the acquitting senators passed.[69] The convention eventually adopted as a plank in the party platform a resolution praising the thirty-five senators who voted for Johnson's conviction, but defeated the attempt to censure the acquitting senators.[70] The convention then nominated U. S. Grant for President and Schuyler Colfax of Indiana for Vice-President.

One telling reason that the convention failed to expel the acquitters was the surge of support in their behalf as a reaction against impeachment set in. In Trumbull's case, after the voting of May 16, he received both a telegram and a letter from Gustave Koerner, in which the German-American leader pledged his support. In reply, Trumbull wrote him a letter which was reported widely in the press. Trumbull reported that at first, after his views had become known, he had received nothing but abusive letters. After two days, the tide changed, and his mail was evenly divided between those praising and condemning his stand.[71] Among the prominent people who wrote Trumbull sympathizing with his stand were the presidents of Princeton and Yale, a senator-elect from Connecticut, and Chicago's mayor.[72]

On May 26, the Senate reconvened as an impeachment court. The Radical leadership passed over the first article as unpromising. A vote was pressed on the second article. Again, the same seven Republicans voted with the Democrats for acquittal.[73] The third article was voted upon with a similar result.[74] At this, even the most ardent impeachers had been sufficiently bruised. Moreover, they faced the prospect of additional Republican senators swelling the acquitters' ranks if they pressed a vote upon the remaining articles. Therefore, they adjourned the impeachment court permanently, 34 to 16; Trumbull stubbornly voted against adjournment, trying to make the Senate pass upon all of the articles.[75]

The failure to convict Johnson meant that for over one hundred years the threat of presidential impeachment became the mere "scarecrow" that Jefferson once had predicted it would be. The impeachment of 1868 injured not the institution of the presidency, but the ability of a Congress to use this instrument against a Chief Executive.[76] After the first reading of opinions by the senators, it was rumored that the acquitting solons would leave the Republicans for the Democrats or, more fantastically, would form a new political party with Chief Justice Chase.[77] None of the seven Republican acquitters left the party; all blew their trumpets for the Republican ticket in 1868.[78] Following impeachment's collapse, the party muffled its denunciation of the seven. With the failure of Johnson's removal, the center and right seized power within the Republican organization.[79]

No one was more relieved than Trumbull.[80] He had no desire to make common cause with the Democrats. To paper over the differences with his party, he voted with recusants Fessenden and Van Winkle for a resolution praising Stanton's services as secretary of war. After the second day of voting at the impeachment trial, Stanton had retired in favor of Schofield.[81]

Loyally doing his party's bidding, as chairman of the judiciary committee, in June and July 1868 Trumbull promptly reported out several bills readmitting the reconstructed Southern states.[82] In general, Trumbull signalled that he continued to be a faithful Republican. Nonetheless, his relations with many individual Radicals reached rock-bottom. Judd blasted Trumbull as a traitor, and Trumbull struck back at his former friend. He had been delaying Senate confirmation of federal appointees unfriendly to Judd. Now, Trumbull stood aside, letting the Senate confirm the appointments. He tried unsuccessfully to discover a rival who could block Judd's renomination as a congressman.[83]

Benjamin F. Wade never forgave Trumbull. Wade was bitter because the acquittal cost him his chance for a place on the 1868 Republican national ticket. Wade needed a new position, since the Democrats controlled the Ohio legislature and he would be retired in 1869. In fact, after Wade left the Senate, he never held a significant office. He took a revenge against Trumbull that was stained with smallness. As Senate presiding officer, during the remainder of the session, he never saw Trumbull when the Illinoisan asked for recognition.[84]

For his part, Trumbull never broke his public impassivity by complaining about his treatment. He wrote Koerner: "I think I am right in coming to the conclusion that no crime or misdemeanor justifying impeachment was made out in the case, but if mistaken in time, I must take the consequences of my error of judgment. . . ."[85]

CHAPTER SIXTEEN

REFORM: THE TONIC KEY

TRUMBULL REPORTED BILLS from the judiciary committee readmitting Arkansas, North Carolina, South Carolina, Florida, Georgia, Louisiana and Alabama. In the end, he supported the readmission of the latter state, despite the fact that the approval of its constitution had not been according to the letter of the law, since it had not ratified the document with the required majority approval of all registered voters. Although the law had been subsequently changed, he did not believe that it could be retroactively applied to Alabama. Yet, in the face of Republican demands for its inclusion in a readmission bill, he reluctantly supported its readmittance on final passage.[1]

Walter wished to go West. With Lyman's active help, he obtained a federal position as assistant assessor of internal revenue in Helena, Montana Territory.[2]

By July 1868, Trumbull turned from all other concerns as his beloved wife became mysteriously and seriously ill. Julia had fallen ill the previous December, but she had recovered. Then her symptoms returned. Although she had little pain, she suffered from abdominal swelling. The most prominent Washington doctors could not diagnose the nature of her sickness. She grew more frail with every passing week,[3] and by June she was bedridden.[4] Driven by his New England concept of duty, Lyman served full days in the Senate until it was obvious that Julia was dying. Then he spent hours at her bedside, reading to her.

With Julia critically ill and Mary Lincoln still suffering from the trauma of Lincoln's assassination, it would be pleasant to chronicle a final reconciliation of these girlhood friends. It was not to be. The antagonistic attitudes of the two women never softened, and although Mrs. Lincoln was visiting in the East in the summer of 1868, she took no notice of Julia's last illness.[5]

Finally, the foremost American specialist in internal medicine was called into Julia's case. He correctly diagnosed her illness as an ovarian tumor, and ordered an immediate operation. Although Julia rallied immediately after this operation, she gradually grew weaker, dying on August 16.[6]

Grief-stricken, Trumbull secluded himself. The campaign of 1868 was in full swing, but he refused to take part in it. He finally weakened in the face of Republican entreaties and on October 12 replied to the Democratic campaigners in a speech at Springfield. In his address, he displayed his Republican orthodoxy. He called for paying government bonds in gold not greenbacks and defended congressional reconstruction.[7] The Republican press enthusiastically hailed Trumbull's belated entry into the campaign.[8] The Illinois state central committee pressed him to accept other speaking engagements. He agreed,[9] delivering short versions of his Springfield speech in Alton and Lincoln.[10] Closing his campaigning in Chicago, he praised the Republican party as the party of internal improvements for building the Union Pacific Railroad.[11]

On November 3, 1868, except for three Southern states still under military rule, the American people voted. Grant easily won the electoral vote count. His popular majority of 300,000 votes was supplied by the newly-freed blacks.[12]

In December, 1868, Trumbull returned to his lonely house in Washington.[13] Senate sergeant-at-arms George T. Brown, who owned the block of houses, moved into the house next door at 492 First Street. He frequently spent evenings with the lonely Trumbull.[14]

The third session of the Fortieth Congress was hectic for Trumbull. The judiciary committee, since the additions of the new members tart George Edmunds of Vermont and vain Roscoe Conkling of New York, proved less responsive to Trumbull's leadership. The committee meetings in the dark basement room in the north wing of the Capitol rang with loud argument.[15] Because of Trumbull's strong feeling that suffrage was a state matter, he took no part in framing the Fifteenth Amendment, guaranteeing the suffrage to all eligible males regardless of race, color, or previous condition of servitude.[16] Only when passage of the amendment seemed inevitable did he vote for its final adoption.[17]

The short congressional session ended on March 4 with the Grant inauguration. This brought a great shuffle of personnel in the executive branch, but the legislative area also witnessed changes. Faithful George T. Brown, who had served Trumbull selflessly for nearly twenty years, was turned out as Senate sergeant-at-arms in favor of a Southern Republican carpetbagger.[18] Brown was ostensibly replaced because he had served two terms, but actually because he was too closely identified with Trumbull in the eyes of Senate Radical leaders. Nor was Brown's loss of his Senate post all that beset him. His fortune dwindled and his health failed.[19] He appealed to Trumbull to get him a place so that he could continue in Washington.[20] Trumbull tried, but the best situation Trumbull could obtain was a seat on the Mexican Treaty Claims Committee. Trumbull's inability to do more caused a deterioration of the relationship between the two men. Failing in purse and health, Brown ultimately retired to Alton, where he died in June 1880.[21]

Trumbull still gathered a share of the political plums. His nephew, Benjamin Trumbull, Jr., continued as Senate postmaster. Restless Walter, whose Western ventures had proved disappointing, returned to Washington to become clerk of the Senate judiciary committee, taking a leave from his assessor's post in Montana.[22]

According to law, the first session of the Forty-First Congress began immediately after the Fortieth had adjourned. In a special message, Grant began his reconstruction program by calling for the completion of reconstruction in Mississippi, Virginia, and Texas.[23] When a bill to set the final stage for the readmission of these three was presented, Indiana's Oliver Morton proposed that these states also ratify the Fifteenth Amendment. Oliver Morton was a typical pragmatic ''New Radical'' in contrast to the more idealistic ''Old Radicals'' such as Wade and Sumner.[24] Trumbull challenged Morton, demanding an end to new conditions exacted from the reconstructed states.[25] The Senate rejected Trumbull's appeal and accepted Morton's proposal.[26]

With this action, Congress adjourned in April 1869. Walter decided to return to his post as assistant assessor of internal revenue for Montana. His father reluctantly agreed that a new sojourn in Montana might strengthen Walter's always frail health.[27] Although the Union Pacific invited Trumbull to travel to California that spring aboard a special sleeping-car for political celebrities, he refused, since he wished to see Walter resettled in Montana. He started West in the late spring of 1869. The emptiness of living without Julia had made him restive, and he decided to try travel as a cure for melancholy. He stopped off with relatives in Nebraska and then continued West over the Union Pacific. He left the new transcontinental railroad to travel north by stage to Montana. There he saw Walter resettled in that territory. Afterwards, he continued by the Union Pacific through Utah and Nevada to California. He made many political friends in the Far West who proved to be useful in 1872 when he tried for a place on the Liberal Republican national ticket. It was September before he returned refreshed to Illinois.[28]

Meanwhile, Lyman's zeal for the Radical cause had ebbed. In the fall of 1869, when he was asked to campaign for the Radical ticket in the local Chicago election, he refused.[29] By December 1869, when Virginia asked for readmittance to the Union, the Conservatives had triumphed in recent state elections. The Radicals were reluctant to readmit Virginia without further guarantees for the blacks. The judiciary committee, under Trumbull's leadership, spurned imposing new conditions and simply passed a resolution proclaiming Virginia's readmittance.[30] In reporting this resolution, Trumbull declared the Northern people were tired of reconstruction.

They wished the South to be fully restored to the Union. In the course of his Senate address, he attacked Charles Sumner for his demand for new conditions guaranteeing the blacks' political status before Virginia's readmission to the Union. Trumbull claimed that Sumner had fallen under the sway of a sinister carpetbagger, Charles H. Porter, on this question.

Sumner was, Trumbull admitted, a true friend of the black people, but in matters affecting them "his zeal outstripped his judgment." To this, Sumner retorted that Trumbull had originally opposed black suffrage.[31] Several days later, Trumbull returned to his attack on Sumner, calling the Massachusetts senator a dupe of Porter's on the Virginia question. For good measure, he called Porter a traitor.[32]

The House agreed with the Senate judiciary committee that Virginia should be unconditionally readmitted, and passed a bill for that purpose. When the House measure reached the Senate for its concurrence, the Radicals amended it to suit their purposes. Trumbull fought all these amendments unsuccessfully[33] and then reluctantly voted *Yes* on the measure's final passage.[34] Trumbull took a similar stance on the readmission of Mississippi, and again failed to achieve his purpose of an unconditional readmittance. Conditions similar to Virginia's were fastened on Mississippi.[35]

The frantic scramble for place which occurred at the start of the Grant administration caused Trumbull to announce in the first session of the Forty-First Congress that unless a more comprehensive plan of civil service was introduced, he would offer a bill at the December session making it a penal offense for a congressman of either House to solicit a position in the executive departments.[36] On December 7, 1869, Trumbull introduced such a civil service reform measure. Senate Republicans unanimously opposed the bill. Only Garrett Davis of the opposition applauded Trumbull's proposal.[37] Trumbull's bill was referred to the judiciary committee, where Lyman, as chairman, struggled to pass it. Eventually, on February 7, 1870, he reported the measure to the Senate after minor amendments. Although he fought for his proposal with flair and determination, he could not press it to a vote.[38] It had, at least, performed Trumbull's purpose of educating public opinion.

Despite his wife's long feud with Mary Lincoln, Trumbull worked successfully to ease the widow's financial distress. He was able to convince doubtful senators away from the Senate floor, so that Mary Lincoln's financial affairs would not be aired in public. Consequently, largely through his efforts, Congress voted Mrs. Lincoln an annual pension.[39]

Trumbull then spent a quiet summer in Ulster County, New York. Thinking over the political situation, he complained to Jayne, "The war pressure is . . . off, and there is now no great principle to hold it [the Republican party] together."[40] He apparently never thought of seizing for the Republican party the issue of railroad and warehouse regulation, issues then agitating Illinois farmers.[41]

Journeying to Chicago for business and political conferences in the summer of 1870, Trumbull returned with nineteen-year-old Perry to New York state. Perry still sought a niche in life; he was at that time attracted to the teaching profession. Lyman unsuccessfully solicited a high school teaching post for the boy. With adolescent indifference, Perry turned to the study of law. Perry always displayed a promise he could never translate into actuality. Later in life, he would be characterized as "indolent."[42]

That fall, Trumbull was unwilling to campaign for the Republican party. He confessed to Jayne, "I do not know partly what to talk about."[43] Still, invitations to speak came to him from local Republican leaders.[44] Finally, on the very eve of the election he made a speech in Chicago. "Coming Issues," he entitled it. As a Jacksonian bullionist, Trumbull advocated the contraction of greenbacks until they became freely convertible into gold. Next, he advocated civil service reform. He wished applicants chosen by competitive examination and once appointed, holding their places by good behavior. Turning to foreign affairs, he advocated asking Britain to cede Canada in order to settle the "Alabama Claims." Britain owed the United States an indemnity not alone because she allowed the Confederates to outfit raiders in her territory, but because the British government had illegally forced the surrender of the captured Southern envoys Mason and Slidell, in 1861.[45]

While newspapers yet debated the merits of his proposals, he left Chicago for Washington.[46] There, he had a long chat with Grant, which confirmed Trumbull's previous opinion of the President as a well-meaning but ill-advised executive.[47]

During the Forty-First Congress, Trumbull became fast friends with a new senator from Missouri, Carl Schurz. A reformer, Schurz had found his native Germany hostile to his ideals, and had migrated to America. He was attracted to the Republican party by its anti-slavery stand, and campaigned for Lincoln. After serving in the army during the Civil War, he settled in Missouri. There, he became disenchanted by Radical reconstruction. When the Missouri Republicans split in 1869, he was elected to the United States Senate by the liberal, i.e., less vindictive wing of the party.[48] In 1870, he joined the Liberal Republican movement in Missouri against the Grant administration.[49] Trumbull tried to keep the Republican party broad enough to encompass both Grant and the Radicals, and Liberals such as Schurz and himself. Therefore, he convinced Schurz to make the traditional courtesy call on Grant when the Missouri senator arrived in Washington for the 1870-1871 congressional session. But when Schurz called at the White House, Grant sent word through a lackey that he could not be disturbed.[50]

In line with Trumbull's feeling that the public (or at least the genteel people he respected) demanded reform, he again pressed a bill making it illegal for congressmen to solicit federal appointments.[51] To gain votes for it, he dropped the controversial provision setting penalties for a President who knowingly appointed an illegally recommended applicant.[52] However, not even Schurz would help Trumbull press this bill, and it died without the saving grace of a formal vote.[53]

Yet Trumbull struck a mighty blow for civil service reform that session. In March 1871, as the session entered its dying hours, Trumbull proposed an amendment to an appropriation bill which authorized the President to establish a commission to set standards for the appointment of federal employees. The reform forces rallied to pass it through the Senate by a vote of 32 to 24.[54] The House accepted the civil service provisions and they became law.[55] Then, although Grant appointed a reformer to head the committee, the unrelenting hostility of Republican regulars and the indifference of Congress to the committee's recommendations prevented significant accomplishment. As the first step toward civil service reform, however, the bill served a useful purpose.[56]

While Congress met in Washington in early 1871, the Illinois legislature voted upon the identity of Yates' senatorial successor. Since Yates had battled Trumbull over patronage, Trumbull at first proclaimed his neutrality in the struggle between the former governor and his principal Republican antagonist for the Senate seat. Only after he had heard that Logan's friends were boasting that "Black Jack" as junior senator would control the future of the Illinois Republican party did he become alarmed.[57] By then it was too late to prevent Logan's election to the Senate.[58]

Disheartened by politics and still suffering from the loneliness caused by Julia's death, Trumbull turned to religion. He frequently attended Julia's church, the New York Avenue Presbyterian. Although he had been raised a Congregationalist, as an adult he had never accepted membership in that sect. In the end, he did not join the Presbyterian church as Julia had done. He seems to have remained a mild, uncertain agnostic. Late in life, Trumbull regularly attended a non-denominational community church in Chicago, but apparently never formally joined it.[59]

On March 4, 1871, the Forty-First Congress died, and the Forty-Second began. Lyman now brought Henry and Perry to Washington to live with him. Perry, who had been listlessly studying law, was sent to a series of legal lectures. Henry, an active boy of nine, played lawn croquet with his father in front of their apartment on sunny days.[60]

The surprise of the new Congress was a Grant ukase that Sumner must be deposed as foreign relations committee chairman. Grant ostensibly asked for Sumner's removal because of the intemperate manner in which Sumner had opposed both the annexation of Santo Domingo and a compromise solution of the Alabama Claims. When a Republican caucus bowing to Grant's wishes deposed Sumner, Trumbull fought the move not alone in the party conclave but upon the floor of the open Senate. He emphasized that Senate usage forbade this cavalier treatment of a veteran senator. He unsuccessfully asked the Senate to reverse the Republican caucus' decision.[61] In gratitude, Sumner embraced Trumbull, his eyes brimming with tears. The breach between the two veteran Republicans had been healed.[62]

Meanwhile, Trumbull reversed his stand on the Alabama Claims, supporting a compromise settlement, the Treaty of Washington.[63] Upon reflection, Trumbull thought the principle of arbitration which Britain had accepted in the treaty a great concession.[64] As tariff reformers, Trumbull and Schurz hoped to effect deep tariff cuts in the March 1871 meeting of Congress.[65] They were soon disappointed to learn that most Republican senators considered this session of the new Congress to be superfluous, and backed a resolution which limited congressional business to a few aspects of Southern reconstruction.[66]

By April 1871, Trumbull had become convinced that the federal government had reached its constitutional limits in the protection of black rights in the South. Therefore, he opposed new legislation on this subject. Disgusted by the excesses of Southern carpetbag regimes, he was willing to liquidate reconstruction and return to a normal federal-state relationship. He believed that an individual must look to state and local governments to protect his civil liberties.[67] Trumbull spent the closing days of the short session pressing without success for a general amnesty bill for Southerners.[68]

After several weeks of vacation in the East, Trumbull returned to Illinois for a Fourth-of-July speaking engagement at Galesburg. He urged that the legal status of women be raised. As before noted, he favored equal pay for equal work. He also declared himself in favor of women's suffrage, which he thought might lessen governmental corruption. Lastly, he called for an end to reconstruction, which he stated had dangerously increased the federal government's power.[69] On September 20, 1871, he addressed the Illinois State Republican convention. In this speech, he advocated lifting the political disabilities imposed by the Fourteenth Amendment upon Southerners. It was time, he said, for experienced political leaders to reassume their guidance of the South. He also stressed the need for civil service reform.[70]

In the fall of 1871, Trumbull left for Congress early so as to tend his growing Washington legal business. He left young Henry Trumbull with Ellen Jayne and her mother in Springfield. Precocious Henry misbehaved. The father tried to guide him by writing chatty letters in which he counselled the boy as he might an equal.[71] The results were unsatisfactory. Meanwhile, Walter returned early from Montana. He had resigned his position because he could not live there on his salary. He resumed his position as judiciary committee clerk.[72]

At the December 1871 session of Congress, rumors swirled through Washington that Trumbull would become a Democrat. This change Trumbull did not wish to accomplish. In a conversation with a former colleague, he complained that the Democratic party was dominated by former secessionists and that he hoped to remain a Republican and reform his party from within.[73] In fact, writing to an old political associate, Trumbull indicated that if Grant could be dissociated from his corrupt advisors he could yet make an acceptable President.[74]

Trumbull's efforts to remain within the Republican party faced two counter-forces. First, there was the group of reformers within and without the GOP who were trying to overcome Grantism. Second, there were Republican party stalwarts who wished to force Trumbull out of the party. The transcendent issues, the relentless march of events, and the idiosyncracies of personal ties combined ultimately to push Trumbull from the Republican party.

CHAPTER SEVENTEEN

LIBERAL FOLLY

IMPORTANT REPUBLICAN ELEMENTS worked to defeat Grant's re-election. On January 24, 1872, an insurgent group, the Missouri Liberal Republican party at its state convention unfurled a statement of principles calling for ex-Confederates' enfranchisement, Southern self-government, and civil service and tariff reform. This convention of dissidents scheduled a national mass meeting of anti-Grant Republicans for the first Monday of May in Cincinnati to project these reforms nationally.[1]

While heeding the call, Trumbull hoped until the Cincinnati convention's eve that it would not select rival candidates against the regular Republican nominees. Trumbull hoped the meeting would not go beyond a statement of principles which the Republican national convention would then be forced to swallow. Also, if Grant were dropped, then Trumbull could answer the many calls for his candidacy for President.[2]

Trumbull's wait-and-see attitude could not restrain his Illinois friends from advocating his nomination at Cincinnati. Included in this group were old-time Trumbull men, who had despaired of his further advancement at Republican hands.[3] Trumbull had captured the imagination of an influential national group, including the Mayor of St. Louis,[4] his former senatorial colleague Ross of Kansas,[5] the California superintendent of public instruction,[6] and the carpetbag governor of Louisiana.[7] Trumbull also had considerable newspaper support,[8] including the powerful New York *Sun*.[9] One of the leading periodicals, the *Nation*, suggested that Trumbull was presidential timber.[10] In addition, dozens of Republican and Democratic officeholders, politicians, and plain citizens urged him to make the national race.[11] Support for his candidacy is all the more amazing when it is realized that his public image was associated with such cold talents as parliamentary skill.

Carl Schurz, the leading architect of Missouri liberalism, would have been the group's logical choice for President except for his foreign birth. Since he was ineligible himself for the prize, it was thought that he would be a kingmaker at the Cincinnati convention. More people urged him to support Trumbull's nomination than that of any rival candidate.[12] Although the Republican Radical Senate leaders, Morton, Chandler, and Conkling, tried to bait Trumbull into admitting his break with the party,[13] Trumbull refused to admit being outside the regular ranks. Only a week before the opening of the Cincinnati convention, he attended an official Republican senatorial caucus.[14]

Meanwhile, Trumbull faced two problems. The first was his own candidacy at Cincinnati, about which he remained ambivalent. The second was the success of the Liberal cause to which his own political future seemed closely linked. Indeed, Trumbull feared to see any Liberal presidential contender emerge too prominently, since the supporters of the others might not then attend the Cincinnati conclave. Therefore, he worked strenuously to obtain a large Illinois delegation, although he realized that many of these delegates would prefer other candidates to himself.[15] On one point, Trumbull was adamant; known Democrats, many of whom were attracted by the possible success of the movement, should stay away from Cincinnati to keep the gathering exclusively for Republican reformers.[16]

David Davis, the wealthy Supreme Court Justice appointed by Lincoln, had hoped to convert the Liberal Republican movement into a presidential boom for himself. Davis disliked Trumbull and saw no reason to step aside for the senator. In February 1872, after Trumbull had spurned feelers from a national labor reform convention,[17] that splinter gathering nominated David Davis for President.

The unclear position of two dominant Illinois politicians complicated the state's political climate. Governor John M. Palmer had wrangled over federal-state relations in the aftermath of the great Chicago fire, yet he hesitated to leave the Republican party. At last, after weighing all the factors, Palmer became an open convert to the Liberal cause.[18] Senator John A. Logan was another matter; he too had had squabbles with Grant. Logan, however, had a sure instinct for political survival. In the end, he remained a regular Republican.[19]

As his thin ties with the regular Republican party frayed, Trumbull made his Liberal presidential candidacy official. Trumbull penned a letter to Horace White for this purpose. He said that he was ''available'' for the nomination on his own terms, but offered his followers no active help.[20] As was his custom, he remained in Washington, hundreds of miles away from the convention. His lieutenants at Cincinnati included Horace White, Gustave Koerner, and Jesse Dubois. Walter Trumbull and William Jayne were present as his personal representatives, but no one was his official spokesman.[21] This group performed their leadership functions poorly. White became a positive brake upon the Trumbull presidential drive, since he believed that the senator could never win. White thought Charles Francis Adams, the son of John Quincy Adams, the certain winner, with Trumbull settling for second place on the ticket.[22]

Thus the stage was set at Cincinnati. Before the convention of Republican reformers could open, the identity of the official delegates from each state had to be determined. Several states, including Illinois, had sent bloated delegations, far in excess of the allotted convention votes. To choose its official delegates, Illinois representatives held a meeting on April 30. The Davis supporters claimed most of the vote since hundreds of men, including many Democrats who were drawn by the possible success of the movement, had come to Cincinnati with the Justice's financial backing. They outnumbered Trumbull's backers, four or five to one. Against these numbers, Trumbull supporters claimed their ranks were composed almost exclusively of Republicans. Also, many Trumbullites held certificates of election from county nominating conventions. The smallest group, the Palmer supporters, insisted upon preference, since they represented the governor as official head of the state party.[23]

At the meeting, a Davis leader read a letter from the judge, urging a compromise. It was speedily done. An eighty-four-man delegation was chosen, with each delegate given half a vote. Forty-two were assigned to Davis men, with twenty-one each given to Palmer and Trumbull backers. At this point, Koerner and White got Palmer to withdraw in Trumbull's favor. This generous act healed the breach between the governor and the senator.[24]

Despite this boost in Trumbull's stock gained from the Palmer support, most reformers still considered Charles Francis Adams to be the front-runner. There were other candidates, but few took them seriously. They included Chief Justice Salmon P. Chase, Missouri Governor B. Gratz Brown, and the quirky editor of the New York *Tribune,* Horace Greeley.[25]

To the true believers of the Liberal cause, the only unwelcome candidate of any stature was Justice David E. Davis. Most Liberals scorned him as an insincere reformer. Accordingly, four leading Liberal editors, Samuel Bowles of the Springfield (Mass.) *Republican,* Horace White of the Chicago *Tribune*, Henry Walterson of the Louisville *Courier-Journal*, and Murat Holstead of the Cincinnati *Commercial* agreed on joint action to stop Davis. At the end of April, they all simultaneously wrote editorials for their newspapers depicting Davis as an impossible candidate. The scheme worked; the Davis boom died. If the editors had considered Greeley a serious candidate, they would have attacked him as well, but since the New York *Tribune* was so popular, no one wished needlessly to offend Greeley.[26]

On May 1, the convention opened. First, the Liberals constructed a platform which provided a consensus of three of the four most vital planks. They were denunciation of the misdeeds of the Grant Administration, declaration for civil service reform, and an appeal for the end of reconstruction. They straddled only on the issue of tariff reduction. The Greeleyites had warned that they would not support a movement which smacked of free trade. Therefore, a meaningless plank was adopted referring the tariff question to the voters in their congressional districts.[27]

On the evening of May 2, a spectacular development occurred. Suddenly, Missouri's governor, B. Gratz Brown, appeared at the convention along with that state's Democratic Senator, Francis Blair, Jr. Immediately after their arrival, they called in Missouri's delegation for a secret conference. Rumors flew about what was transpiring. At last, reliable reports declared that a second Missouri Compromise had occurred. Brown, irked that the Schurzites had persuaded the Missouri delegation to vote for Adams instead of him, came to Cincinnati to bargain with the Greeley forces. While the Adams and Trumbull men confusedly pondered these developments, the Greeley forces, led by the editor's clever lieutenant, Whitelaw Reid, gained strength among vital state delegations.[28]

On Friday morning, May 3, the convention reconvened to choose the national ticket. After a slight pause, while the platform was officially accepted, the roll call of thirty-seven states began. On the first ballot, Adams led with 204 to Greeley's 147, Trumbull's 110, Brown's 95, and Davis' 92½. The rest of the votes were scattered.[29] Trumbull had received support from seventeen of the thirty-seven delegations. Before the balloting's result could be announced, Brown asked the presiding officer if he could make a statement. Schurz would have ruled him out of order, but being confused, did not. Brown then announced his withdrawal from the race in favor of Greeley.[30]

After order was restored, the convention cast a second ballot. Greeley gained in this voting, but it was not so much Brown's votes transferring to the New York editor (outside of the South) as it was a general shift in the vote totals. Thus Greeley still trailed Adams, with Trumbull third, and Davis a poor fourth.[31] California then shifted from Davis to Greeley, and the editor led. In dribs and drabs, Trumbull made a modest gain of 38 votes on this ballot.[32] The importance of the Brown deal was not the votes that the Missouri governor delivered to Greeley, but the Greeleyites' demonstration of being realists. Practical politicians felt more at home with this type of behavior than with the stiff, uncompromising stance exhibited by the Adams and Trumbull men.

On the third ballot, Trumbull failed to gain, and with 146 votes, trailed the leaders, Adams with 264 and Greeley with 258. Despite Davis' poor showing, the Justice's half of the Illinois delegation stubbornly voted for him.[33] The fourth ballot showed no real change.[34] Then, it became clear that the Adams-Trumbull forces must reach an accommodation. Both sides eschewed deals; each bowed the other to the nomination. Horace White wondered how he could deliver the Trumbull strength to Adams despite Koerner and Jayne.[35] Meanwhile, tariff reformer David A. Wells wished to swing Adams' New England votes behind Trumbull, but because of White's unresponsive attitude, never could.[36]

While the Adams and Trumbull supporters fidgeted indecisively, a fifth ballot was called. This ballot showed Adams about 50 votes short of a decision, with 309 to Greeley's 258. Trumbull's cause had collapsed, as his supporters outside of Illinois moved to Adams.[37] At this, the convention went into an uproar. The Illinois delegates left the hall to caucus. At last, Koerner tried to swing the delegates as a bloc to Adams. The Davisites mostly declared their preference for Greeley. As a result, the Illinois delegation split, 27 for Adams and 15 for Greeley.[38]

The convention, refusing to wait for the Illinoisans, went ahead with the balloting. A trend for Greeley developed. Although the roll call was completed before the Illinois vote was tabulated, it was included in the announced result. Two Illinois delegates, repudiating the caucus arrangement, stubbornly voted for Trumbull. The ballot's result was 332 for Greeley and Adams 324. Trumbull garnered 19 die-hard votes. For just a second, Greeley teetered, 30 votes short of the nomination. Then, a switch of votes in the Pennsylvania delegation nominated Greeley. Schurz officially proclaimed Greeley the convention's choice.[39]

In the balloting that followed, most Greeleyites supported B. Gratz Brown for the vice-presidential nomination. Yet, started by the Delaware delegation, a movement to nominate Trumbull erupted. One Ohio delegate asked Koerner if Trumbull would accept second place on the ticket behind Greeley. Disgusted, Koerner snapped, "A man cannot swim with a millstone [Greeley] around his neck." With that, the Trumbull boom died.[40] Nevertheless, Trumbull received 158 votes to Brown's 237, the rest scattering.[41] At this point, Koerner reiterated that Trumbull was unavailable for the vice-presidential nomination. Since several delegates had challenged Koerner's right to speak for Trumbull, a telegram was sent directly to him at Washington. Trumbull replied, "positively declining." On the next ballot, Brown was easily nominated.[42]

The convention adjourned in grave disarray. A movement dominated by free traders had nominated a spokesman for protection; civil service reformers had chosen as its candidate a lifelong confidant of spoilsmen. A movement whose future depended upon Democratic assistance had selected a man who had castigated Democrats all his adult life. Definitely, many Liberals felt that Greeley was an impossible candidate. Soon, the rebels moved in every direction, searching for a winner.[43] Quickly, Carl Schurz joined hands with editor William Cullen Bryant of the New York *Post* and E. L. Godkin of the *Nation* to demand a new nomination.[44]

As a practical politician of thirty-five years' standing, Trumbull was critical of attempts to get new nominations. Rather, in a letter to Greeley he sought pledges from the editor concerning the tariff and civil service reform that would make him an acceptable candidate.[45] In his reply, Greeley assured Trumbull that he favored a genuine reform of American political life and that during the campaign, he would be careful not to offend tariff revisionists.[46] When Horace White proposed uniting the splintered Liberal groups, several prominent Liberals proposed a June meeting at the New York City Fifth Avenue Hotel.[47] At this time, since the regular Republicans had renominated Grant upon a platform that conceded little to reform, the prospects of any compromise with the regulars had evaporated. Consequently, White appealed to Trumbull to attend the Fifth Avenue Hotel Conference and convince the recalcitrant Liberals that they must support Greeley.[48]

Trumbull attended the conference, taking the floor early to declare that Greeley was the only practical alternative to Grant.[49] In the end, the conference agreed with him, refusing to name a new national ticket.[50] Meanwhile, Greeley gained vital adherents — the Democrats, who accepted him and the Cincinnati platform at their July convention.[51] In Illinois, as nationally, the Liberals and Democrats faced enormous organizational problems. To facilitate cooperation, there was considerable sentiment among both Liberals[52] and Democrats[53] for Trumbull to run for governor. After much soul-searching, Trumbull refused the gubernatorial nomination,[54] since he desired a new senatorial term.

On June 26, the Illinois Liberal Republicans and Democrats held separate state conventions in Springfield, which divided the state nominations between the two parties. After Trumbull had again refused the gubernatorial nomination, a joint nominating committee selected Koerner as the candidate for governor. Many Liberals insisted that Koerner, as a German-American leader, would be the victim of nativist prejudice, and that only Trumbull could win.[55] At the Liberal convention, a motion was made to drop Koerner from the gubernatorial nomination and replace him with Trumbull. Koerner agreed, and he was arising to second the motion, when word came that the Democrats had ratified the agreed-upon slate. Since it was too late to effect the change, the motion to nominate Trumbull was voted down.[56]

The Liberals-Democrats needed to wage a strong campaign, since the Republican regulars had undercut their appeal. The regulars had hastily pushed a general amnesty act through Congress, lifting the officeholding disabilities from most Confederate leaders affected by the Fourteenth Amendment.[57] Also, they revised the tariff downward.[58] The Republicans had displayed an ability to sway with reform gales.

Disregarding the petty squabbles between the Liberals and Democrats in Illinois,[59] Trumbull opened the fall campaign in his home state.[60] He interrupted it only for a quick trip to address the Michigan Liberal state convention.[61] Returning to Illinois, he began stumping one small town after another, including many that he had not visited since the 1850's.[62] Then the Maine Liberals appealed to Trumbull to campaign there. Maine's early

September election was, as usual, heavy with psychological importance. Trumbull entrained for the East, appearing at rallies at Biddeford, Lewiston, Portland, Augusta and Bangor. The theme of Trumbull's speeches was the necessity for a change, as the Republican party masked its corruption behind appeals to Lincoln's memory.[63]

During his return trip to Illinois, Trumbull stopped over in Ohio. There, he hit at administration graft to crowds at Columbus, Dayton, and Cincinnati, who flocked to hear the Republican apostate, billed as "Lincoln's friend."[64] Back in Illinois, during a ten-day period, he spoke at eight different towns in the central part of the state.[65] Then, Illinoisans took their politics with deadly seriousness. One town, Carlock, had a cemetery for Republicans a safe quarter of a mile away from the last resting place for Democrats.[66] Trumbull found his former Republican friends bitter and their heckling savage.[67]

The Indiana October election was also psychologically vital to the Illinois Liberals' cause, so Trumbull carried his fight to the Hoosier state. There, he charged that the Republicans refused to face current problems, but instead hid behind patriotic appeals. At the end of his Indiana tour, his voice cracked and hoarse, he took a short rest.[68] In response to frantic appeals, he returned to the stump in Illinois. Newspaper correspondents noted that he never stopped his campaigning each day until he was physically exhausted.[69]

While Trumbull continued his tireless campaigning, the Liberal cause met stinging defeats in the early elections in North Carolina, Maine, Vermont, Ohio, and Pennsylvania. Only in Indiana did the Liberals find cheer when they elected a governor. Even here, the Republicans captured the legislature, so that Morton would be returned to the Senate.[70] With heckles cracking the air, Trumbull continued on the hustings in southern and central Illinois until the November election day.[71] He had to contend with the heavy clouds of despondency that settled over the Illinois Liberals. Some disappointed Liberals, particularly the Davisites, returned to the Republicans.[72] Many Illinois Democrats, as was the case with Democrats nationally, could not bring themselves to support Greeley.[73] Trumbull refused to despair, doing more than his share. He spoke in five states, making over forty major speeches and traveling over six thousand miles during the campaign.

In Illinois, as nationally, the Liberal cause met with disaster on election day. Grant scored a smashing victory, carrying the Northern and Western states.[74] Grant swept Illinois by more than 50,000 votes, the Republican tide engulfing Koerner. On a joint ballot, the legislature was securely Republican.[75] To reward his strenuous exertions during the campaign, although it was only a gesture, in January 1873, the Liberals and Democrats united behind Trumbull. The Republican caucus chose the newly-elected Republican Governor Richard J. Oglesby to succeed Trumbull. He did what Trumbull refused to do, that is, seek the governorship as an immediate gateway to the Senate. In the formal vote in the legislature, Oglesby was elected over Trumbull in a joint legislative session.[76]

In December, although Trumbull maintained a tight-lipped silence, rumors were rife that he would resign. Nonetheless, he left for Washington as usual.[77] He stopped off in New York to serve as a pallbearer for Horace Greeley, who had died a few weeks after the election.[78] Although the administration wished to treat the Senate Liberal leaders, Schurz, Sumner (who had belatedly endorsed the Liberal movement), and Trumbull as traitors, this prickly question was remanded to the Republican caucus. That body jettisoned Trumbull as chairman of the judiciary committee, replacing him with George Edmunds.[79] Trumbull was placed on the committee of privileges and elections, and given a seat on the inactive committee of investigation and retrenchment.[80] The other Liberals were similarly disciplined.

Reconstruction backwash complicated the election of 1872. In Louisiana, the carpetbag Governor Henry C. Warmoth defected to the Liberal Republicans. In an election marred by frauds, a returning board, so called since it judged the validity of the election returns, counted in the entire Democratic ticket. With the help of the federal courts and the army, the Republicans created their own returning board, which proclaimed a GOP triumph.[81] The question was which set of electors was to count in the congressional joint session. Trumbull, arguing for the Democrats, said, "I question . . . whether . . . the United States has any right to go behind the appointment of the electors."[82] In four years, Trumbull would be arguing the opposite opinion in regard to the Louisiana election vote.

Late in the session, Congress considered a measure referred to as the "salary grab." Enacted with bipartisan support, this bill raised congressmen's salaries from $5,000 to $7,500. This generous raise might not have created the uproar it did had it not been made retroactive for two years, giving congressmen a bonus of $5,000 for the past Congress.[83] Trumbull supported the measure actively on the Senate floor, and consistently voted for it.[84] The Senate and House having passed the bill, Grant signed it into law.[85] Some congressmen, from scruples or sound political judgment, refused the extra $5,000. Trumbull collected this additional salary. He never explained his stand. It was legal, but hardly the action of a reformer. The best explanation was that he simply needed the money. By neglecting his law practice during the Greeley campaign, he had piled up heavy debts.[86]

Stifling any impulse to make a farewell speech, Trumbull sat quietly in his place until the session ended. Then he unobtrusively cleaned the papers from his desk and left the Senate chamber after eighteen years' service.[87] He left Washington for his Chicago home and his law practice, a bitterly disappointed man.

CHAPTER EIGHTEEN

CITIZEN TRUMBULL

THE CHICAGO to which Trumbull returned in 1873 was a city of three hundred thousand. Chicago's business flourished, and along with it, the legal profession. Trumbull had as large and varied practice as he cared to handle. He formed a partnership, Trumbull, Church, and Trumbull.[1] Firman Church, an active Democratic politician, was the middle partner,[2] and Perry, who had passed the bar, served as the third member. Changes occurred. Church moved to California and was replaced by Henry S. Robbins. Later, Hempstead Washburne, son of veteran congressman Elihu B. Washburne, joined the firm.[3]

Trumbull remained a man without a party until 1876. The Republicans proved unforgiving and the Democrats slow to accept Liberals into their party. By 1876, hope of a permanent Liberal organization evaporated. Outside of the tiny one-issue parties — the Prohibition and Greenback — the choice lay between the corrupt Republicans and the mossbacked Democrats. The splinter parties had no attraction for Trumbull, since he disapproved of their basic principles. Therefore, in 1876, when the Democrats picked reformer Samuel J. Tilden as their presidential candidate, Trumbull rejoined them.

Although not a candidate for anything, he stumped Illinois for the Democrats in the fall in 1876. Trumbull's theme: the Republican party had lost its principles, while the Democrats had been purged of their pro-slavery ideas.[4]

Although the Democrats lost Illinois, the national results were indecisive. Tilden had 184 undisputed electoral votes to Republican Rutherford B. Hayes' 165. The electoral votes of three Southern states, under carpetbag rule, were in dispute, as was one electoral vote from Oregon. If all disputed votes went to Hayes, he could yet win.[5]

As the realization dawned on politicians that the returning boards of the disputed Southern states held the election's key, the two national committees sent prominent Northerners as unofficial observers to witness the count. Trumbull was sent to observe that area of his legal and political expertise — Louisiana.[6] In the November election, the Democrats had what seemed to be a popular majority, but the Republican governor claimed Democratic coercion in five parishes.[7] Trumbull was extremely active for an observer,[8] but to no avail, as the Republican-controlled board counted in the GOP electors.[9] The other two Southern states decided their electoral disputes in a similar manner.[10]

To count the disputed votes, a compromise solution was evolved, setting up an electoral commission which ultimately consisted of eight Republicans to seven Democrats.[11] When the Louisiana case came before the electoral commission, Lyman Trumbull appeared as counsel for the Democrats. He made an elaborate, polished constitutional argument, claiming that the federal government had the authority to go behind the state returns to render justice. His argument changed no Republican commissioners' minds, and Louisiana was awarded to the GOP,[12] as were all disputed electoral votes.[13] Consequently, Hayes won, erasing Trumbull's chance for a Tilden cabinet post.[14]

Trumbull's extensive legal practice allowed him to maintain a comfortable standard of living, but there was a drain on his resources. Henry, still a schoolboy, Walter, an unsuccessful commodity broker, and Perry, a ne'er-do-well lawyer — all required heavy allowances from their father.[15]

On Trumbull's Eastern summer visits he had grown romantically attached to a much younger woman, Mary Jane Ingraham, daughter of his first cousin, Captain Jonas Ingraham. Lyman saw her often, as one year succeeded another. Their courtship was casual — relatives and friends assuming that some day they would marry. On November 3, 1877, they did. Mary Jane differed from the intellectual Julia in many ways. She cared nothing for books or politics; her hobbies were singing and conversational French. She was an impulse-buyer of clothing and home furnishings. Thirty years younger than Lyman, she survived him by nearly twenty years.[16]

The Trumbulls settled down to the busy social life of the late 1870's, despite the fact that Lyman despised the newly-rich captains of commerce that dominated it. In 1879, Perry left his father's household when he married Caroline Peck,[17] a daughter of Trumbull's old friend.

In 1880, the Democrats drafted Lyman to run for governor. The problem was that the Democrats had no strong issue against Governor Shelby Cullom.[18] Trumbull spurned any accommodation with the third party soft money Greenbackers, who went over to the Republicans.[19] Trumbull lost by some 37,000 votes, and Cullom was re-elected.[20] To his wife, off visiting Connecticut relatives, Trumbull laconically wired, "Illinois goes Republican as usual."[21] After forty years, his office-seeking days were over; he knew it and accepted it.

Before November 1880 had finished, Trumbull returned to the practice of law with the same dedication as if he had never been away. He upgraded his profession by helping to organize both the Chicago Bar Association[22] and the American Bar Association.[23] But as he settled back into private life, troubles continued to bedevil him. Walter, now a realtor, was felled by tuberculosis in 1881. After this attack, for several years Walter went West each fall, first to Colorado and then to New Mexico, in an attempt to regain his health.[24] Perry was the "leg man" of the Trumbull firm. He had a tendency to rattle under pressure.[25] Henry finished preparatory school and entered Yale.[26]

In 1884, Trumbull backed Democrat Grover Cleveland for President. To Trumbull's disgust, when Cleveland was successful, he refused to appoint any of Trumbull's deserving friends to office. Trumbull attributed this to the influence of border and Southern Democrats, who thought that no one who had been a Republican during the war years was sufficiently deserving of rewards.[27]

Meanwhile, Henry had not applied himself at Yale. His father disapproved of his rollicking conduct and summoned him home to study law under his steely eye. He thought Henry needed the sobering influence of an industrious young man his own age. Therefore, in 1881, when an old political friend asked that his son, William Jennings Bryan, already the quintessence of wooden respectability, be allowed to study law with the Trumbull firm, Lyman agreed.[28]

Trumbull enrolled the young men in Union College, Chicago's law school, where he himself was a part-time faculty member.[29] Early mornings and late afternoons, William Bryan worked six hours a day in Trumbull's law office. He and Trumbull had many chats. Although Lyman, as a specialized technician, may not have had much law to impart to the novice of immediate benefit, he could and did talk politics by the hour.[30] Bryan could exert only a minimal influence upon fun-loving Henry Trumbull, who occasionally drank too much and frequented professional baseball games.[31] Judge Trumbull had more impact on William than young Bryan had upon Henry. Bryan afterward maintained that next to his parents, Lyman Trumbull had most shaped his humanitarian views.[32]

Meanwhile, tragedy shadowed Lyman's personal life. His second marriage resulted in two daughters — Mae, born in 1878, and Alma in 1883. Both children were a delight to Trumbull.[33] In the summer of 1884, Mae was injured in a coach accident and then accidentally scalded. Despite the best medical care, she died on August 17. The Trumbulls were desolate.[34]

Walter, finding his tuberculosis had worsened, returned to Chicago for medical attention. Despite tender care and a relay of physicians, he died at Lyman's home on October 25, 1891.[35] Lyman invited Walter's widow and her two young sons to live with him. He played football and baseball with his grandsons, although he was then nearly eighty.[36] The Trumbulls' surviving daughter, Alma, was coddled and anxiously watched over. Nonetheless, in mid-March, 1894, she fell ill with "something like malaria" and died. Although Lyman bore his burden with quiet grace, his wife was inconsolable for years.[37] Henry had finished his law course and effortlessly passed the bar. When he showed signs of tubercular tendencies, he practiced law for several years in the milder climate of Albuquerque, New Mexico. He now returned to Chicago, only to become much worse. He practiced law when he could, but finally died on January 20, 1895, with Lyman at his bedside.[38] Brilliant Henry was dead; only Perry survived of all the children.

Lyman never complained about his health. In his diary for 1894, he remarks upon the health of members of his family — never about his own. Only from his wife's diary can one learn about the painful "rheumatism" from which he suffered in the 1880's and 1890's. He never consulted physicians, but doctored himself with home remedies and patent medicines.[39]

Over the years, Trumbull had grown bitter over what he dubbed the "money power." As early as 1877, he railed against those who demanded "the meanest sort of deference because they have wealth."[40] He also inveighed against the accumulation of great fortunes "by inheritance . . . by the vulgar, the ignorant and the depraved."[41] In 1893, at the Congress of Jurisprudence and Law Reform, held at Chicago in connection with the Columbian Exposition, Trumbull uttered many of the caustic criticisms of the existing society that he did the next year when they caused a sensation. The audience was small and press coverage confined to legal journals and his speech drew little notice.[42]

Thus, his social attitude should not have been the shock it was to contemporaries in 1894. He stuck closely to the Jacksonian principles of his youth. Koerner, a longtime observer of Trumbull, noted two salient points about him. First, "He hates monopolists more than monopolies. . . ." Second, "He likes to be independent."[43] The events which drew Trumbull again into the public eye were caused by the severe depression of 1893. The following year, business conditions and the reaction to them caused the Pullman Company workers to strike. Making little headway against Pullman, his workers appealed to the American Railway Union, headed by Eugene V. Debs. When the Railway Union supported the strikers, the railroad managers stood behind Pullman. A railroad strike resulted which was broken by President Cleveland's use of court injunctions and federal troops. Debs and his principal lieutenants were imprisoned on contempt of court charges.[44]

Trumbull was appalled by Cleveland's action, which smacked to him of "big government." To denounce Cleveland's actions, Trumbull turned for a forum to the third party, the Populists. They appealed to Trumbull as reformers, and for their monetary solution, the free coinage of silver, which accorded with his long-held bullionist principles.[45] Consequently, on October 6, 1894, he made a speech, "The Rights of Man as Affected by Accumulated Wealth and Favored Monopolies."[46] In it, Trumbull declaimed against the terribly unequal distribution of wealth in America. This condition he blamed on "the aid of statutes . . . providing for the transmission of property by . . . will or the creation of monopolies." To get relief, the workers need not turn to violence, but simply organize politically to take over control of Congress and the state legislatures. They could then pass the needed legal reforms to break up monopolies and redistribute America's wealth.[47] After this speech, Trumbull made his way from the hall in Chicago where he had spoken to the plaudits of a foot-stomping, handkerchief-waving crowd.[48]

The press reaction to Trumbull's address was nation-wide. Predictably, newspapers of the two old parties castigated him as a senile radical,[49] while Populist sheets hailed him as the fount of wisdom.[50]

Although the Populists did poorly in the elections of 1894 in Illinois, they were undaunted. To prepare for 1896, they wished to draw up a fresh statement of principles to bring to a regional conclave of the party in St. Louis. Because of Henry's last illness, Trumbull could not attend, but he authored nine resolutions which called for rescuing the federal government "from the control of the monopolists," criticized Cleveland's actions in the Debs case, denounced international bankers, and called for the free coinage of silver at the ratio of 16 to 1. The last resolution thundered, "Down with monopolies and millionaire control: Up with the rights of man and the masses."[51] The press response to Trumbull was furious. The conservative press denounced him as simply too shocking to understand.[52]

Then, through the influence of a young attorney with offices in his building, Clarence Darrow, Trumbull entered the Debs case. Darrow was a Populist sympathizer who easily persuaded Trumbull to aid Debs' legal cause. In December 1894, Debs drew a six-month jail term on the contempt charges.[53] Debs' counsel Darrow and Stephen S. Gregory were then appealing his jail sentence to the United States Supreme Court. When that body agreed to hear the case, Trumbull agreed to argue before it as Debs' counsel. Since the Union treasury was exhausted, Trumbull agreed to work only for actual expenses.[54]

On March 25, 1895, the Debs case was argued in the Supreme Court. Trumbull was given the opportunity to open the case for Debs. He penetrated to the heart of the controversy. Did the lower court have the right to grant a blanket injunction and then imprison Debs and his associates for violating it? Trumbull attacked various defects of the bill in equity filed with the lower court. His voice unusually heavy, he stated the basic values which should decide the case, asking the judges to look over the tops of their law books and to recognize that punishing Debs without a jury trial was unconstitutional.[55] Gregory followed with a more technical argument,[56] while Darrow echoed Trumbull's emotional arguments.[57] Cleveland's Attorney General Richard Olney headed the three-man team of government attorneys.[58]

After the counsel finshed the arguments, the Supreme Court took the case under advisement until its decision in May 1895. At that time, it rendered a unanimous opinion for the government,[59] a fact that surprised even Olney.[60] The use of an injunction in labor disputes was not new, but one so sweeping in scope seldom had been obtained before. For his part, Trumbull greeted the decision with disgust. He growled that the doctrine enunciated by the Supreme Court placed every citizen at the mercy of a prejudiced federal judge.[61]

By the spring of 1896, Trumbull felt vague pains and a debilitating weakness. When Gustave Koerner died, he insisted upon attending the funeral in Belleville. While eulogizing Koerner, he collapsed. Local physicians decided that Trumbull should return home at once. In Chicago, his doctor decided upon an exploratory operation, which revealed that Trumbull was suffering from an advanced stage of cancer of the bladder.[62] Grimly, Trumbull clung to life. After several rallies, he died on the morning of June 25, surrounded by his family.[63]

Trumbull's life had been exceedingly busy. For nearly thirty years, he had held public office. In his officeholding, he had always filled his posts with distinction. Yet, since he was never President or even governor, he was not widely known. He has gradually faded from the history books.

The history of the United States would have been different had Trumbull never entered politics. He aided mightily in the revolt against Douglas and the founding of the Republican party. In the Senate, between 1861 and 1872, as chairman of the important judiciary committee, he stopped thousands of bills from becoming law, and shaped hundreds more to his liking before they could pass.

For a long time, it was believed that the Thirteenth Amendment was Trumbull's only very significant piece of legislation. Yet the Civil Rights Act of 1866, which long seemed a dead letter, has grown in significance over the years; it should now be mentioned along with the Thirteenth Amendment as an important contribution to American constitutional history. In recent years, the Supreme Court has given the Civil Rights Act of 1866 a new meaning. The Court, in 1948, in the case of *Hurd* v. *Hodge,*[64] held that judicial enforcement of restrictive covenants in the District of Columbia was contrary to Trumbull's Civil Rights Act. In 1969 in *Jones* v. *Mayer Co.,* the court held that a portion of the federal code, originally enacted as a part of the Civil Rights Act of 1866, prohibited racial discrimination, private as well as public, in the rental or sale of property.[65] In 1976, the Court decided, in *Runyon* v. *McCrary,* that private schools could not discriminate in admission policies because of race, since this also was contrary to Trumbull's Civil Rights Act.[66] And that same year in *McDonald* v. *Santa Fe Trail Company,* it was held that whites as well as non-whites could challenge racial discrimination in private employment under a section of the Civil Rights Act of 1866.[67]

Trumbull was out of power for the last twenty-three years of his life, but even then, his Populist pronouncements had impact. It is true that his independence left him an excommunicated leader in the eyes of both political parties. In the main, however, he made a contribution to American life which has grown rather than diminished over the years.

NOTES

Notes to Chapter One

1. Walter Trumbull, "The Life and Time of Lyman Trumbull," I, ch. 1, pp. 1-2. This unfinished and largely unpublished biography of Lyman Trumbull begun by his elder son, Walter, is an invaluable source for Trumbull's life to 1872. When consulted it was in possession of Edward Trumbull, Seattle, Wash.
2. Ibid., 1-2; New Haven *Daily Journal and Courier,* February 5, 14, 1890, clippings then in possession of Edward Trumbull, Seattle, Wash.
3. Trumbull, "Trumbull," I, ch. 1, pp. 1-3.
4. John Warner Barber, *Connecticut Historical Collections* (New Haven, Durrie & Peck and J. W. Barber, 1846), 303-304; *Return of the Whole Number of Persons Within the Several Districts of the United States* (1800), 18.
5. Trumbull, "Trumbull," I, ch. 1, pp. 3-4.
6. Ibid., I, 3; Lyman to Julia Jayne Trumbull, September 24, 1857, Lyman Trumbull Family MSS, Illinois State Historical Library.
7. Lyman to Julia Jayne Trumbull, October 20, 1857, Trumbull Family MSS.
8. Chicago *Tribune,* June 25, 1896; Trumbull, "Trumbull," I, ch. 1, p. 4.
9. Trumbull, "Trumbull," I, ch. 1, p. 4.
10. Ibid., I, 5-6.
11. Charles S. Sydnor, *The Development of Southern Sectionalism,* 1819-1848 (E. Merton Coulter and Wendell H. Stephenson, eds., *A History of the South, V*) (Baton Rouge: Louisiana State University Press, 1948), 58-59, 61.
12. Mark M. Krug, *Lyman Trumbull, Conservative Radical* (New York: A. S. Barnes, 1965), 23. Krug believes that part of the reason Trumbull left teaching was his lack of formal preparation, but considering the educational qualifications of the time, this does not appear very plausible.
13. Trumbull, "Trumbull," I, ch. 1, pp. 5-6. See also Trumbull's pronouncements concerning the constitutionality of slavery within southern states in the *Congressional Globe* between 1855 and 1860.
14. Trumbull, "Trumbull," I, ch. 1, pp. 5-6.
15. Stewart Holbrook, *The Yankee Exodus, An Account of Migration from New England* (New York: Macmillan, 1950), 62, 64, 71; Theodore Calvin Pease, *The Story of Illinois* (Chicago: University of Chicago Press, 1949), 117, 118, 270.
16. Trumbull, "Trumbull," I, ch. 1, p. 7.
17. Thomas J. McCormack, ed., *The Memoirs of Gustave Koerner, 1809-1895: Life-Sketches Written at the Suggestion of His Children* (Cedar Rapids, Iowa: Torch Press, 1909), I, 425-426.
18. David Trumbull to Lyman Trumbull, April 20, 1836, Trumbull Family MSS; "Trumbull," I, ch. 1, p. 7.
19. Trumbull, "Trumbull," I, ch. 1, pp. 7-8; McCormack, ed., *Memoirs of Koerner,* I, 425;

Josephine L. Harper, "John Reynolds, 'The Old Ranger' of Illinois, 1788-1865," MSS doctoral dissertation, University of Illinois, 1949, p. 167.

20. Trumbull, "Trumbull," I, ch. 1, p. 8.

21. McCormack, ed., *Memoirs of Koerner,* I, 425.

22. Trumbull, "Trumbull," I, ch. 1, p. 4.

23. Albert Beveridge, *Abraham Lincoln* (Boston and New York: Houghton Mifflin, Co., 1928), I, 272; McCormack, ed., *Memoirs of Koerner,* I, 440, 444; Democratic State Central Committee to Democratic Party of Illinois in Robert W. Johannsen, ed., *The Letters of Stephen Douglas* (Urbana: University of Illinois Press, 1961), 82.

24. McCormack, ed., *Memoirs of Koerner,* I, 444.

25. Theodore C. Pease, ed., *Illinois Election Returns, 1818-1848 (Collections of the State of Illinois State Historical Library,* XVIII) (Springfield, Ill.: The Trustees of the Illinois State Historical Library, 1923), 340.

26. Trumbull, "Trumbull," I, ch. 3, p. 8.

27. McCormack, ed., *Memoirs of Koerner,* I, 425-426.

28. Trumbull, "Trumbull," I, ch. 3, p. 1.

29. McCormack, ed., *Memoirs of Koerner,* I, 425-426.

30. Evarts Boutwell Greene and Charles Manfred Thompson, eds., *Governors' Letter-Books,* 1840-1853 *(Collections of the Illinois State Historical Library,* VII) (Springfield, Ill.: The Trustees of the Illinois State Historical Library, 1911), xli-xliii; Theodore Calvin Pease, *The Frontier State, 1818-1848 (Centennial History of Illinois)* II, (Springfield: Illinois Centennial Commission, 1918), II, 310; John H. Krenkel, *Illinois Internal Improvements, 1818-1848* (Cedar Rapids, Iowa: Torch Press, 1958), 126-143; G. S. Boritt, *Lincoln and the Economics of the American Dream* (Memphis: Memphis State University Press, 1978), 8-10.

31. Greene and Thompson, eds., *Governors' Letter-Books,* xlii-xliv.

32. Pease, ed., *Illinois Election Returns,* xlii-xlv.

33. *Illinois House Journal,* 12 General Assembly, 2nd Session, 460, 468-469, 480, 482, 485, 507.

34. *Ibid.,* 468, 485.

35. *Ibid.,* 538-539.

36. Greene and Thompson, eds., *Governors' Letter-Books,* li-liii; Krenkel, *Illinois Internal Improvements,* 26-40, 66-72; *Laws of Illinois, 1836-1837,* pp. 121-153.

37. Greene and Thompson, eds., *Governors' Letter-Books,* liii; John Jay Knox, *A History of Banking in the United States* (New York: B. Rhodes & Co., 1900), 719-720; Krenkel, *Illinois Internal Improvements,* 166-184.

38. Beveridge, *Abraham Lincoln,* I, 283.

39. *Illinois House,* 12 Gen. Assembly, 2nd Sess., 500.

40. *Sangamo Journal,* February 9, 1841.

41. Beveridge, *Abraham Lincoln,* I, 284.

42. *Illinois House Journal,* 12 Gen. Assembly, 2nd Sess., 161.

43. *Laws of Illinois, 1840-1841,* pp. 189-190.

44. Newton D. Harris, "Negro Servitude in Illinois," *Illinois State Historical Society Transactions* (1906), 53.

45. Thomas Ford, *A History of Illinois from its Commencement as a State in 1818 to 1847* (Chicago: S. C. Griggs & Co., 1854), 338.

46. *Illinois House Journal,* 12 Gen. Assembly, 2nd Sess., 568-569.

47. 2 Illinois Reports, 79-185; Robert W. Johannsen, *Stephen A. Douglas* (New York: Oxford University Press, 1973), 84-85.

48. *Blue Book of Illinois, 1943-1944,* p. 612; Pease, *Frontier State,* 278-281; John Moses, *Illinois Historical and Statistical* (Chicago: Fergus Printing Co., 1889-1892), I, 444; S. A.

Douglass [sic] to John A. McClernand, January 29, 1841 in Johannsen, ed., *Letters of Douglas,* 95-96; Johannsen, *Douglas,* 92-95.

49. Moses, *Illinois,* I, 444; Allen Johnson, *Life of Stephen A. Douglas, A Study in American Politics* (New York: The Macmillan Co., 1908), p. 56; Douglas to Thomas Carlin, February 16, 1841 in Johannsen, ed., *Letters of Douglas,* 97; Johannsen, *Douglas,* 97.

50. Lyman Trumbull to David Trumbull, October 12, 1841, Trumbull Family MSS.

51. Ford, *History of Illinois,* 306.

52. *Illinois Senate Journal,* 12 Gen. Assembly, 2nd Sess., 443.

Notes to Chapter Two

1. *Blue Book of Illinois, 1943-1944,* pp. 607-610; Johannsen, *Douglas,* 92; Lyman Trumbull to David Trumbull, October 12, 1841, Trumbull Family MSS; Lyman Trumbull to Julia Trumbull, March 20, 1842, ibid.; Sally Trumbull to John S. Trumbull, June 16, 1841, ibid.

2. Pease, *The Frontier State,* 286-287; McCormack, ed., *Memoirs of Koerner,* I, 463; Johnson, *Life of Stephen A. Douglas,* 56; Greene and Thompson, eds., *Governors' Letter-Books,* xxxiii-xxxvii; William Gerald Shade, *Banks or No Banks: The Money Issue in Western Politics, 1832-1865* (Detroit: Wayne State University Press, 1972), 101; Krenkel, *Illinois Internal Improvements,* 175-180.

3. Greene and Thompson, eds., *Governors' Letter-Books,* xlv-xlviii.

4. Ford, *History of Illinois,* 306, 308; Pease, *Frontier State,* 314; Krenkel, *Illinois Internal Improvements,* 175-176; Greene and Thompson, eds., *Governors' Letter-Books,* xxxvii.

5. Ford, *History of Illinois,* 308-309; Krenkel, *Illinois Internal Improvements,* 177-180; *Illinois State Journal,* 13 Gen. Assembly, 1 Sess., 527-528.

6. Moses, *Illinois, Historical and Statistical,* I, 458.

7. Trumbull, "Trumbull," I, ch. 2, p. 1.

8. Ibid., p. 2.

9. Carl Sandburg and Paul M. Angle, *Mary Lincoln, Wife and Widow* (New York: Harcourt, Brace & Co., 1932), pt. 2, pp. 184-185.

10. Trumbull, "Trumbull," I, ch. 2, p. 5. There are variant versions of bridesmaids in attendance, see Ruth Painter Randall, *Mary Lincoln, Biography of a Marriage* (Boston: Little, Brown, 1953), 72, and Krug, *Trumbull,* 43.

11. Lyman Trumbull to Julia Trumbull, March 20, 1842, Trumbull Family MSS.

12. Trumbull, "Trumbull," I, ch. 2, pp. 5-6.

13. Julia Trumbull to John Trumbull, November 16, 1843; when consulted, in possession of Edward Trumbull, Seattle, Wash.; Lyman Trumbull to David Trumbull, June 27, 1844, Trumbull Family MSS.

14. Julia Jayne Trumbull to Lyman Trumbull, May 13, 1844, Trumbull Family MSS; Julia Jayne Trumbull to Lyman Trumbull, May 15, 1844, ibid.; Julia Jayne Trumbull to Lyman Trumbull, May 20, 1844, ibid.; Benjamin Trumbull to David Trumbull, July 2, 1844, then in possession of Edward Trumbull, Seattle, Wash.

15. Genealogical Table in handwriting of Walter Trumbull, then in possession of Edward Trumbull, Seattle, Wash.

16. Pease, *The Story of Illinois,* 127-128, 133-134, 270.

17. Alexander Davidson and Bernard Stuve, *A Complete History of Illinois from 1673 to 1873* (Springfield: Illinois Journal Co., 1894), 309-314, 321-327; Pease, *Frontier State,* 377; Newton D. Harris, *Negro Servitude in Illinois and of the Slavery Agitation in that State, 1719-1864* (Chicago: A. C. McClurg Co., 1904), 1-15, 27-49; Moses, *Illinois Historical and Statistical,* I, 310-324.

18. Pease, ed., *Illinois Election Returns,* 27; Merton Lynn Dillon, "The Antislavery Movement

in Illinois, 1824-1835," *Illinois State Historical Society Journal,* XLVII (Summer, 1954), 149-156.

19. Harris, *Negro Servitude in Illinois,* 103-104; Pease, ed., *The Frontier State,* 378; John P. Hand, "Negro Slavery in Illinois," *Transactions of the Illinois State Historical Society* (1910), 44-45.

20. 4 *Illinois Reports,* 1-25; Harris, *Negro Servitude in Illinois,* 108-109, 122-123; Pease, *Frontier State,* 378.

21. 7 *Illinois Reports,* 354-364; Hand, "Negro Slavery in Illinois," 45-46; Pease, *Frontier State,* 378-379; Harris, *Negro Servitude in Illinois,* 116-118.

22. Alton *Telegraph & Democratic Review,* March 11, 1843.

23. McCormack, ed., *Memoirs of Koerner,* I, 486.

24. *Ibid.,* I, 486; Alton *Telegraph & Democratic Review,* May 6, 1843.

25. Harper, "John Reynolds," 192.

26. Alton *Telegraph & Democratic Review,* January 13, 1844.

27. Pease, *Frontier State,* 195-197.

28. Alton *Telegraph & Democratic Review,* November 8, 1845.

29. Pease, *Frontier State,* 299; Lyman Trumbull to Charles Lanphier, September 2, 1846, Charles Lanphier MSS, Illinois State Historical Library.

30. Alton *Telegraph & Democratic Review,* December 27, 1845; Trumbull, "Trumbull," I, 3; Krug, *Trumbull,* 50-51.

31. Trumbull, "Trumbull," I, ch. 3, p. 3; Pease, *Frontier State,* 301; Moses, *Illinois, Historical and Statistical,* I, 505; S. A. Douglass [sic] to Augustus C. French, February 20, 1846 in Johannsen, ed., *The Letters of Stephen A. Douglas,* 134.

32. Trumbull, "Trumbull," I, ch. 3, pp. 6-7.

33. Ibid., 5.

34. Ibid.; Lyman Trumbull to Julia Trumbull, April 11, 1846, Trumbull Family MSS; Lyman Trumbull to Julia Trumbull, April 25, 1846, ibid.; Lyman Trumbull to Julia Jayne Trumbull, April 28, 1856, ibid.

35. *Illinois State Register,* May 8, 1846; Ibid., June 19, 1846; Ibid., July 17, 1846; Alton *Telegraph & Democratic Review,* May 23, 1846; Trumbull, "Trumbull," I, ch. 3, pp. 6-7; *Sangamo Journal,* July 16, 1846 as reprinted in *Illinois State Register,* July 17, 1846; Ibid., July 24, 1846; Lyman Trumbull to Julia Trumbull, May 3, 1846, Trumbull Family MSS; Lyman Trumbull to Julia Trumbull, June 19, 1846, ibid.; McCormack, ed., *Memoirs of Koerner,* I, 187.

36. Pease, ed., *Illinois Election Returns, 1818-1848,* p. 153.

37. *Ibid.*

38. *Sangamo Journal,* July 16, 1846 as reprinted in *Illinois State Register,* July 17, 1846.

39. Genealogical Table, then in possession of Edward Trumbull, Seattle, Wash.; Lyman Trumbull to Benjamin Trumbull, November 20, 1846, Trumbull Family MSS.

Notes to Chapter Three

1. McCormack, ed., *Memoirs of Koerner,* I, 425; John J. Duff, *A. Lincoln: Prairie Lawyer* (New York: Rhinehart, 1960), 254-255.

2. See the Nicholas Perrin Collection, St. Clair County Records, 1839-1847, Illinois State Archives.

3. Lyman Trumbull to Julia Jayne Trumbull, March 4, 1847, Trumbull Family MSS; Lyman Trumbull to Julia Jayne Trumbull, January 30, 1848, ibid.

4. See 1-9 *Illinois Reports;* Duff, *Lincoln,* 254-258.

5. Trumbull to Augustus C. French, April 2, 1848, Augustus C. French MSS, Illinois State Historical Library.

6. Ibid.

7. Trumbull, "Trumbull," I, ch. 3, p. 7.

8. Trumbull to French, August 12, 1848, French MSS.
9. Alton *Telegraph & Democratic Review,* September 15, 1848; Trumbull, "Trumbull," I, ch. 3, p. 7.
10. Trumbull to French, October 14, 1848, French MSS.
11. John Dean Caton, *Early Bench and Bar of Illinois* (Chicago: Chicago Legal News Co., 1893), p. 93; Lyman Trumbull to Julia Jayne Trumbull, December 5, 1848, Trumbull Family MSS.
12. Lyman Trumbull to Benjamin Trumbull, November 20, 1846, Trumbull Family MSS.
13. Lyman Trumbull to Julia Jayne Trumbull, February 6, 1848, ibid.
14. White, *Trumbull,* 21; Krug, *Trumbull,* 69.
15. Trumbull, "Trumbull," I, ch. 3, p. 8; Alton *Telegraph & Democratic Review,* February 11, 1848; White, *Trumbull,* 20-21; Lyman Trumbull to Julia Jayne Trumbull, Alton, February 10, 1849, ibid.
16. Genealogical list of the Trumbulls; when consulted, in possession of Edward Trumbull, Seattle, Wash.; *Illinois State Register* as reported in Alton *Telegraph & Democratic Review,* July 26, 1850.
17. Genealogical list of the Trumbulls, then in possession of Edward Trumbull, Seattle, Wash.
18. For example see *Martin Tubbs* v. *Abby Van Klee,* 12 *Illinois Reports,* 450-451.
19. *Hone* v. *Ammons,* 14 *Illinois Reports,* 29.
20. 10-14 *Illinois Reports.*
21. Trumbull to John Dean Caton, May 19, 1853, John Dean Caton MSS, manuscripts division, Library of Congress.
22. Lyman Trumbull to Julia Jayne Trumbull, March 4, 1847, Trumbull Family MSS.
23. Lyman Trumbull to Julia Jayne Trumbull, December 4, 1848, ibid.; Lyman Trumbull to Julia Jayne Trumbull, June 11, 1849, ibid.; Lyman Trumbull to Julia Jayne Trumbull, November 15, 1849, ibid.; Lyman Trumbull to Julia Jayne Trumbull, June 10, 1850, ibid.
24. Mount Carmel *Register* as reprinted in Alton *Telegraph & Democratic Review,* April 2, 1852; Alton *Telegraph & Democratic Review,* May 7, 1852.
25. Alton *Telegraph & Democratic Review,* June 10, 1852.
26. Emil Joseph Verlie, ed., *Illinois Constitutions* (Collections of the Illinois State Historical Library, XII, *Constitutional Series,* I) (Springfield, Ill.: Trustees of the Illinois State Historical Library, 1919), 73.
27. Alton *Weekly Telegraph,* May 23, 1851.
28. Alton *Telegraph,* June 4, 1852.
29. *Ibid.,* May 10, 1855.
30. Alton *Courier,* August 3, 1852; Alton *Weekly Courier,* November 8, 1855.
31. Alton *Courier,* 1852-1855; W. T. Norton, ed., *Centennial History of Madison County and its People, 1812-1912* (Chicago and New York: The Lewis Publishing Co., 1912), 113-114; Alton Daily *Democrat,* June 10, 1880.
32. McCormack, ed., *Memoirs of Koerner,* I, 617.
33. Trumbull to Governor Joel A. Matteson, May 18, 1853, copy in Trumbull Family MSS.
34. Julia Jayne Trumbull to Julia Wetherbee Jayne, June 6, 1853, William Jayne Family MSS, Illinois State Historical Library; Lyman Trumbull to Julia Trumbull, May 9, 1850, Trumbull Family MSS. Krug, *Trumbull,* 76-77, stresses Trumbull's desire to return to politics to oppose the growing slave power, but the evidence for this is weak.
35. Gershom Jayne to Julia Wetherbee Jayne, Alton, Ill., June 20, 1853, Jayne Family MSS; Trumbull, "Trumbull," I, ch. 3, p. 9.
36. Alton *Courier,* June 18, 21, 22, 1853.
37. Trumbull to Caton, June 25, 1853, Caton MSS; Trumbull to Caton, June 27, 1853, ibid.; Alton *Courier,* July 8, 1853.
38. Chief Justice B. D. Magruder as quoted in White, *Trumbull,* 21-22.
39. Trumbull, "Trumbull," I, ch. 3, p. 10. Lyman traveled at great inconvenience to his dying

father's side. Lyman Trumbull to Julia Jayne Trumbull, June 14, 1850, Trumbull Family MSS; Lyman Trumbull to Julia Jayne Trumbull, June 21, 1850, ibid.
40. Trumbull, "Trumbull," I, ch. 3, p. 10.
41. Ibid., 11.
42. Ibid.; White, *Trumbull,* 38; Krug, *Trumbull,* seems to have missed Trumbull's illness at this time and writes instead that he "on the whole enjoyed good health."
43. 16 *Illinois Reports,* 53-58, 149-150.
44. Alton *Telegraph,* May 2, 1855; Alton *Weekly Courier,* July 1854-February 1856.
45. See the full accounts of the passage of the Kansas-Nebraska bill in Allan Nevins, *Ordeal of the Union* (New York: Scribner, 1947), II, 94-121 and Johannsen, *Douglas,* 401-434.
46. Michael F. Holt, *The Political Crisis of the 1820's* (New York: John Wiley & Sons, 1978), 144-155.

Notes to Chapter Four

1. Don E. Fehrenbacher, *Prelude to Greatness: Lincoln in the 1850's* (Stanford, Calif.: Stanford University Press, 1962), 20-21, gives the traditional account. G. S. Borit, "Lincoln's Opposition to the Mexican War," *Journal of the Illinois State Historical Society,* LXVII, No. 1 (February, 1974), 79-100, argues convincingly that Lincoln's Mexican War stand did not seriously damage Lincoln's political career.
2. Samuel Ashton to Stephen A. Douglas, March 18, 1854, Stephen A. Douglas MSS, University of Chicago Library; Johannsen, *Douglas,* 450; Damon Wells, *Stephen Douglas: Last Years, 1857-1861* (Austin: University of Texas Press, 1971), 31; David M. Potter, *The Impending Crisis, 1848-1861,* completed and edited by Don E. Fehrenbacher (New York: Harper & Row, 1976), 163-165.
3. Fehrenbacher, *Prelude,* 6; Frank L. Klement, *The Copperheads in the Middle West* (Chicago: University of Chicago Press, 1960), 6, 12; Stanley L. Jones, "Agrarian Radicalism in Illinois Constitutional Convention of 1862," *Journal of the Illinois State Historical Society,* XLVIII (Autumn, 1955), 271-273. On midwestern negrophobia, see Eugene H. Berwanger, *The Frontier Against Slavery: Western Anti-Negro Prejudice and the Slavery Controversy* (Urbana: University of Illinois Press, 1967), 30-59.
4. Trumbull, "Trumbull," I, ch. 4, pp. 4-5; Julia Jayne Trumbull to Lyman Trumbull, April 10, 1856, Trumbull Family MSS.
5. Trumbull, "Trumbull," I, ch. 4, pp. 5-6; Julia Jayne Trumbull to Lyman Trumbull, April 10, 1856, Trumbull Family MSS.
6. Trumbull, "Trumbull," I, ch. 4, p. 5; I, ch. 5, p. 1; John S. Wright, *Lincoln and the Politics of Slavery* (Reno: University of Nevada Press, 1970), 60-61, 70-72; Harris, *Negro Servitude,* 190-192.
7. White, *Trumbull,* 37-38.
8. *Ibid.,* 38; *Illinois State Journal,* September 28, 1854; Beveridge, *Lincoln,* II, 239-240.
9. Alton *Weekly Courier,* September 14, 1854; *Illinois State Register,* September 14, 1854.
10. Trumbull, "Trumbull," I, ch. 4, pp. 4-5.
11. Arthur C. Cole, *The Era of the Civil War* (Centennial History of Illinois, III) (Chicago: A. C. McClurg Co., 1922), 131; Alton *Telegraph,* October 26, 1854.
12. Trumbull, "Trumbull," I, ch. 4, p. 5; *Biographical Congressional Directory of the American Congress, 1774-1961,* p. 909; *Illinois State Register,* September 14, 1854.
13. Alton *Weekly Courier,* October 12, 19, 26, 1854; Chester *Herald* as reprinted in Alton *Weekly Courier,* October 26, 1854; Alton *Telegraph,* October 26, 1854.
14. Beveridge, *Lincoln,* II, 242.
15. Boston *Transcript,* September 7, 1854; Johannsen, *Douglas,* 456-457.
16. Beveridge, *Lincoln,* II, 241-242; Ronald D. Rietveld, "Lincoln and the Politics of Morality," *Journal of the Illinois State Historical Society,* LXVIII, No. 1 (February 1975), 33-36.

17. Cole, *Era of the Civil War,* 132; Beveridge, *Lincoln,* II, 242; Johannsen, *Douglas,* 457.
18. Paul M. Angle, *"Here I Have Lived": A History of Lincoln's Springfield, 1821-1865* (Springfield, Ill.: The Abraham Lincoln Association, 1935), 212; Alton *Weekly Courier,* October 12, 1854; Stephen B. Oates, *With Malice Toward None: The Life of Abraham Lincoln* (New York: Harper & Row, 1977), 114.
19. Beveridge, *Lincoln,* II, 243-244; Roy P. Basler, Marion Dolores Pratt, and Lloyd A. Dunlap, eds., *The Collected Works of Abraham Lincoln,* II, 240-247; Oates, *With Malice Toward None,* 114.
20. Beveridge, *Lincoln,* II, 262-263; Fehrenbacher, *Prelude,* 34; Johannsen, *Douglas,* 458.
21. *Illinois State Journal,* September 28, 1854.
22. Alton *Weekly Courier,* October 12, 1854.
23. Trumbull, "Trumbull," I, ch. 5, p. 1; George H. Mayer, *The Republican Party, 1854-1964* (New York: Oxford University Press, 1964), 38.
24. *Illinois State Register,* October 12, 1854; Harris, *Negro Servitude,* 193-194; Fehrenbacher, *Prelude,* 35; Willard King, *Lincoln's Manager, David Davis* (Cambridge: Harvard University Press, 1960), 104.
25. Alton *Weekly Courier,* October 12, 19, 26, November 2, 1854.
26. Rietveld, "Lincoln and the Politics of Morality," 40; Beveridge, *Lincoln,* II, 273; A. Lincoln to O. H. Browning, November 12, 1854 in Basler, Pratt, and Dunlap, eds., *Collected Works,* II, 286-287; Fehrenbacher, *Prelude,* 36-37.
27. *Congressional Globe,* 34 Congress, 1 Session, part 1, p. 656.
28. *Ibid.;* Harris, *Negro Servitude,* Appendix IV, 267; slightly variant figures are given in Alton *Weekly Courier,* November 16, 1854; *Cong. Globe,* 34 Cong., 1 Sess., pt. 1, p. 656; James A. Rawley, *Race and Politics: "Bleeding Kansas" and the Coming of the Civil War* (Philadelphia: Lippincott, 1969), 78.
29. Trumbull, "Trumbull," I, ch. 4, p. 4.
30. Ibid., ch. 5, pp. 1-2; White, *Trumbull,* 41-42; Fehrenbacher, *Prelude,* 32-33, 35-36.
31. Thomas L. Harris to Stephen A. Douglas, January 25, 1855, Douglas MSS; Krug, *Trumbull,* 96-97.
32. John M. Palmer to Malinda Ann Palmer, January 31, 1855, John M. Palmer MSS, Illinois State Historical Library.
33. Lincoln to Jacob Harding, November 11, 1854 in Basler, Pratt, and Dunlap, eds., *Collected Works,* II, 286; Lincoln to Thomas J. Henderson, November 27, 1854 in *ibid.,* 288; Lincoln to Joseph Gillespie, December 1, 1855 in *ibid.,* 288.
34. George Thomas Palmer, *A Conscientious Turncoat, The Story of John M. Palmer, 1817-1900* (New Haven: Yale University Press, 1941), 32.
35. Beveridge, *Lincoln,* II, 282.
36. *Ibid.,* 283.
37. Trumbull, "Trumbull," I, ch. 5, p. 5; Lincoln to Washburne, December [January] 6, 1855 in Basler, Pratt, and Dunlap, eds., *Collected Works,* II, 303.
38. Beveridge, *Lincoln,* II, 283.
39. *Illinois State Register,* February 7, 1855; McCormack, ed., *Memoirs of Koerner,* I, 623; Trumbull, "Trumbull," I, ch. 5, pp. 3-4.
40. *House Journal,* 19 Gen. Assembly, 1 Sess., 348.
41. *Ibid.,* 351.
42. *Ibid.,* 353.
43. Trumbull, "Trumbull," I, ch. 5, p. 7.
44. *House Journal,* 19 Gen. Assembly, 1 Sess., 353.
45. *Ibid.,* 354.
46. *Ibid.,* 355.
47. Lincoln to Elihu Washburne, February 9, 1855 in Basler, Pratt, and Dunlap, eds., *Collected Works,* II, 304-305; Johannsen, *Douglas,* 463.

48. Trumbull, "Trumbull," I, ch. 5, p. 9.
49. *House Journal,* 19 Gen. Assembly, 1 Sess., 357.
50. *Ibid.,* 358.
51. Trumbull, "Trumbull," I, ch. 5, p. 9.
52. Beveridge, *Lincoln,* II, 286.
53. *House Journal,* 19 Gen. Assembly, 1 Sess., 359.
54. Trumbull, "Trumbull," I, ch. 5, pp. 4, 10; Jane Martin Johns, "A Momentous Incident in the History of Illinois," *Journal of the Illinois State Historical Society,* X (January 1918), 556-558.
55. Chicago *Weekly Democrat,* August 11, 1855.
56. Trumbull, "Trumbull," I, ch. 5, p. 10; Lincoln to Washburne, February 7, 1855 in Basler, Pratt, and Dunlap, eds., *Collected Works,* II, 306. Lincoln had also become convinced that Matteson was a callous politician indifferent to the sufferings of individuals, Duff, *Lincoln,* 274-275.
57. *House Journal,* 19 Gen. Assembly, 1 Sess., 360.
58. *Illinois State Journal,* February 9, 1855.
59. Lincoln to Washburne, February 9, 1855 in Basler, Pratt, and Dunlap, eds., *Collected Works,* II, 304-306.
60. Trumbull, "Trumbull," I, ch. 5, p. 11. Horace White related the same incident, but said it happened at Ninion W. Edwards' house, "Lincoln in 1854," *Transactions of the Illinois Historical Society* (1908), 41.
61. Katherine Helm, *The True Story of Mary, Wife of Lincoln* (New York and London: Harper & Bros., 1928), 107-108; Randall, *Mary Lincoln,* 164.
62. Beveridge, *Lincoln,* I, fn. p. 323. Sandburg accepted this story, see Sandburg and Angle, *Mary Lincoln,* pt. 1, p. 78.
63. See the discussion in Randall, *Mary Lincoln,* 165, for the complex factors which figured in the Julia Jayne Trumbull-Mary Lincoln estrangement.
64. Mrs. Mary Lincoln to Dr. A. G. Henry, Chicago, July 26, 1865 in Sandburg and Angle, *Mary Lincoln,* pt. 2, p. 237.
65. Lincoln to Washburne, February 9, 1855 in Basler, Pratt, and Dunlap, eds., *Collected Works,* II, 306.
66. King, *Lincoln's Manager,* 108.
67. *Illinois State Register,* February 14, 1855; Beveridge, *Lincoln,* II, 292; Lincoln to Trumbull, February 3, 1859, in *ibid.,* III, 355-356.
68. Francis O'Shaughnessy, "General James Shields," *Transactions of the Illinois State Historical Society* (1915), 113-122; Johannsen, *Douglas,* 464.
69. J. C. Cunningham, "The Bloomington Convention of 1856 and Those Who Participated in It," *Transactions of the Illinois State Historical Society* (1915), 102.
70. W. D. French, "Men and Manners of the Early Days in Illinois," ibid. (1904), 74; Palmer to Malinda Ann Palmer, February 10, 1855, Palmer MSS; Alton *Telegraph* as clipped in "Walter Trumbull's Writing Book," 4; when consulted, in possession of Mrs. James L. Worrall, Indianapolis, Ind.

Notes to Chapter Five

1. *Illinois State Register,* February 21, 1855.
2. Trumbull to A. P. Butler, April 9, 1855, copy in Trumbull Family MSS.
3. Butler to Trumbull, April 20, 1855, ibid.
4. Alton *Courier,* July 23, 1855.
5. Belleville *Advocate,* July 4, 1855; Aurora *Beacon,* July 5, 1855.
6. *Cong. Globe,* 34 Cong., 1 Sess., pt. 1, pp. 655, 657; Alton *Weekly Courier,* October 4, 1856; *Illinois State Register,* October 4, 1856; Chicago *Weekly Democrat,* October 6, 1855.

7. See "Both Sides" in Alton *Weekly Courier,* October 11, 1855. Johannsen, *Douglas,* 482, writes that Douglas cancelled the debate arrangement because Trumbull did not confine himself to the Kansas-Nebraska Act, but tried to prove himself a "better Democrat" than Douglas.
8. Alton *Weekly Courier,* October 11, 1855.
9. Chicago *Daily Democratic Press,* October 12, 1855; Cairo City *Times,* October 24, 1855.
10. Trumbull to Owen Lovejoy, August 20, 1855, copy in Trumbull Family MSS.
11. Shelby M. Cullom to William Jayne, October 28, 1911, William Jayne MSS, Illinois State Historical Library.
12. See the Julia Jayne Trumbull letters to Lyman Trumbull in April 1856 in Trumbull Family MSS.
13. *A Sketch of the Life of Mrs. Lyman Trumbull* (privately printed pamphlet), 7, 14.
14. Trumbull, "Trumbull," I, ch. 6, p. 1.
15. *Illinois State Register,* November 29, 1855; Ottawa *Free Trader,* December 8, 1855.
16. Trumbull, "Trumbull," I, ch. 7, p. 1; *Cong. Globe,* 34 Cong., 1 Sess., pt. 1, pp. 1-2.
17. *Cong. Globe,* 34 Cong., 1 Sess., pt. 1, p. 58.
18. *Ibid.,* 136, 302.
19. *Ibid.,* 514.
20. *Ibid.,* 515.
21. *Ibid.,* 549-552, 562, 564.
22. Samuel Ashton to Stephen A. Douglas, March 5, 1856, Stephen A. Douglas MSS; Julia Trumbull to Mrs. Gershom Jayne, as quoted in Trumbull, "Trumbull," I, ch. 7, p. 3; Johannsen, *Douglas,* 494, believes that Douglas did not exert himself against Trumbull as he believed that Lyman would surely be seated.
23. *Cong. Globe,* 34 Cong., 1 Sess., pt. 1, p. 584.
24. Alton *Weekly Courier,* February 21, 1856, March 13, 1856; *Biographical Directory of Congress, 1774-1961,* fn. 162.
25. James D. Richardson, ed., *A Compilation of the Messages and Papers of the Presidents* (New York: Bureau of National Literature, Inc., 1897), V, 352-360; Johannsen, *Douglas,* 490; Berwanger, *The Frontier Against Slavery,* 99-101; Rawley, *Race & Politics,* 79-99.
26. Trumbull, "Trumbull," I, ch. 8, pp. 2-3.
27. *Cong. Globe,* 34 Cong., 1 Sess., app. 200-206.
28. *Ibid.,* pt. 1, pp. 654-658.
29. Alton *Daily Courier,* March 20, 1856; Alton *Weekly Courier,* April 3, 1856; *Illinois State Journal* as reprinted in *ibid.;* Palmer to Trumbull, March 24, 1856, Trumbull MSS; W. H. Herndon to Trumbull, March 28, 1856, ibid. The Eastern press took particular notice of Trumbull's joust with Douglas. See the many clippings in "Walter Trumbull's Writing Book," 6-9.
30. Herndon to Trumbull, March 28, 1856, Trumbull MSS; Anson S. Miller to Trumbull, March 27, 1856, ibid.; M. Concannon to Trumbull, March 30, 1956, ibid.
31. *Cong. Globe,* 34 Cong., 1 Sess., app. 288-289.
32. Johnson, *Douglas,* 294.
33. See the many letters of Julia Jayne Trumbull to Lyman Trumbull between March and May 1856 in the Trumbull Family MSS. On Springfield developments, see Julia Jayne Trumbull to Lyman Trumbull, May 5, 1856, ibid.
34. Ibid.
35. Julia Jayne Trumbull to Lyman Trumbull, May 11, 1856, ibid.

Notes to Chapter Six

1. See the many letters concerning the political situation in February and March 1856 in the Trumbull MSS. Also see Richard H. Sewell, *Ballots for Freedom: Antislavery Politics in the United States, 1837-1860* (New York: Oxford University Press, 1976), 263.
2. Trumbull, "Trumbull," I, ch. 8, p. 1; Fehrenbacher, *Prelude to Greatness,* 19.

3. Trumbull to Palmer, January 24, 1856, Palmer MSS.
4. Cole, *The Era of the Civil War,* 142; Wright, *Lincoln and the Politics of Slavery,* 85-87.
5. Fred Harvey Harrington, *Fighting Politician: Major General N. P. Banks* (Philadelphia: University of Pennsylvania Press, 1948), 155; Johannsen, *Douglas,* 448-489; Sewell, *Ballots for Freedom,* 275-276.
6. David L. Smiley, *Lion of White Hall: The Life of Cassius M. Clay* (Madison: University of Wisconsin Press, 1962), 155; Louis Filler, *The Crusade against Slavery, 1830-1860* (New York: Harper, 1960), 247; Sewell, *Ballots for Freedom,* 278-279.
7. Saul Sigelschiffer, *The American Conscience: The Drama of the Lincoln-Douglas Debates* (New York: Horizon Press, 1973), 130.
8. See the letters of approval in the Trumbull MSS, for late March, April, and early May 1856.
9. See H. Prather to Trumbull, February 11, 1856, ibid.
10. See the letters January-April 1856 in ibid.; *Illinois State Journal,* August 9, 1856; Alton *Weekly Courier,* April 3, 1856.
11. Herndon to Trumbull, April 24, 1856, Trumbull MSS.
12. Brown to Trumbull, April 24, 1856, May 12, 1856, ibid.
13. Brown to Trumbull, May 12, 1856, June 2, 1856, ibid.; Trumbull, "Trumbull," I, ch. 9, p. 1.
14. Lyman Trumbull to Julia Jayne Trumbull, April 25, 1856, Trumbull Family MSS; New York *Times,* April 30, 1856; Sewell, *Ballots for Freedom,* 282.
15. Trumbull, "Trumbull," I, ch. 12, p. 19.
16. Trumbull to A. Lincoln, June 15, 1856, Trumbull Family MSS. The Quincy *Whig* favored Trumbull's nomination for the presidency and claimed "western men" talked of his availability. Trumbull did not take this support seriously. See the *Whig* clipping in "Walter Trumbull's Writing Book," 10; Sewell, *Ballots for Freedom,* 283-284.
17. Lincoln to Trumbull, June 7, 1856 in Basler, Pratt, and Dunlap, eds., *Collected Works of Lincoln,* II, 342-343.
18. Trumbull to Lincoln, June 15, 1856, Trumbull Family MSS.
19. Trumbull, "Trumbull," I, ch. 9, p. 1.
20. Potter, *The Impending Crisis,* 260; Rawley, *Race & Politics,* 150.
21. David Donald, *Charles Sumner and the Coming of the Civil War* (New York: Knopf, 1967), 282-301; Potter, *The Impending Crisis,* 209-211, 220-221.
22. Trumbull, "Trumbull," I, ch. 6, pp. 6-19; New York *Tribune,* May 23, 24, 1856; *Cong. Globe,* 34 Cong., 1 Sess., pt. 2, p. 1280.
23. Trumbull, "Trumbull," I, ch. 6, pp. 6-19; Donald, *Sumner,* 298-302.
24. *Cong. Globe,* 34 Cong., 1 Sess., pt. 2, p. 1369.
25. *Ibid.,* 1373-1375.
26. Trumbull to Lincoln, June 15, 1856, Trumbull Family MSS.
27. Fehrenbacher, *Prelude to Greatness,* 121-142.
28. *Cong. Globe,* 34 Cong., 1 Sess., pt. 2, p. 1375.
29. Nevins, *Ordeal of the Union,* II, 471-472; Glyndon G. Van Deusen, *William Henry Seward* (New York: Oxford University Press, 1967), 172; Johannsen, *Douglas,* 524; Potter, *The Impending Crisis,* 215.
30. *Cong. Globe,* 34 Cong., 1 Sess., pt. 2, pp. 1506-1507.
31. *Ibid.,* app. 778-779.
32. *Ibid.,* 796, 798, 803-804.
33. *Ibid.,* 805.
34. Nevins, *Ordeal of the Union,* II, 472; Charles A. Jellison, *Fessenden of Maine, Civil War Senator* (Syracuse: Syracuse University Press, 1962), 94-95.
35. *Cong. Globe,* 34 Cong., 1 Sess., pt. 2, pp. 1286, 1666-1667.
36. *Ibid.,* 1574; Roy Nichols, *Franklin Pierce: Young Hickory of the Granite Hills* (Philadelphia: University of Pennsylvania Press, 1958), 475-477.

37. *Cong. Globe,* 34 Cong., 1 Sess., pt. 2, pp. 1968-1969.
38. *Ibid.,* 2230-2232.
39. *Ibid.,* 2235-2236; Lyman Trumbull to John Trumbull, August 17, 1856, Trumbull Family MSS.
40. New York *Times,* August 20, 1856. The Pennsylvania state party did not then use the name of Republican.
41. *Cong. Globe,* 34 Cong., 2 Sess., pt. 1, pp. 21, 78.
42. See the Washington correspondence of the Cincinnati *Commercial* as quoted in Carl Sandburg, *Abraham Lincoln: The War Years* (New York: Harcourt, Brace & Co., 1939), II, 556.
43. *Cong. Globe,* 34 Cong., 2 Sess., app. 797-798.
44. *Ibid.,* app. 868.
45. *Ibid.,* pt. 2, pp. 2062, 2225.
46. *Ibid.,* pt. 2, pp. 2100, 2169, 2205, 2206.
47. *Ibid.,* 2023.
48. Lyman Trumbull to Julia Jayne Trumbull, April 3, 1856, Trumbull Family MSS.
49. Julia Jayne Trumbull to Lyman Trumbull, April 27, 1856, ibid.
50. See the many letters on the campaign of 1856 in Trumbull MSS.
51. See James C. Conkling to Trumbull, July 26, 1856, ibid.; Brown to Trumbull, July 28, 1856, ibid.; Trumbull to Palmer, August 3, 1856, Palmer MSS.
52. Lincoln to Trumbull, August 11, 1856 in Basler, Pratt, and Dunlap, eds., *Collected Works of Lincoln,* II, 359-360.
53. Chicago *Democrat* as reprinted in *Illinois State Journal,* September 11, 1856.
54. *Illinois State Journal,* September 18, 1856.
55. *Ibid.,* September 29, 1856; *Ibid.,* October 3, 1856.
56. Peoria *Daily Democratic Press,* October 11, 1856.
57. Alton *Weekly Courier,* October 23, 1856.
58. Trumbull to Palmer, October 17, 1856, Palmer MSS.
59. Belleville *Advocate,* October 22, 1856.
60. Potter, *The Impending Crisis,* 264-265; Rawley, *Race & Politics,* 168-172.
61. W. Dean Burnham, *Presidential Ballots, 1836-1892* (Baltimore: Johns Hopkins Press, 1955), 368; Fehrenbacher, *Prelude to Greatness,* 47.
62. Trumbull to Palmer, December 2, 1856, Palmer MSS.
63. Richardson, ed., *Compilation of the Messages and Papers of the Presidents,* V, 404-407; Nichols, *Franklin Pierce,* 439; Frank Zornow, *Kansas: A History of the Jayhawk State* (Norman: University of Oklahoma Press, 1957), 75-76.
64. *Cong. Globe,* 34 Cong., 3 Sess., pt. 1, pp. 15-16; newspaper clippings in ''Walter Trumbull's Writing Book,'' 10-11.
65. *Cong. Globe,* 34 Cong., 3 Sess., pt. 1, p. 43.
66. *Ibid.,* app., 351; *Ibid.,* pt. 1, p. 1062.
67. Poore, *Perley's Reminiscences,* I, 516.
68. John B. Ellis, *The Sights and Secrets of the Nation's Capital* (Chicago: Jones, Junkin & Co., 1869), 138; Nevins, *The Emergence of Lincoln,* I, 81.
69. Detroit *Post & Tribune, Zachariah Chandler: An Outline of his Life and Public Services* (Detroit: The Post & Tribune Co., 1880), 19-132; Sister Mary Karl George, *Zachariah Chandler: A Political Biography* (East Lansing: Michigan State University Press, 1969), 2.
70. *Cong. Globe,* Special Session of Senate in 34 Cong., 3 Sess., app., 384.
71. George A. Nourse to Trumbull, March 30, 1857, Trumbull MSS.
72. Lincoln to Charles A. Gilfillan, May 9, 1857 in Basler, Pratt, and Dunlap, eds., *Collected Works of Lincoln,* II, 395.
73. N. B. Judd to Trumbull, May 12, 1857, Trumbull MSS.
74. Nourse to Trumbull, July 24, 1857, August 24, 1857, November 5, 1857, ibid.; Gilfillan to Trumbull, June 17, 1857, ibid.

75. Gilfillan to Trumbull, June 17, 1857, ibid.; Theodore C. Blegen, *Minnesota: A History of the State* (Minneapolis: University of Minnesota Press, 1963), 222.
76. Chicago *Press,* May 19, May 20, 1857. For the persistent anti-black bias of many Illinoisans, see Berwanger, *The Frontier Against Slavery,* 48-51.
77. Alton *Weekly Courier,* July 9, 1857; *Illinois State Journal,* July 8, 1857.
78. An example of many is C. D. Hay to Trumbull, July 10, 1857, Trumbull MSS.
79. Koerner to Trumbull, July 4, 1857, ibid.
80. Alton *Weekly Courier,* November 12, 1857; O. M. Hatch to Trumbull, July 13, 1857, Trumbull MSS.
81. Johannsen, *Douglas,* 568-571; Damon Wells, *Stephen Douglas: The Last Years, 1857-1861* (Austin: University of Texas Press, 1971), 27-28.
82. Wells, *Douglas,* 22-24; Filler, *The Crusade against Slavery,* 261.
83. Alton *Weekly Courier,* November 12, 1857.
84. Trumbull, "Trumbull," I, ch. 10, p. 1.
85. Elbert B. Smith, *The Presidency of James Buchanan* (Lawrence: University of Kansas Press, 1975), 40-41; Richardson, ed., *Messages and Papers of the Presidents,* V, 436-463; Holt, *The Political Crisis of the 1850's,* p. 204.
86. *Cong. Globe,* 35 Cong., 1 Sess., pt. 5, pp. 7-8.
87. Douglas to Buchanan, September 4, 1857 in Johannsen, ed., *Letters of Douglas.* 397-398.
88. Nevins, *The Emergence of Lincoln,* I, 255; Phillip Klein, *James Buchanan* (University Park: Pennsylvania State University Press, 1962), 301-303; Wells, *Douglas,* 34.
89. Glyndon G. Van Deusen, *Horace Greeley: Nineteenth Century Crusader* (Philadelphia: University of Pennsylvania Press, 1953), 225-226; Jeter Allen Isely, *Horace Greeley and the Republican Party, 1853-1861: A Study of the New York Tribune* (Princeton: Princeton University Press, 1947), 235; Sewell, *Ballots for Freedom,* 346-348.
90. Alton *Weekly Courier,* December 7, 1857.
91. See the letters written to Trumbull during December 1857 in Trumbull MSS.
92. Trumbull to Lincoln, December 25, 1857, Trumbull Family MSS.
93. Lincoln to Trumbull, December 26, 1857 in Basler, Pratt, and Dunlap, eds., *Collected Works of Lincoln,* II, 430.
94. Trumbull to Lincoln, Washington, January 3, 1858, Robert Todd Lincoln Collection, manuscripts division, Library of Congress.
95. Trumbull to Colonel W. B. Archer, January 8, 1858, Gilpin Library, Chicago Historical Society; Trumbull to W. C. Flagg, January 8, 1858, copy in W. C. Flagg MSS, Illinois Historical Survey, Urbana, Ill.
96. Hatch to Trumbull, January 14, 1858, Trumbull MSS.
97. Klein, *Buchanan,* 302; Van Deusen, *Seward,* 184.
98. Nevins, *The Emergence of Lincoln,* I, 269-270; Klein, *Buchanan,* 302.
99. Richardson, ed., *Messages and Papers of the Presidents,* V, 471-481.
100. *Cong. Globe,* 35 Cong., 1 Sess., pt. 2, pp. 1159-1165; Alton *Weekly Courier,* April 1, April 8, 1858.
101. *Cong. Globe,* 35 Cong., 1 Sess., pt. 2, pp. 1264-1265.
102. Nevins, *The Emergence of Lincoln,* I, 288; Wells, *Douglas,* 43-44.
103. Klein, *Buchanan,* 311-312; Wells, *Douglas,* 44.
104. Nevins, *The Emergence of Lincoln,* I, 297-298; Wells, *Douglas,* 44-46; Zorrow, *Kansas,* 78; Alice Nichols, *Bleeding Kansas* (New York: Oxford University Press, 1954), 211.
105. Nevins, *The Emergence of Lincoln,* I, 299-301; Wells, *Douglas,* 46.
106. *Cong. Globe,* 35 Cong., 1 Sess., pt. 2, pp. 1827-1828, 1899.
107. Potter, *The Impending Crisis,* 325; Rawley, *Race & Politics,* 250.
108. *Cong. Globe,* 35 Cong., 1 Sess., app., 105.
109. *Ibid.,* pt. 2, p. 1647.

110. *Ibid.*, pt. 3, p. 2230.
111. *Ibid.*, 2230, 2233, 2234.
112. *Ibid.*, 2426.
113. *Ibid.*, 2349, 2403, 2404, 2426.
114. *Ibid.*, 2527.
115. *Ibid.*, app., 363.
116. Doolittle to wife, May 1858, as quoted in Duane Mowry, ed., "An Appreciation of James Rood Doolittle," *Proceedings of the State Historical Society of Wisconsin at its Fifty-Seventh Annual Meeting Held October 21, 1909*, p. 288.

Notes to Chapter Seven

1. William Pickering to Trumbull, April 21, 1858, Trumbull MSS.
2. Herndon to Trumbull, April 24, 1858, ibid.
3. New York *Semi-Weekly Tribune*, June 11, 1858. Two of Trumbull's friends in the Democratic party of the 1840's were "Danites," as the National Democrats were styled. See John Y. Simon, "Union County in 1858 and the Lincoln-Douglas Debates," *Journal of the Illinois State Historical Society*, LXII (Autumn, 1969), 268, 277-278.
4. Nevins, *The Emergence of Lincoln*, I, 350; Harry E. Pratt, ed., *Concerning Mr. Lincoln* (Springfield: The Abraham Lincoln Association, 1944), 13.
5. Lincoln to Trumbull, June 23, 1858 in Basler, Pratt, and Dunlap, eds., *Collected Works of Lincoln*, II, 471-472.
6. Mildred C. Stoler, "The Democratic Element in the Republican Party in Illinois, 1856-1860," *Papers in Illinois History and Transactions of the Illinois State Historical Society* (1942), 46; Mark W. Delahay to Trumbull, May 22, 1858, Trumbull MSS.
7. Brown to Trumbull, April 25, 1858, Trumbull MSS; Sigelschiffer, *The American Conscience*, 139.
8. *Illinois State Journal*, June 16, 1858.
9. Trumbull to Lincoln, June 12, 1858, Robert Todd Lincoln Collection.
10. J. McClea to Trumbull, July 11, 1858, Trumbull MSS.
11. Chicago *Press & Tribune*, August 8, 1858; Chicago *Weekly Times*, August 12, 1858.
12. See the newspaper clippings in "Walter Trumbull's Writing Book."
13. Ottawa *Free Trader*, August 14, 1858.
14. *Illinois State Journal*, August 16, 1858.
15. *Illinois State Journal*, September 29, 1858; Sigelschiffer, *The American Conscience*, 213.
16. Edward Erle Sparks, ed., *The Lincoln-Douglas Debates of 1858 (Collections of Illinois State Historical Library*, III) (Springfield: The Trustees of Illinois State Historical Library, 1908), 20-21; Johannsen, *Douglas*, 662.
17. *Illinois State Journal*, August 14, October 9, 1858; *The Chicago Democrat* as reprinted in *ibid.*, August 10, 1858; Louisville *Journal* as reprinted in *ibid.*, August 19, 1858.
18. Sparks, ed., *Lincoln-Douglas Debates*, 58; Johannsen, *Douglas*, 663.
19. Sparks, ed., *Lincoln-Douglas Debates*, 59-60; Douglas to Lincoln, July 24, 1858 in Johannsen, ed., *Letters of Douglas*.
20. Sparks, ed., *Lincoln-Douglas Debates*, 88-93; Paul M. Angle, ed., *Created Equal? The Complete Lincoln-Douglas Debates of 1858* (Chicago: University of Chicago Press, 1958), 103-114.
21. Sparks, ed., *Lincoln-Douglas Debates*, 98-100; Angle, ed., *Created Equal?*, 114-130.
22. New York *Semi-Weekly Tribune*, September 10, 1858; *Illinois State Journal*, October 2, 1858.
23. *Illinois State Journal*, September 3, 1858.
24. Henry Clay Whitney to Lincoln, August 26, 1858, Robert Todd Lincoln Collection.
25. Angle, ed., *Created Equal?*, 236.

26. Sparks, ed., *Lincoln-Douglas Debates,* 152; Angle, ed., *Created Equal?,* 229.
27. Sparks, ed., *Lincoln-Douglas Debates,* 161; Angle, ed., *Created Equal?,* 152. As Fehrenbacher has pointed out, Douglas' standing in the eyes of most Southern Democratic politicans had already sunk so low since his Lecompton apostasy that the Freeport Doctrine had probably little effect on his popularity in the South. Don E. Fehrenbacher, "Lincoln, Douglas and the 'Freeport Question,' " *American Historical Review,* LXVI (April 1961), 605-612; Fehrenbacher, *Prelude,* 136-139.
28. Trumbull to Lincoln, September 14, 1858, Robert Todd Lincoln Collection.
29. Sparks, ed., *Lincoln-Douglas Debates,* 246; Angle, ed., *Created Equal?,* 219-220.
30. Sparks, ed., *Lincoln-Douglas Debates,* 258; Angle, ed., *Created Equal?,* 229.
31. Sparks, ed., *Lincoln-Douglas Debates,* 269-281; Angle, ed., *Created Equal?,* 235-247.
32. Sparks, ed., *Lincoln-Douglas Debates,* 281-302; Angle, ed., *Created Equal?,* 247-267.
33. Angle, ed., *Created Equal?,* 270.
34. *Ibid.,* 264-265.
35. *Ibid.,* 285.
36. *Ibid.,* 293; Sparks, ed., *Lincoln-Douglas Debates,* 341.
37. Sparks, ed., *Lincoln-Douglas Debates,* 347; Angle, ed., *Created Equal?,* 298-299.
38. Sparks, ed., *Lincoln-Douglas Debates,* 395-407; Angle, ed., *Created Equal?,* 324-335.
39. Sparks, ed., *Lincoln-Douglas Debates,* 407-427; Angle, ed., *Created Equal?,* 335-353.
40. Sparks, ed., *Lincoln-Douglas Debates,* 450-496; Angle, ed., *Created Equal?,* 362-402.
41. Henry E. Pratt, "The Great Debates," in *Illinois Blue Book, 1953-1954,* pp. 26-27.
42. Pratt, *Concerning Mr. Lincoln,* 17.
43. Judd to Trumbull, April 19, 1858, Trumbull MSS; Wright, *Lincoln and the Politics of Slavery,* 145.
44. Fehrenbacher, *Prelude,* 118-119.
45. Pease, *Illinois,* 165; Johannsen, *Douglas,* 677.
46. Nevins, *The Emergence of Lincoln,* I, 415-429.
47. *Cong. Globe,* 35 Cong., 2 Sess., pt. 1, pp. 264-266; Aurora *Weekly Beacon* in "Walter Trumbull's Writing Book," 31.
48. *Cong. Globe,* 35 Cong., 2 Sess., pt. 1, p. 627.
49. *Ibid.,* 326, 332, 373, 374, 375-376, 418, 420, 442, 477-478, 577-578, 602-609, 624, 627; Nevins, *The Emergence of Lincoln,* I, 440-444; Jellison, *Fessenden,* 116.
50. *Cong. Globe,* 35 Cong., 2 Sess., pt. 1, p. 627.
51. Richardson, ed., *Messages and the Papers of the Presidents,* VII, 3074-3081; Klein, *Buchanan,* 338.
52. *Cong. Globe,* 35 Cong., 2 Sess., pt. 2, pp. 1274-1275.
53. Trumbull to John Dean Caton, March 1, 1859, John Dean Caton MSS, manuscripts division, Library of Congress.
54. *Cong. Globe,* 35 Cong., 2 Sess., pt. 2, Special Session of the Senate, 1686.
55. Trumbull to Thurlow Weed, April 11, 1859, Stuart Collection, Henry E. Huntington Library, San Marino, Calif.; Nevins, *The Emergence of Lincoln,* II, fn. 230.
56. *Illinois State Journal,* May 25, 1859.
57. Trumbull to Lincoln, August 29, 1859, Robert Todd Lincoln Collection.
58. Lincoln to Hawkins Taylor, September 8, 1859 in Basler, Pratt, and Dunlap, eds., *Collected Works of Lincoln,* III, 399-400; Lincoln to Peter Zinn, September 6, 1859, *ibid.,* 400.
59. Wells, *Douglas,* 81; Johannsen, ed., *Letters of Douglas,* fn. 76.
60. See speeches in Basler, Pratt, and Dunlap, eds., *Collected Works of Lincoln,* III, 400-462; Johannsen, ed., *Letters of Douglas,* fn. 476.
61. Douglas, "The Dividing Line between Federal and Local Authority: Popular Sovereignty in the Territories," *Harper's New Monthly Magazine,* XIX (September 1859), 519-537.
62. Washington *National Era,* October 13, 1859.

63. New York *Times,* October 14, 1859; Wells, *Douglas,* fn. 182.
64. Trumbull to Palmer, December 19, 1858, Palmer MSS.
65. Ibid. Krug described Trumbull's campaigning for Palmer as "furious." Krug, *Trumbull,* 156.
66. Nevins, *The Emergence of Lincoln,* II, 5-27, 70-105, 181; Stephen B. Oates, *To Purge This Land with Blood: A Biography of John Brown* (New York: Harper & Row, 1970), 290-302, 310-312.
67. Trumbull to Yates, November 2, 1859, Reavis MSS, Gilpin Library, Chicago Historical Society.
68. Trumbull to Lincoln, November 23, 1859, Robert Todd Lincoln Collection.
69. 22 Howard v.
70. *Cong. Globe,* 36 Cong., 1 Sess., pt. 1, p. 1.
71. *Ibid.,* 5-7.
72. *Ibid.,* 27-32.
73. *Ibid.,* 32-38.
74. *Ibid.,* 38-40, 54-62.
75. C. D. Hay to Trumbull, December 25, 1859, Trumbull MSS.
76. Lincoln to Trumbull, December 25, 1859 in Basler, Pratt, and Dunlap, eds., *Complete Works of Lincoln,* III, 512-513.
77. L. Maria Child to Trumbull, December 25, 1859, Trumbull MSS.
78. *Cong. Globe,* 36 Cong., 1 Sess., pt. 1, p. 152.
79. Reinhard H. Luthin, *The First Lincoln Campaign* (Gloucester, Mass.: P. Smith, 1964), 19; Potter, *The Impending Crisis,* 388.
80. *Cong. Globe,* 36 Cong., 1 Sess., pt. 2, pp. 1118-1119, 1507, 1508, 1550, 1551; pt. 3, pp. 1997-2008, 2040, 2043.
81. *Ibid.,* 3263-3264; Klein, *Buchanan,* 346-347; Smith, *Presidency of James Buchanan,* 121.
82. *Cong. Globe,* 36 Cong., 1 Sess., pt. 4, p. 3272.
83. *Ibid.,* pt. 1, pp. 918-921.
84. Lincoln to Trumbull, March 16, 1860 in Basler, Pratt, and Dunlap, eds., *Complete Works of Lincoln,* IV, 32.
85. See the Trumbull MSS for December 1859-May 1860.
86. Lincoln to Richard M. Corwine, April 6, 1860 in Basler, Pratt, and Dunlap, eds., *Complete Works of Lincoln,* IV, 36.
87. Hinckley to Brother, March 28, 1860, Trumbull MSS.
88. White, *Trumbull,* 103.
89. Trumbull to Lincoln, April 24, 1860, Robert Todd Lincoln Collection.
90. See Trumbull MSS for many letters between 1857 and 1860.
91. J. R. Bulion to Trumbull, April 9, 1860, Trumbull MSS.
92. Trumbull to Lincoln, April 24, 1860, Robert Todd Lincoln Collection. For Trumbull's attitude, see Fehrenbacher, *Prelude,* 152-154.
93. Trumbull to Lincoln, April 24, 1860, Robert Todd Lincoln Collection; Fehrenbacher, *Prelude,* 153; Wright, *Lincoln and the Politics of Slavery,* 177.
94. Trumbull, "Trumbull," I, ch. 12, pp. 18-19.
95. Carl Sandburg, *Abraham Lincoln: The Prairie Years,* II (New York: Harcourt Brace, 1944), 43.
96. Lincoln to Trumbull, April 29, 1860 in Basler, Pratt, and Dunlap, eds., *Complete Works of Lincoln,* IV, 45-46.
97. Trumbull to Lincoln, April 24, 1860, Robert Todd Lincoln Collection.
98. King, *Lincoln's Manager,* 136-141.
99. Lincoln to Trumbull, April 29, 1860 in Basler, Pratt, and Dunlap, eds., *Complete Works of Lincoln,* IV, 59.

100. Lincoln to Trumbull, April 7, 1860 in Basler, Pratt, and Dunlap, eds., *Complete Works of Lincoln,* IV, 40; Don E. Fehrenbacher, *Chicago Giant: A Biography of "Long John" Wentworth* (Madison, Wisc.: American History Research Center, 1957), 127.
101. Trumbull, "Trumbull," I, ch. 10, pp. 5-7; William Jayne to Trumbull, May 20, 1860, Trumbull MSS; Fehrenbacher, *Chicago Giant,* 178.
102. Nevins, *The Emergence of Lincoln,* II, 256, 258; Fehrenbacher, *Chicago Giant,* 178.
103. Trumbull to Lincoln, May 18, 1860, Robert Todd Lincoln Collection.
104. Trumbull, "Trumbull," I, ch. 10, p. 10; Lincoln to Trumbull, May 31, 1860 in Basler, Pratt, and Dunlap, eds., *Complete Works of Lincoln,* IV, 59.
105. H. G. McPike to Trumbull, June 26, 1860, Trumbull MSS.
106. *Cong. Globe,* 36 Cong., 1 Sess., pt. 3, pp. 2455-2456.
107. Trumbull to Lincoln, May 31, 1860, Robert Todd Lincoln Collection.
108. Lincoln to Trumbull, May 26, May 31, June 5, 1860 in Basler, Pratt, and Dunlap, eds., *Complete Works of Lincoln,* IV, 55, 59, 71.
109. Stoler, "The Democratic Element in the New Republican Party," 69-70.
110. Judd to Trumbull, June 15, 1860, Trumbull MSS.
111. *Illinois State Journal,* July 10, 1860.
112. *Ibid.*
113. *Ibid.,* July 12, 1860.
114. Howard K. Beale, ed., *The Diary of Edward Bates, 1859-1866 (Annual Report of the American Historical Association,* 1930, IV), 158.
115. *Illinois State Journal,* July 24, 1860.
116. Chicago *Press & Tribune,* July 30, 1860; Oquawka *Spectator,* August 2, 1860.
117. *Illinois State Journal,* August 8, 1860.
118. *Ibid.,* August 13, 1860; New York *Semi-Weekly Tribune,* August 10, 1860.
119. James G. Randall and Theodore Calvin Pease, eds., *The Diary of Orville Hickman Browning, 1850-1864,* I *(Collections of the Illinois State Historical Library,* XX) (Springfield: The Trustees of the Illinois State Historical Library, 1925), 422; New York *Semi-Weekly Tribune,* August 28, 1860; Amos C. Babcock to Trumbull, August 27, 1860, Trumbull MSS; Rushville *Schuyler Citizen,* August 29, 1860.
120. *Illinois State Journal,* September 4, 1860.
121. *Ibid.,* September 6, 1860.
122. *Ibid.,* September 25, 1860.
123. *Ibid.*
124. *Ibid.,* October 10, October 11, 1860; Genealogy in writing of Walter Trumbull.
125. Trumbull, "Trumbull," ch. 12, p. 5.
126. Lincoln to William Fithian, August 15, 1860 in Basler, Pratt, and Dunlap eds., *Complete Works of Lincoln,* IV, 95.
127. Hannibal Hamlin to Trumbull, Hampden, August 29, 1860, Trumbull MSS.
128. Elihu B. Washburne to Trumbull, September 9, 1860, ibid.
129. McCormack, ed., *Memoirs of Koerner,* II, 99.
130. William Salter, *The Life of James W. Grimes, Governor of Iowa, 1854-1858, Senator of the United States, 1859-1869* (New York: Appleton and Company, 1876), 128.
131. Committee of Arrangements to Trumbull, September 14, 1860, Trumbull MSS; Van Deusen, *Seward,* 233.
132. *Illinois State Journal,* October 18, October 20, 1860, Trumbull MSS.
133. Yates to Trumbull, October 20, 1860, Trumbull MSS.
134. Cameron to Trumbull, October 25, 1860, ibid.
135. White, *Trumbull,* 109.
136. Harry J. Carman and Reinhard H. Luthin, *Lincoln and the Patronage* (Gloucester, Mass.: P. Smith, 1964), 86-87.
137. Bessie Louise Pierce, *A History of Chicago,* II (New York: Knopf, 1937), 253.

138. New York *Tribune,* November 12, 1860; New York *Semi-Weekly Tribune,* November 13, 1860; William E. Baringer, *A House Dividing: Lincoln as President-Elect* (Springfield: The Abraham Lincoln Association, 1945), 5-6.
139. Rushville *Schuyler Citizen,* November 14, 1860.
140. William Jayne, *Personal Reminiscences of the Martyred Abraham Lincoln* (Chicago: Grand Army Hall and Memorial Association, c. 1908), 31; *Illinois State Journal,* November 12, 1860.
141. Jayne, *Personal Reminiscences,* 45; Trumbull, "Trumbull," I, ch. 12, p. 5; White, *Trumbull,* 109; New York *Tribune,* November 14, 1860.
142. *Illinois State Journal,* November 10, 1860.

Notes to Chapter Eight

1. Baringer, *A House Dividing,* 32; Basler, Pratt, and Dunlap, eds., *Collected Works of Lincoln,* IV, 141-142.
2. New York *Herald,* November 20, 1860.
3. *Illinois State Journal,* November 21, 1860.
4. *Ibid.;* New York *Times,* November 21, 1860.
5. Baltimore *Patriot* as reprinted in *Illinois State Journal,* November 29, 1860; New York *Times,* November 21, 22, 1860.
6. New Orleans *Crescent,* November 28, 1860 as reprinted in Dwight L. Dumond, ed., *Southern Editorials on Secession* (New York: The Century Co., 1931), 272-274.
7. New York *Times,* November 22, 24, 1860; James G. Randall, *Lincoln the President: From Springfield to Gettysburg,* I (New York: Dodd Mead & Co., 1945), 233.
8. Lincoln to Henry J. Raymond, November 28, 1860 in Basler, Pratt, and Dunlap, eds., *Collected Works of Lincoln,* IV, 145-146. For a full treatment, see Ralph J. Roske, "Lincoln's Peace 'Puff,' " *Abraham Lincoln Quarterly,* VI (December 1950), 239-245.
9. New York *Herald,* November 22, 1860; New York *Tribune,* November 23, 1860.
10. New York *Herald,* November 24, 1860; H. Draper Hunt, *Hannibal Hamlin of Maine: Lincoln's First Vice-President* (Syracuse: University of Syracuse Press, 1969), 127-128.
11. Baringer, *A House Dividing,* 84.
12. New York *Herald,* November 29, 1860.
13. Baringer, *A House Dividing,* 90.
14. *Ibid.,* 87-88; Hunt, *Hamlin,* 128-129.
15. Trumbull to Lincoln, December 2, 1860, copy in Lincoln Collection, Gilpin Library, Chicago Historical Society.
16. White, *Trumbull,* 149.
17. Baringer, *A House Dividing,* 181.
18. H. B. Stanton to S. P. Chase, November 30, 1860 in A. B. Hart, ed., *Diary and Correspondence of Salmon P. Chase (Annual Report of the American Historical Association,* 1902, II), 485.
19. Trumbull to Lincoln, December 2, 1860, copy in Lincoln Collection, Gilpin Library.
20. Lincoln to Trumbull, December 8, 1860 in Basler, Pratt, and Dunlap, eds., *Collected Works of Lincoln,* IV, 149; Baringer, *A House Dividing,* 100-101, 109; Carman and Luthin, *Lincoln and the Patronage,* 14-15; Hunt, *Hamlin,* 130-131.
21. Baringer, *A House Dividing,* 129-130; Van Deusen, *Seward,* 240; Hunt, *Hamlin,* 128-129, 131.
22. Baringer, *A House Dividing,* 132-133; Ervin Stanley Bradley, *Simon Cameron: Lincoln's Secretary of War: A Political Biography* (Philadelphia: University of Pennsylvania Press, 1966), 164-168.
23. Trumbull to Lincoln, December 31, 1860, Robert Todd Lincoln Collection; Trumbull to Lincoln, January 3, 1861, ibid.; Trumbull to Lincoln, January 20, 1861, ibid.

24. Trumbull to Lincoln, December 31, 1860, ibid.
25. Henry Clay Whitney, *Life on the Circuit with Lincoln* (Boston: Estes and Lauriat, 1892), 2; Baringer, *A House Dividing,* 76-77.
26. New York *Herald,* November 26, 1860; Baringer, *A House Dividing,* 76-77.
27. Leonard Swett to Lincoln, January 5, 1860 [actually 1861], Robert Todd Lincoln Collection.
28. New York *Herald,* January 22, 23, 1861; Randall, *Lincoln the President,* I, 269.
29. Krug, *Trumbull,* 168; Ralph J. Roske, "Lincoln and Lyman Trumbull," in *Lincoln Images* (Rock Island, Ill.: Augustana College Library, 1960), 74, 77.
30. Brown to Trumbull, November 26, 1860, Trumbull MSS.
31. Trumbull to Lincoln, December 27, 1860, Robert Todd Lincoln Collection.
32. Trumbull to Lincoln, January 7, 1861, ibid.
33. Carman and Luthin, *Lincoln and the Patronage,* 31-33.
34. J. O. Glover to William Butler, December 10, 1860, Trumbull MSS.
35. Brown to Trumbull, December 10, 1860, ibid.; Judd to Trumbull, December 1, 1860, ibid.
36. Yates to Trumbull, December 21, 1860, ibid.
37. Edwin Beecher to Trumbull, December 31, 1860, ibid.
38. *House Journal,* 19 Gen. Assembly, 1 Sess., 31.
39. Jonas Notestine to Trumbull, December 12, 1860, Trumbull MSS; David M. Potter, *Lincoln and His Party in the Secession Crisis* (New Haven: Yale University Press, 1942), 1-19, 69-70, 77; Kenneth M. Stampp, *And the War Came: The North and the Secession Crisis* (Baton Rouge: Louisiana State University Press, 1950), 17.
40. *Cong. Globe,* 36 Cong., 2 Sess., pt 1, p. 73.
41. *Ibid.,* 156.
42. Nevins, *The Emergence of Lincoln,* II, 396, 399; Frederic Bancroft, *The Life of William H. Seward* (New York: Harper and Bros., 1900), 11, 10.
43. New York *Times,* December 25, 1860; Boston *Courier,* December 27, 28, 1860.
44. Trumbull, "Trumbull," I, ch. 13, p. 14.
45. *Cong. Globe,* 36 Cong., 2 Sess., pt. 1, p. 312.
46. *Ibid.,* 156.
47. *Ibid.,* 409.
48. *Ibid.,* 327, 404, 521, 543.
49. See the Trumbull MSS for many letters in December and January urging no concessions to the South and applauding Trumbull's rock-like stand. See also Richard H. Sewell, *Ballots for Freedom: Anti-Slavery Politics in the United States, 1837-1860* (New York: Oxford University Press, 1976), 364.
50. *Cong. Globe,* 36 Cong., 2 Sess., pt. 1, pp. 484-487.
51. *Ibid.,* 698.
52. *Ibid.,* 740.
53. *Ibid.,* 884-885.
54. Trumbull to Jayne, February 17, 1861, Trumbull Family MSS.
55. Baringer, *A House Dividing,* 294-295; Sandburg, *Lincoln: The War Years,* I, 288-289; Potter, *The Impending Crisis,* 561-562.
56. Nevins, *The Emergence of Lincoln,* II, 451; Randall, *Lincoln the President,* I, 289.
57. Washburne to Lincoln, February 19, 1861, Robert Todd Lincoln Collection.
58. Carman and Luthin, *Lincoln and the Patronage,* 49-50; Randall, *Lincoln the President,* I, 288.
59. Trumbull to Lincoln, February 25, 1861, William Butler MSS, Gilpin Library, Chicago Historical Society.
60. Paul M. Angle, ed., *New Letters and Papers of Lincoln* (Boston: Houghton Mifflin Co., 1930), 261-262.
61. Nevins, *The Emergence of Lincoln,* II, 411; Potter, *Lincoln and His Party,* 307-308.

62. Trumbull to Yates, February 4, 1861, Richard Yates MSS, Illinois State Historical Library.
63. *Cong. Globe,* 36 Cong., 2 Sess., pt. 1, p. 864; James E. Hendrickson, *Lane of Oregon: Machine Politics in the Sectional Crisis* (New Haven: Yale University Press, 1967), 246.
64. Nevins, *The Emergence of Lincoln,* II, 412; James G. Randall and David Donald, *The Civil War and Reconstruction* (Boston: D. C. Heath & Co., 1961), 152.
65. *Cong. Globe,* 36 Cong., 2 Sess., pt. 2, p. 1255; Van Deusen, *Seward,* 249.
66. Julia Jayne Trumbull to Walter Trumbull, February 3, 1861 in Trumbull, "Trumbull," I, ch. 12, p. 22; Trumbull, "Trumbull," I, ch. 13, p. 22.
67. Potter, *The Impending Crisis,* 525; S. York to Trumbull, January 9, 1860 [actually 1861], Trumbull MSS; Trumbull to Lincoln, December 2, 1860, Robert Todd Lincoln Collection.
68. *Cong. Globe,* 36 Cong., 2 Sess., pt. 2, pp. 1267-70.
69. *Ibid.,* 1270; Van Deusen, *Seward,* 249.
70. *Cong. Globe,* 36 Cong., 2 Sess., pt. 2, pp. 1356, 1358.
71. *Ibid.,* 1360.
72. *Ibid.,* 1361.
73. *Ibid.,* 1363.
74. *Ibid.,* 1367, 1374.
75. *Ibid.,* 1380-1383.
76. *Ibid.,* 1386-7, 1401.
77. *Ibid.,* 1403.
78. *Ibid.,* 1405.
79. *Ibid.,* 1413; New York *Semi-Weekly Tribune,* March 5, 1861.
80. Baringer, *A House Dividing,* 332, 333.
81. Anson G. Henry to Wife, February 18(?), 1863, Anson G. Henry MSS, Illinois State Historical Library.
82. Carman and Luthin, *Lincoln and the Patronage,* 68; Ralph J. Roske, *Everyman's Eden: A History of California* (New York: Macmillan, 1968), 287, 300; Hendrickson, *Lane,* 234-236.
83. Carman and Luthin, *Lincoln and the Patronage,* 69-70, 75.
84. Trumbull to Ozias Hatch, March 24, 1861, Ozias Hatch MSS, Illinois State Historical Library.
85. Jayne to Butler, March 21, 1861, Butler MSS.
86. See the many appeals for office by place-seekers to Trumbull in Trumbull Family MSS, Illinois State Historical Library.
87. Jayne to Butler, March 21, 1861, Butler MSS.
88. Henry to Wife, February 18(?), 1863, Henry MSS.
89. Mrs. Elizabeth J. Grimsley to John T. Stuart, March 20, 1861 as quoted in Pratt, *Concerning Mr. Lincoln,* 75.
90. Carman and Luthin, *Lincoln and the Patronage,* 100.
91. *Ibid.,* 79.
92. *Ibid.,* 103.
93. *Ibid.,* 117.
94. *Senate Executive Journal,* XI, 312.
95. Hatch to Trumbull, March 21, 1861, Trumbull MSS; Hatch to Trumbull, March 30, 1861, ibid.
96. *Senate Executive Journal,* XI, 312.
97. Lincoln to Stuart, March 30, 1861 in Basler, Pratt, and Dunlap, eds., *Collected Works of Lincoln,* IV, 303.
98. New York *Semi-Weekly Tribune,* March 8, 1861; Special Session of the Senate, *Cong. Globe,* 36 Cong., 2 Sess., pt. 2, p. 1433.
99. *Cong. Globe,* 36 Cong., 2 Sess., pt. 2, pp. 1519.
100. *Ibid.,* 1519-1520.

101. New York *Herald,* March 11, 12, 1861; New York *Evening Post,* March 11, 1861; New York *Evening Post,* March 11, 1861; New York *Tribune,* March 14, 1861; Springfield (Mass.) *Republican,* March 13, 1861.
102. Mrs. Grimsley to Stuart, March 20, 1861, as quoted in Pratt, *Concerning Mr. Lincoln,* 75.
103. New York *Evening Post,* April 3, 1861; Cincinnati *Commercial,* April 6, 1861; Chicago *Tribune,* April 5, 13, 1861.
104. L. Rosette to John G. Nicolay, April 13, 1861 in David C. Mearns, ed., *The Lincoln Papers; the Story of the Collection, with Selections to July 4, 1861,* II (Garden City, N.Y.: Doubleday, 1948), 551.

Notes to Chapter Nine

1. L. Rosette to John G. Nicolay, April 13, 1861 in Mearns, ed., *The Lincoln Papers,* II, 551; Yates, Trumbull *et al.* to Lincoln, April 17, 1861 in *War of the Rebellion: . . . Official Records of the Union and Confederate Armies,* Series III, Vol. 1, 80-81.
2. Trumbull to C. H. Ray, April 19, 1861, C. H. Ray MSS, Henry E. Huntington Library; Cole, *The Era of the Civil War,* 261-262.
3. Trumbull to Ray, April 19, 1861, Ray MSS; Hans Christian Adamson, *Rebellion in Missouri: 1861, Nathaniel Lyon and his Army of the West* (Philadelphia: Chilton Co., 1961), 1-78; Edward Conrad Smith, *The Borderland in the Civil War* (Freeport, N. Y.: Books for Library Press, 1961), 116-132, 149-154, 221-239.
4. Trumbull to Doolittle, May 16, 1861 in "A Statesman's Letters of the Civil War Period," *Journal of the Illinois State Historical Society,* II (July 1909), 47.
5. General orders 5 of Brigadier General Lyon, May 31, 1861 in *War of the Rebellion,* Series I, Vol. III, 381; "Trumbull," I, ch. 14, p. 5.
6. Col. Thomas L. Sneed, "The First Year of the War," Clarence C. Buel and Robert Underwood Johnson, eds., *Battles and Leaders of the Civil War,* I (New York: The Century Co., 1884), 166-173; Adamson, *Rebellion,* 97-285; Smith, *The Borderland,* 226-230, 245-246, 261; Stephen B. Oates, *With Malice Toward None: The Life of Abraham Lincoln* (New York: Harper & Row, 1977), 250.
7. Trumbull to Doolittle, April 27, 1861 in "A Statesman's Letters of the Civil War Period," 45; Trumbull to Doolittle, May 16, 1861 in ibid; Oates, *With Malice Toward None,* 250.
8. Randall, *Lincoln the President,* I, 354-380; Randall and Donald, *The Civil War and Reconstruction,* 274.
9. Trumbull, "Trumbull," I, ch. 12, pp. 14, 23; Lincoln to Gideon Welles, May 21, 1861 in Basler, Pratt, and Dunlap, eds., *The Collected Works of Lincoln,* IV, 381.
10. White, *Trumbull,* 165.
11. Pease and Randall, eds., *Diary of Browning,* I, ch. 14, p. 5; Johannsen, *Douglas,* 871-872.
12. Pease and Randall, eds., *Diary of Browning,* I, 475.
13. *Cong. Globe,* 37 Cong., 1 Sess., pt. 1, p. 1.
14. *Ibid.,* 17; *Illinois State Journal,* January 5, August 24, 1860.
15. *Cong. Globe,* 37 Cong., 1 Sess., pt. 1, pp. 27-28.
16. Pease and Randall, eds., *Diary of Browning,* I, 479, 481; New York *Herald,* July 27, 31, 1861.
17. Pease and Randall, eds., *Diary of Browning,* I, 479.
18. *Ibid.,* 479, 481.
19. *Cong. Globe,* 37 Cong., 1 Sess., pt. 1, p. 134.
20. James B. Fry, "McDowell's Advance to Bull Run," Buel and Johnson, eds., *Battles and Leaders,* I, fn. p. 183; Bruce Catton, *This Hallowed Ground: The Story of the Union Side of the Civil War* (Garden City, N.Y.: Doubleday, 1956), 57-58.

21. Lyman Trumbull to Julia Trumbull, July 22, 1861 in White, *Trumbull*, 166-167; Trumbull, "Trumbull," I, ch. 5, pp. 3-4.
22. Trumbull to Koerner as quoted in McCormack, ed., *Memoirs of Koerner,* II, 162-163.
23. New York *Herald,* July 26, 1861.
24. White, *Trumbull,* 168, 172-173; Hans L. Trefousse, *The Radical Republicans: Lincoln's Vanguard for Racial Justice* (New York: Knopf, 1969), 205-206.
25. James G. Randall, *Constitutional Problems under Lincoln* (Urbana: University of Illinois Press, 1954, rev. ed.), 275-276.
26. *Cong. Globe,* 37 Cong., 1 Sess., pt. 1, p. 120.
27. *Ibid.,* 218-219.
28. *Ibid.*, 218-219.
29. William Reddick to Trumbull, July 25, 1861, Trumbull MSS; Thomas G. Shearman to Trumbull, July 30, 1861, ibid.
30. *Cong. Globe,* 37 Cong., 1 Sess., pt. 1, p. 415.
31. *Ibid.,* 430-431.
32. *Ibid.,* 431.
33. *Ibid.,* 427.
34. *Ibid.,* 434.
35. *Cong. Globe,* 37 Cong., 1 Sess., pt. 2, p. 1313; Oates, *With Malice Toward None,* 254.
36. *Cong. Globe,* 37 Cong., 1 Sess., pt. 1. pp. 167, 275.
37. *Ibid.,* 340-341, 372-373, 376-380.
38. *Ibid.,* 339, 376-380, 382-383.
39. *Ibid.,* 383.
40. *Ibid.,* 257-260, 265; Trefousse, *The Radical Republicans,* 173.
41. James G. Blaine, *Twenty Years of Congress: From Lincoln to Garfield,* I (Norwich, Conn.: The Henry Hill Publishing Co., 1884-86), 341.
42. *Congressional Directory,* I, 36.
43. Leonard P. Curry, *Blueprint for Modern America: Non-Military Legislation of the First Civil War Congress* (Nashville: Vanderbilt University Press, 1968), 16.
44. Trefousse, *The Radical Republicans,* xiii-xiv.
45. Glenn M. Linden, " 'Radicals' and Economic Policies: The Senate: 1861-1873," *Journal of Southern History,* XXXII (May 1966), 193.
46. Krug, *Lyman Trumbull, Conservative Radical.*
47. Trumbull to Doolittle, August 31, 1861 in "A Statesman's Letters of the Civil War Period," 49.
48. Trefousse, *The Radical Republicans,* 175-177; Hans L. Trefousse, *Benjamin F. Wade, Radical Republican from Ohio* (New York: Twayne Publishers, 1963), 152.
49. Trumbull to Lincoln, October 1, 1861, Robert Todd Lincoln Collection.
50. Smith, *The Borderland,* 280; Trefousse, *The Radical Republicans,* 177.
51. James Grimes to Elizabeth Sarah Grimes, November 6, 1861 as quoted in Salter, *Grimes*, 153; James Grimes to Elizabeth Sarah Grimes, November 10, 1861 as quoted in ibid., 153-154. Oates argues that Fremont's removal did not cause a rift between Lincoln and the Radicals, but his is a minority view, Oates, *With Malice Toward None,* 262-263.
52. *Congressional Directory,* I, 46.
53. Trumbull to Lincoln, May 31, 1860, Robert Todd Lincoln Collection.
54. *Cong. Globe,* 36 Cong., 1 Sess., pt. 3, p. 2403; George, *Chandler,* 8-9, 17-18.
55. George B. McClellan, *McClellan's Own Story* (New York: C. L. Webster & Co., 1887), 171; George, *Chandler,* 56; Trefousse, *Wade,* 154, 342, fn. 32.
56. Tyler Dennett, ed., *Lincoln and the Civil War in the Diaries and Letters of John Hay* (New York: Dodd, Mead & Co., 1939), 31; George, *Chandler,* 56-57; Trefousse, *Wade*, 154; Oates, *With Malice Toward None,* 164-165.

57. Trefousse, *Wade,* 155.
58. Oates, *With Malice Toward None,* 266.

Notes to Chapter Ten

1. White, *Trumbull,* 168-169.
2. Van Deusen, *Seward,* 289-291; Randall and Donald, *The Civil War and Reconstruction,* 305-307.
3. F. K. Howard to Trumbull, December 8, 1861, Trumbull MSS.
4. *Cong. Globe,* 37 Cong., 2 Sess., pt. 1, p. 6.
5. *Ibid.,* 90-93.
6. *Ibid.,* 93-98.
7. Randall and Donald, *The Civil War and Reconstruction,* 320-324; White, *Trumbull,* 184-186; Oates, *With Malice Toward None,* 262-276, 277.
8. Pease and Randall, eds., *Diary of Browning,* I, 524.
9. *Ibid.;* White, *Trumbull,* 187; Irwin Stanley Bradley, *The Triumph of Militant Republicanism: A Study of Pennsylvania and Presidential Politics, 1860-1872* (Philadelphia: University of Pennsylvania, 1960), 187.
10. *Senate Executive Journal,* XII, 87; Randall, *Lincoln the President,* II, 60-61.
11. White, *Trumbull,* 189.
12. Trumbull to Jesse W. Fell, Washington, February 1, 1862 in "Trumbull Correspondence," *Mississippi Valley Historical Review,* I (June 1914), 103.
13. *Cong. Globe,* 37 Cong., 2 Sess., pt. 1, pp. 18-19.
14. *Ibid.*
15. *Ibid.,* 19.
16. See the letters in Trumbull MSS, manuscripts division, Library of Congress, dated from December 1 to 18, 1861.
17. *Cong. Globe,* 37 Cong., 2 Sess., pt. 1, pp. 153, 181, 219; Trumbull, "Trumbull," I, ch. 17, p. 6; Curry, *Blueprint for Modern America,* 78.
18. *Cong. Globe,* 37 Cong., 2 Sess., pt. 1, p. 334.
19. *Ibid.,* 849-850, pt. 2, pp. 941-942.
20. *Ibid.,* 942-944.
21. *Ibid.,* 944-946; Trefousse, *The Radical Republicans,* 218-219; Oates, *With Malice Toward None,* 182.
22. *Cong. Globe,* 37 Cong., 2 Sess., pt. 2, pp. 963-964, 1014-1015, 1097.
23. *Ibid.,* 1136-1141; Pease and Randall, eds., *Diary of Browning,* I, 533.
24. Pease and Randall, eds., *Diary of Browning,* I, 534; Trefousse, *Wade,* 184.
25. Randall, *Lincoln the President: Midstream* (New York: Dodd, Mead & Co., 1952), 119-120; Oates, *With Malice Toward None,* 309-310.
26. *Cong. Globe,* 37 Cong., 2 Sess., pt. 2, pp. 1557-1562.
27. T. Harry Williams, *Lincoln and the Radicals* (Madison: University of Wisconsin, 1941), 163-164; Trefousse, *The Radical Republicans,* 218-219.
28. *Cong. Globe,* 37 Cong., 2 Sess., pt. 2, pp. 1603-1607, 1665, 1742.
29. *Ibid.,* 1782.
30. *Ibid.,* 1783-1785.
31. *Ibid.,* 1809-1813; Pease and Randall, eds., *Diary of Browning,* I, 542.
32. *Cong. Globe,* 37 Cong., 2 Sess., pt. 2, pp. 1813-1814.
33. *Ibid.,* 1814.
34. Pease and Randall, eds., *Diary of Browning,* I, 534.
35. *Cong. Globe,* 37 Cong., 2 Sess., pt. 2, p. 1886.
36. *Ibid.,* pt. 3, p. 1922.
37. *Ibid.,* pt. 3, p. 1954.

38. *Ibid.*, 1958.
39. *Ibid.*, 1965; Randall, *Lincoln the President,* II, 226.
40. *Cong. Globe,* 37 Cong., 2 Sess., pt. 2, p. 1991; Trumbull, "Trumbull," I, ch. 17, p. 8.
41. *Cong. Globe,* 37 Cong., 2 Sess., pt. 3, p. 2112.
42. Trumbull, "Trumbull," I, ch. 17, p. 10.
43. *Cong. Globe,* 37 Cong., 2 Sess., pt. 3, pp. 2165-2166.
44. *Ibid.*, 2170-2171.
45. *Ibid.*, 2173.
46. *Ibid.*, 2202.
47. *Ibid.*, 2226.
48. *Ibid.*, 2227.
49. *Ibid.*, 2252-2253.
50. *Ibid.*, 2253-2254.
51. *Ibid.*, 261; Randall, *Lincoln the President,* II, 226.
52. *Cong. Globe,* 37 Cong., 2 Sess., pt. 3, p. 2878.
53. *Ibid.*, 2864.
54. *Ibid.*, pt. 4, pp. 2902-2903.
55. *Ibid.*, 2970-2973.
56. *Ibid.*, 2973-2975.
57. *Illinois State Journal,* July 7, 1862.
58. *Cong. Globe,* 37 Cong., 2 Sess., pt. 3, p. 2995-2996.
59. *Ibid.*, 2998, 3000.
60. *Ibid.*, 3000.
61. *Ibid.*, 3006.
62. *Ibid.*, 3166.
63. *Ibid.*
64. *Ibid.*, 3276.
65. For Trumbull's bill as perfected in the judiciary committee, see *ibid.*, pt. 1, p. 942; the final form of the confiscation act is found in *ibid.*, pt. 4, appendix 412.
66. "Message of Abraham Lincoln to the House of Representatives," July 17, 1862 in Basler, Pratt, and Dunlap, eds., *The Collected Works of Lincoln,* V, 330.
67. Francis Fessenden, *Life and Public Service of William Pitt Fessenden,* I (Boston: Houghton Mifflin and Co., 1907), 173; Nevins, *The War for the Union,* II, 146.
68. *Cong. Globe,* 37 Cong., 2 Sess., pt. 4, pp. 3373-3374.
69. *Ibid.*, 3374-3375.
70. *Ibid.*, 3375-3379; Trefousse, *Wade,* 189.
71. *Ibid.*, 3383.
72. Randall, *Constitutional Problems,* 280; Randall, *Lincoln the President: Midstream,* 119-120; Oates, *With Malice Toward None,* 309-310.
73. *Cong. Globe,* 37 Cong., 2 Sess., pt. 4, p. 3406.
74. See *Senate Document* No. 58, 40 Congress, 2 Session; Randall, *Constitutional Problems,* 280-281, 288-291, 361, 363; Randall, *Lincoln the President: Midstream,* 120.
75. *Ibid.*, pt. 4, pp. 3042-3043.
76. *Ibid.*, 3219.
77. *Ibid.*, 3221, 3223-3224, 3224-3225.
78. *Ibid.*, 3227.
79. *Ibid.*, pt. 2, pp. 1285, 1517-1518, 1523-1524, 1526; Nevins, *The War for the Union,* II, 93-94.
80. *Cong. Globe,* 37 Cong., 2 Sess., pt. 4, p. 3138.
81. *Ibid.*, pt. 2, pp. 1142-1143.
82. *Ibid.*, pt. 3, 2618.
83. *Ibid.*, 2491.

84. *Ibid.*, 1951; Curry, *Modern America,* 101-108.

85. *Cong. Globe,* 37 Cong., 2 Sess., pt. 3, pp. 2626, 2627, 2629, 2631; Curry, *Modern America,* 108-115.

86. *Cong. Globe,* 37 Cong., 2 Sess., pt. 3, p. 2840; Curry, *Modern America,* 116-136.

87. *Cong. Globe,* 37 Cong., 2 Sess., pt. 4, pp. 3271, 3335-3336, 3354.

88. Arthur Charles Cole Notes, Box 18, Illinois Historical Survey, Urbana, Illinois.

89. "An Illinois Farmer During the Civil War: Extracts from the Journal of John Edward Young," *Journal of the Illinois State Historical Society,* XXVI (April 1933-January 1934), 90.

90. William Jayne to Trumbull, Quincy, Ill., June 22, 1862, Trumbull MSS; J. Notestine to Trumbull, Olney, Ill., June 24, 1862, ibid.; *Illinois State Journal,* February 27, 1862, April 30, 1862; New York *Tribune* as reprinted in Chicago *Tribune,* July 2, 1862.

91. Jayne to Trumbull, Quincy, Ill., June 22, 1862, Trumbull MSS; Robert D. Holt, "The Political Career of William A. Richardson," *Journal of the Illinois State Historical Society,* XXVI (April 1933-January 1934), 254-255.

92. Randall, *Lincoln the President: Midstream,* 232-233.

93. Chicago *Tribune* as reprinted in *Illinois State Journal,* July 23, 1862.

94. *Illinois State Journal,* August 26, 1862; Randall and Donald, *Civil War and Reconstruction,* 459; Holt, "Richardson," 254-255.

95. Medill to Trumbull, Chicago, August 26, 1861, Trumbull MSS; The Chicago *Tribune, . . . Pictured Encyclopedia of the World's Greatest Newspaper . . .*, 318-325, 470-472.

96. Trumbull to Chandler, Alton, Ill., September 28, 1862, copy in Trumbull MSS, manuscripts division, Library of Congress.

97. *Illinois State Register,* September 25, 1862.

98. New York *Semi-Weekly Tribune,* October 7, 1862.

99. Pease and Randall, eds., *Diary of Browning,* I, fn. 582.

100. Trumbull to Chandler, Alton, Ill., September 28, 1862, copy in Trumbull MSS, manuscripts division, Library of Congress; Trumbull to Chandler, Springfield, Ill., November 9, 1862, Zachariah Chandler MSS, ibid.

101. *Illinois State Journal,* September-November 1862.

102. See the *Illinois State Journal,* September-November 1862.

103. St. Louis *Union* as reprinted in *Illinois State Journal,* November 1, 1862.

104. Randall and Donald, *Civil War and Reconstruction,* 458-460; Randall, *Lincoln the President,* II, 233-234; Nevins, *The War for the Union,* II, 318-322; Oates, *With Malice Toward None,* 322-323.

105. Trumbull to Chandler, Springfield, Ill., November 9, 1862, Chandler MSS. Trumbull attributed the Republican defeat to military and political factors, but a recent work, Christopher Dell, *Lincoln and the War Democrats; The Grand Erosion of Conservative Tradition* (Rutherford, N. J.: Fairleigh Dickinson University Press, 1975), 179, blames economic factors, including particularly the poor corn crop, for the Republican 1862 debacle.

Notes to Chapter Eleven

1. *Congressional Directory,* 38 Cong., 1 Sess., I, 45.

2. Trumbull to Butler, November 26(?), 1862, Butler MSS.

3. *Cong. Globe,* 36 Cong., 1 Sess., pt. 1, pp. 54-62.

4. Julia Jayne Trumbull to Walter Trumbull, February 3, 1861 in Trumbull, "Trumbull," I, ch. 12, p. 21.

5. Randall and Pease, eds., *Diary of Browning,* I, 558.

6. Burton J. Hendrick, *Lincoln's War Cabinet* (Gloucester, Mass.: Peter Smith, 1965), 328-329; Randall, *Lincoln the President,* II, 241; White, *Trumbull,* 210-211; Van Deusen, *Seward,* 344; David Donald, *Charles Sumner & the Rights of Man* (New York: Alfred A. Knopf, 1970), 90-91.

7. Randall and Pease, eds., *Diary of Browning,* I, 596-598; Van Deusen, *Seward,* 344; Oates, *With Malice Toward None,* 327-328.
8. Randall and Pease, eds., *Diary of Browning,* I, 598-599; Van Deusen, *Seward,* 344-345; Donald, *Sumner & Rights,* 91-92.
9. Randall and Pease, eds., *Diary of Browning,* I, 599; Fessenden, *Fessenden,* I, 231-240.
10. Beale, ed., *Diary of Bates,* 269; Howard K. Beale, ed., *Diary of Gideon Welles, Secretary of Navy under Lincoln and Johnson,* I (New York: W. W. Norton Co., 1960), 194; John G. Nicolay and John Hay, *Abraham Lincoln: A History,* VI (New York: The Century Co., 1917), 264; Van Deusen, *Seward,* 345; Hans L. Trefousse, *Benjamin Franklin Wade: Radical Republican from Ohio* (New York: Twayne Publishers, 1963), 91.
11. Hendrick, *Lincoln's War Cabinet,* 335-336; Fessenden, *Fessenden,* I, 240-242; Randall, *Lincoln the President,* II, 246; Beale, ed., *Diary of Bates,* 269; Beale, ed., *Diary of Welles,* I, 194-195; Van Deusen, *Seward,* 345; Donald, *Sumner & Rights,* 92-93; Oates, *With Malice Toward None,* 329.
12. Beale, ed., *Diary of Welles,* I, 196-198; Fessenden, *Fessenden,* I, 243-248; Beale, ed., *Diary of Bates,* 269-270; Van Deusen, *Seward,* 345-346; Donald, *Sumner & Rights,* 94-95; Oates, *With Malice Toward None,* 329.
13. Beale, ed., *Diary of Bates,* 220.
14. Nicolay and Hay, *Lincoln,* VI, 267; Hendrick, *Lincoln's War Cabinet,* 403-404.
15. Nicolay and Hay, *Lincoln,* VI, 267-271; Beale, ed., *Diary of Bates,* I, 201-202; Van Deusen, *Seward,* 346-348; Oates, *With Malice Toward None,* 329.
16. *Cong. Globe,* 37 Cong., 3 Sess., pt. 1, p. 608; Holt, "Richardson," 222-268; Joel H. Sibley, *A Respectable Minority: The Democratic Party in the Civil War Era, 1860-1868* (New York: W. W. Norton & Co., Inc., 1977), 38-39, 62-63.
17. *Cong. Globe,* 37 Cong., 3 Sess., pt. 1, pp. 709-711; Sibley, *A Respectable Minority,* 63.
18. *Cong. Globe,* 37 Cong., 3 Sess., pt. 2, pp. 1507-1509.
19. *Ibid.,* 1512, 1523, 1526, 1527-1528, 1529-1531.
20. *Ibid.,* pt. 1, pp. 26, 31.
21. *Ibid.,* 529.
22. *Ibid.,* 529, 538.
23. *Ibid.,* p. 552.
24. *Ibid.,* 554.
25. *Ibid.,* pt. 2, pp. 1090-1092.
26. *Ibid.,* 1095, 1097, 1102, 1140, 1158, 1185, 1186, 1205-1207.
27. *Ibid.,* 1208.
28. *Ibid.,* 1435-1436.
29. *Ibid.,* 1435-1436.
30. *Ibid.,* 1436.
31. *Ibid.,* 1437-1438.
32. *Ibid.,* 1459.
33. *Ibid.,* 1459-1477.
34. *Ibid.,* 1477.
35. *Ibid.*
36. *Ibid.*
37. *Ibid.,* 1493.
38. See *ibid.,* 1357 and the following pages for the filibuster, and 1479 for the vote.
39. Randall, *Constitutional Problems,* 166-168.
40. *Ibid.,* 193-214.
41. Samuel S. Cox, *Union – Division – Reunion: Three Decades of Federal Legislation, 1855-1885* (Providence, R. I.: J. A. and R. A. Reid, 1885), 229.
42. Randall, *Constitutional Problems,* 180-183.
43. Trumbull to Chandler, August 4, 1863, Chandler MSS.
44. Wyatt Winton Belcher, *The Economic Rivalry between St. Louis and Chicago, 1850-1880*

(New York: Columbia University Press, 1947), 138-157; Mabel McIlwaine, comp., *Reminiscences of Chicago During the Civil War* (New York: Citadel Press, 1967), intro., xi-xii.
45. Chicago *Tribune,* January 10, 1867.
46. George Trumbull to Koerner, May 4, 1863 in "Letters to Gustave Koerner," *Illinois State Historical Society Transactions* (1907), 245; Trumbull to Chandler, August 4, 1863, Chandler MSS.
47. Randall, *Constitutional Problems,* 493-494; Robert S. Harper, *Lincoln and the Press* (New York: McGraw-Hill, 1951), 7, 257-260; *War of the Rebellion: A Compilation of the Official Records of the Union and Confederate Armies,* Series I, Volume XXIII, pt. 2, p. 385; Trumbull, "Trumbull," I, ch. 16, pp. 6-7.
48. *War of the Rebellion: A Compilation of the Official Records of the Union and Confederate Armies,* Series J, Volume XXIII, pt. 2, p. 385; Frederick Francis Cook, "Suppression of the Times," in McIlwaine, comp., *Reminiscences,* 157.
49. Isaac N. Arnold to Lincoln, June 11, 1863, copy in Isaac N. Arnold MSS, Gilpin Library, Chicago Historical Society.
50. Randall and Pease, eds., *Diary of Browning,* I, 633; Krug, *Trumbull,* 209.
51. New York *Semi-Weekly Tribune,* June 5, 1863; Harper, *Lincoln and the Press,* 260; Cook, "Suppression of the Times," 154.
52. New York *Semi-Weekly Tribune,* June 5, 1863; White, Trumbull, 207-208; Trumbull, "Trumbull," I, ch. 16, p. 6.
53. Lincoln to Arnold, May 25, 1864 in Basler, Pratt, and Dunlap, eds., *Collected Works of Lincoln,* VII, 361; Oates, *With Malice Toward None,* 344.
54. Harper, *Lincoln and the Press,* 262; Cook, "Suppression of the Times," 159.
55. Chicago *Journal,* June 5, 1863 as reprinted in *Illinois State Journal,* June 8, 1863; Trumbull, "Trumbull," I, ch. 16, p. 8.
56. Chicago *Times,* October 13, 1863; George M. Maston (?) to Trumbull, June 11, 1863, Trumbull MSS.
57. Peoria *Daily Transcript,* June 10, 1863.
58. Peter L. Jay to Trumbull, June 11, 1863, Trumbull MSS.
59. Maston (?) to Trumbull, June 11, 1863, ibid.
60. J. H. Mayborne to Trumbull, July 13, 1863, ibid.
61. See the invitations to Trumbull, August-October 1863, ibid.
62. Horace Roblee, state central committee chairman, to Trumbull, October 9, 1863, ibid.
63. *Illinois State Journal,* September 4, 1863.
64. Chicago *Times*, September 22, 1863.
65. *Ibid.,* October 13, 1863.
66. *Illinois State Journal,* December 7, 1863; Oates, *With Malice Toward None,* 360.
67. *Congressional Directory,* 38 Cong., 1 Sess., I, 69, 70-73.
68. *Ibid.,* 22.
69. *Cong. Globe,* 38 Cong., 1 Sess., February 21, March 15, 1864.
70. *Ibid.,* pt. 3, pp. 2543-2545; Donald, *Sumner & Rights,* 180-181.
71. *Cong. Globe,* 38 Cong., 1 Sess., pt. 2, pp. 1175-1176.
72. *Ibid.,* 1715.
73. *Ibid.,* pt. 4, p. 3191.
74. *Ibid.,* pt. 3, pp. 2786-2787; *ibid.,* 2931; *ibid.,* pt. 4, p. 2970; Donald, *Sumner & Rights,* 176-177.
75. *Cong. Globe,* 38 Cong., 1 Sess., pt. 4, p. 3304.
76. *Ibid.,* 3306-3307.
77. *Ibid.,* 3307.
78. *Ibid.,* pt. 4, p. 3327.
79. *Ibid.,* 3350.

80. *Ibid.*
81. Bentley, *A History of the Freedmen's Bureau,* 36-73.
82. *Cong. Globe,* 38 Cong., 1 Sess., pt. 4, p. 3131.
83. *Ibid.,* 3132; Donald, *Sumner & Rights,* 156.
84. *Cong. Globe,* 38 Cong., 1 Sess., pt. 4, pp. 3133-3137; Donald, *Sumner & Rights,* 160-161.
85. *Cong. Globe,* 38 Cong., 1 Sess., pt. 4, pp. 3257-3265; Donald, *Sumner & Rights,* 153-154.
86. On Sumner's self-righteous attitude, see Donald, *Sumner & Rights,* 9-12, 25-29, 135, 146-147, 152, 164.
87. *Cong. Globe,* 38 Cong., 1 Sess., pt. 3, p. 2392; William B. Hesseltine, *Lincoln's Plan of Reconstruction* (Chicago: Quadrangle Books, 1967), 106-107.
88. *Cong. Globe,* 38 Cong., 1 Sess., pt. 3, p. 2842.
89. *Ibid.,* 2906.
90. Trumbull to Lincoln, June 15, 1864, Robert Todd Lincoln Collection.
91. Lincoln to Trumbull, June 17, 1864 in Basler, Pratt, and Dunlap, eds., *Collected Works of Lincoln,* VII, 398.
92. *Cong. Globe,* 38 Cong., 1 Sess., pt. 4, pp. 3284-3285.
93. *Ibid.,* 3361.
94. *Ibid.,* 3361-3368.
95. *Ibid.,* 3461.
96. James G. Randall and Richard N. Current, *Last Full Measure: Lincoln the President* (New York: Dodd, Mead & Company, 1955), 207-208; Trefousse, *The Radical Republicans,* 286-289; Oates, *With Malice Toward None,* 391-393.
97. Benjamin Quarles, *The Negro in the Civil War* (New York: Russell & Russell, 1968), 103-104, 248; Donald, *Sumner & Rights,* 147-149; Richard H. Abbott, *Cobbler in Congress: The Life of Henry Wilson, 1812-1875* (Lexington: University of Kentucky Press, 1972), 145-146.
98. *Cong. Globe,* 38 Cong., 1 Sess., pt. 1, p. 145; John B. Henderson, "Emancipation and Impeachment," *Century,* LXXXV (December 1912), 196-209.
99. *Cong. Globe,* 38 Cong., 1 Sess., pt. 1, p. 145.
100. *Ibid.,* 521-522; Donald, *Sumner & Rights,* 149-150.
101. *Cong. Globe,* 38 Cong., 1 Sess., pt. 1, p. 553.
102. White, *Trumbull,* 224.
103. *Cong. Globe,* 38 Cong., 1 Sess., pt. 1, p. 694.
104. *Ibid.,* pt. 2, p. 1130.
105. *Ibid.,* 1175; Donald, *Sumner & Rights,* 151-152.
106. *Cong. Globe,* 38 Cong., 1 Sess., pt. 2, pp. 1364-1367.
107. *Ibid.,* 1250-1251, 1258.
108. *Ibid.,* 1313-1314.
109. *Ibid.,* 1419-1424.
110. *Ibid.,* 1424, 1425, 1445-1446, 1447.
111. *Ibid.,* 1447.
112. *Ibid.,* 1456-1459.
113. *Ibid.,* 1459-1465.
114. *Ibid.,* 1465; Donald, *Sumner & Rights,* 150-151.
115. *Cong. Globe,* 38 Cong., 1 Sess., pt. 2, pp. 1479-1483.
116. *Ibid.,* 1488; Donald, *Sumner & Rights,* 151.
117. *Cong. Globe,* 38 Cong., 1 Sess., pt. 2, p. 2995.
118. *Ibid.,* 1490.
119. Randall and Current, *Last Full Measure,* 289-307; Oates, *With Malice Toward None,* 388-389.

120. *Cong. Globe,* 38 Cong., 1 Sess., pt. 4, p. 2995.
121. *Ibid.,* 2 Sess., pt. 1, p. 531. For Lincoln's part in pushing the Thirteenth Amendment, see Charles A. Dana, *Recollections of the Civil War with the Leaders at Washington and in the Field in the Sixties* (New York: Collier Books, 1963), 174-178 and Randall and Current, *Last Full Measure,* 308-313.
122. Willard L. King, "Lectures, November 14, 1952 at Amherst College, 'The Debs Case' " in Colston E. Warne, ed., *The Pullman Boycott of 1898: The Problem of Federal Intervention* (Boston: D. C. Heath, 1955), 93-94.

Notes to Chapter Twelve

1. Basler, Pratt, and Dunlap, *Collected Works of Lincoln,* VII, 427.
2. Ishbel Ross, *Proud Kate: Portrait of an Ambitious Woman* (New York: Harper & Bros., 1953), 148; Albert Bushnell Hart, *Salmon P. Chase* (Boston: Houghton Mifflin Co., 1909), 420.
3. Oates, *With Malice Toward None,* 328-329; Nicolay and Hay, *Lincoln,* VI, 267.
4. Trumbull, "Trumbull," I, ch. 20, pp. 5-6.
5. Ross, *Proud Kate,* 148; Hart, *Chase,* 420.
6. Alexander K. McClure, *Abraham Lincoln and Men of War-Times* (Philadelphia: The Times Publishing Co., 1892), 62; Nevins, *The War for the Union: The Organized War to Victory, 1864-1865,* IV, 61-62.
7. Judd to Trumbull, January 2, 1864, Trumbull MSS.
8. Yates to Trumbull, February 21, 1864, ibid.
9. Trumbull to N. P. Banks, February 18, 1864, Nathaniel Banks MSS, Illinois State Library.
10. William Frank Zornow, *Lincoln & the Party Divided* (Norman: University of Oklahoma Press, 1954), 47.
11. Oates, *With Malice Toward None,* 382-383; Zornow, *Lincoln,* 39-63.
12. Oates, *With Malice Toward None,* 382-383; Nevins, *The War for the Union,* IV, 67-70.
13. David Donald, *Lincoln Reconsidered* (New York: Knopf, 1956), 123-124; Donald, *Sumner & Rights,* 162-166.
14. *Cong. Globe,* 38 Cong., 1 Sess., pt. 2, pp. 1313-1314, 1445.
15. See Trumbull MSS for September-October 1864.
16. Trumbull, "Trumbull," I, ch. 19, p. 9.
17. George T. Allen to Trumbull, October 4, 1864, Trumbull MSS.
18. *Illinois State Journal,* September 6, 1864.
19. *Ibid.,* October 6, 1864; New York *Semi-Weekly Tribune,* October 14, 1864.
20. McCormack, ed., *Memoirs of Koerner,* II, 435.
21. *Illinois State Journal,* October 6, 1864.
22. Nevins, *War for the Union,* IV, 136-140; Oates, *With Malice Toward None,* 400-401.
23. *Congressional Directory,* 38 Cong., 2 Sess., I, 53; Lyman Trumbull to nephew Lyman Trumbull, January 2, 1865, Trumbull Family MSS; Lyman Trumbull to Julia Jayne Trumbull, December 3, 1863, ibid.
24. *Cong. Globe,* 38 Cong., 2 Sess., pt. 1, p. 5. For the Louisiana government in 1864 see James M. McPherson, *The Struggle for Equality: Abolitionists and the Negro in the Civil War and Reconstruction* (Princeton, N. J.: Princeton University Press, 1964), 243; Hesseltine, *Lincoln's Plan of Reconstruction,* 65-68.
25. *Cong. Globe,* 38 Cong., 2 Sess., pt. 1, pp. 5, 8.
26. Trumbull, "Trumbull," I, ch. 20, pp. 3-5.
27. Ibid., ch. 19, p. 13; Nicolay and Hay, *Lincoln,* IX, 453; Trumbull to Lincoln, January 9, 1865, Robert Todd Lincoln Collection; Donald, *Sumner & Rights,* 203.
28. Chicago *Record,* June 26, 1896.
29. Fred Harvey Harrington, *Fighting Politician: Major General N. P. Banks* (Philadelphia:

University of Pennsylvania Press, 1948), 164-165; Lincoln to Trumbull, January 9, 1865 in Basler, Pratt, and Dunlap, eds., *Collected Works of Lincoln,* VIII, 207-208; Hesseltine, *Lincoln's Plan of Reconstruction,* 134. For Banks' testimony, see 38 Cong., 2 Sess., *Miscellaneous Document* No. 7.

30. *Cong. Globe,* 38 Cong., 2 Sess., pt. 2, p. 908.

31. *Ibid.,* 1007; Donald, *Lincoln Reconsidered,* 118-119; Donald, *Sumner & Rights,* 200-202; Hesseltine, *Lincoln's Plan of Reconstruction,* 134.

32. *Cong. Globe,* 38 Cong., 2 Sess., pt. 2, p. 1008.

33. *Ibid.,* 1009.

34. *Ibid.*

35. *Ibid.,* 1010, 1011; Krug, *Trumbull,* 224.

36. Wendell Holmes Stephenson, *The Political Career of James H. Lane (Publications of the Kansas State Historical Society,* III) (Topeka: Kansas State Printing Plant, 1930), fn. on bottom of 252; *Cong. Globe,* 38 Cong., 2 Sess., pt. 2. pp. 1011-1012.

37. *Cong. Globe,* 38 Cong., 2 Sess., pt. 2, pp. 1048-1049.

38. *Ibid.,* 1058; George, *Chandler,* 123.

39. *Cong. Globe,* 38 Cong., 2 Sess., pt. 2, pp. 1061-1064.

40. *Ibid.,* 1064-1070.

41. *Ibid.,* 1089, 1091-1099.

42. *Ibid.*

43. *Ibid.*

44. *Ibid.,* 1127.

45. *Ibid.*

46. *Ibid.,* 1128.

47. *Ibid.*

48. Fawn M. Brodie, *Thaddeus Steven: Scourge of the South* (New York: W. W. Norton Co., 1966), 212; Trefousse, *The Radical Republicans,* 302.

49. *Cong. Globe,* 38 Cong., 2 Sess., pt. 2, p. 1348.

50. George Fort Milton, *The Age of Hate, Andrew Johnson and the Radicals* (Hamden, Conn.: Anchor Books, 1965), 139-140; Trefousse, *The Radical Republicans,* 302-303; Donald, *Sumner & Rights,* 203-205; Hesseltine, *Lincoln's Plan,* 134-135; Oates, *With Malice Toward None,* 406-407.

51. *Cong. Globe,* 38 Cong., 2 Sess., pt. 2, p. 1348.

52. *Ibid.,* pt. 2, p. 1307. The need for additional conservative votes for the measure caused the joint resolution's deletion, see La Wanda Cox, "The Promise of Land for the Freedmen," *Mississippi Valley Historical Review,* XLV (December 1958), 432-434, Bentley, *Freedmen's Bureau,* 46-49.

53. *Cong. Globe,* 38 Cong., 2 Sess., pt. 2, p. 1348.

54. *Ibid.,* pt. 1, pp. 361-362; *ibid.,* pt. 2, p. 1017. For a recent discussion of the freedmen's bureau bill, see Herman Belz, *A New Birth of Freedom: The Republican Party and Freedmen's Rights, 1861-1866* (Westport, Conn.: Greenwood Press, 1976). 69-108.

55. Thomas Weber, *The Northern Railroads in the Civil War,* 1861-1865 (Westport, Conn.: Greenwood Press, 1970), 108-109, 123-125; David F. Trask, "Charles Sumner and the New Jersey Railroad Monopoly during the Civil War," *New Jersey Historical Society Proceedings* (1957), 259-275.

56. *Cong. Globe,* 38 Cong., 2 Sess., pt. 2, pp. 1393-1394.

57. *Ibid.,* 1394.

58. *Ibid.,* 1236, 1294.

59. Trumbull, "Trumbull," II, ch. 1, pp. 2-3; Margaret Leech, *Reveille in Washington,* 1860-1865 (New York: Harper & Bros., 1941), 367; Sandburg, *Lincoln: The War Years,* IV, 90: *Cong. Globe,* 38 Cong., 2 Sess., pt. 2, pp. 1394-1395.

60. Oates, *With Malice Toward None,* 410-411.

61. Special Session of the Senate of 39th Congress, bound with *Cong. Globe,* 38 Cong., 2 Sess., pt. 2, pp. 1431-1435.
62. Trumbull, "Trumbull," I, ch. 19, p. 17.
63. *Ibid.*, 18.
64. William H. Bradley to Trumbull, April 18, 1865, Trumbull MSS; Julia Kirby to Joseph Duncan, May 7, 1865 in Pratt, *Concerning Mr. Lincoln,* 131.

Notes to Chapter Thirteen

1. Newton D. Bateman to Trumbull, January 15, 1866, Trumbull MSS.
2. Trumbull to Johnson, April 21, 1865, Andrew Johnson MSS, manuscripts division, Library of Congress.
3. Julia Jayne Trumbull to Lyman, June 13, 1865, Trumbull Family MSS.
4. Beale, ed., *Diary of Welles,* II, 322.
5. J. K. Morehouse to Trumbull, August 3, 1865, Trumbull MSS.
6. Trumbull to Jayne, August 21, 1865, Trumbull Family MSS. On Trumbull's unpopularity, see the clippings in Trumbull's scrapbooks, ibid.
7. Trumbull to Jayne, December 24, 1865, ibid. For Lyman's gold speculations, see ibid. in January and February 1865. On Lyman's oil speculation, see letters in September 1865 and June 1866, ibid.
8. Trumbull to Julia Trumbull, May 3, 1866, ibid.; Lyman Trumbull to Julia Trumbull, May 6, 1866, ibid.
9. Richardson, ed., *Messages and Papers of the Presidents*, VI, 353-371; Trumbull, "Trumbull," II, ch. 1, p. 5.
10. *Cong. Globe*, 39 Cong., 1 Sess., pt. 1, pp. 61, 68.
11. *Ibid.*, 129; Avery Craven, *Reconstruction: The Ending of the Civil War* (New York: Holt, Rinehart and Winston, Inc., 1969), 144, 148-149.
12. Record Group 46, Records of the U.S. Senate, Minutes of the Judiciary Committee, 39 Cong., 1 Sess., January 10, 11, 1866 in National Archives.
13. Oliver Otis Howard, *Autobiography of Oliver Otis Howard*, II (New York: Baker & Taylor Co., 1907), 280-281; Bentley, *Freedmen's Bureau*, 115-116; William S. McFeely, *Yankee Stepfather: General O. O. Howard and the Freedmen* (New York: W. W. Norton & Co., 1970), 199.
14. Trumbull, "Trumbull," II, ch. 2, p. 4.
15. *Cong. Globe*, 39 Cong., 1 Sess, pt. 1, p. 299; McFeely, *Yankee Stepfather,* 213-215.
16. *Cong. Globe*, 39 Cong., 1 Sess., pt. 1, pp. 334-349.
17. *Ibid.*, 314-323.
18. *Ibid.*, 349, 374, 415-427.
19. Howard, *Autobiography*, II, 281; Brodie, *Stevens*, 247-248.
20. Record Group 46, Records of the U.S. Senate, Minutes of the Judiciary Committee, February 7, 1866.
21. *Cong. Globe*, 39 Cong., 1 Sess., pt. 1, p. 746.
22. *Ibid.*
23. Record Group 46, Records of the U.S. Senate, Minutes of the Judiciary Committee, February 7, 1866.
24. *Cong. Globe*, 39 Cong., 1 Sess., pt. 1, pp. 211-212; W. R. Brock, *An American Crisis: Congress and Reconstruction, 1865* (New York: Harper & Row, 1966), 111-112.
25. Trumbull to Jayne, January 11, 1866, Trumbull Family MSS.
26. *Cong. Globe*, 39 Cong., 1 Sess., pt. 1, pp. 474-480.
27. *Ibid.*, 498.
28. *Ibid.*, 594-606.

29. *Ibid.*, pt. 2, pp. 1123, 1291, 1293; Eric L. McKitrick, *Andrew Johnson and Reconstruction* (Chicago: University of Chicago Press, 1960), 339.
30. New York *Herald*, March 12, 1866.
31. Trumbull to Jayne, January 11, 1866, Trumbull Family MSS.
32. Bentley, *Freedmen's Bureau*, 118-119; La Wanda Cox and John H. Cox, *Politics, Principle and Prejudice, 1865-1866* (New York: Atheneum, 1969), 178-179.
33. *Cong. Globe*, 39 Cong., 1 Sess., pt. 1, p. 917; John H. Cox and La Wanda Cox, "Andrew Johnson and his Ghost Writers: An Analysis of the Freedmen's Bureau and Civil Rights Veto Messages," *Mississippi Valley Historical Review,* XLV.C (December 1958), 462-465.
34. Trumbull, "Trumbull," II, ch. 2, p. 11.
35. *Cong. Globe*, 39 Cong., 1 Sess., pt. 1, pp. 936-943; Krug, *Trumbull*, 239-240.
36. *Nation*, II (March 1, 1866), 257.
37. White to Trumbull, February 21, 1866, Trumbull MSS; Benjamin Walsh to Yates, February 22, 1866, Yates MSS; Chicago *Tribune*, February 22, 1866.
38. New York *Herald*, February 22, 1866.
39. *Cong. Globe*, 39 Cong., 1 Sess., pt. 1, p. 943; A. Nourse to Trumbull, February 22, 1866; D. L. Phillips to Trumbull, March 5, 1866, ibid.
40. Bentley, *Freedmen's Bureau*, 120; McFeely, *Yankee Stepfather*, 246.
41. *Cong. Globe*, 39 Cong., 1 Sess., pt. 3, pp. 2743, 2772-2773, 2808, 2873; pt. 4, pp. 3839-3842, 3849-3850; McKitrick, *Johnson*, 357; Bentley, *Freedmen's Bureau*, 69.
42. Bentley, *Freedmen's Bureau*,134; Brock, *An American Crisis*, 238.
43. Blaine, *Twenty Years of Congress*, II, 181; Brodie, *Stevens*, 254-255.
44. Phillips to Trumbull, March 20, 1866, Trumbull MSS.
45. *Cong. Globe*, 39 Cong., 1 Sess., pt. 1, pp. 1679-1681; Cox and Cox, "Johnson and his Ghost Writers," 473-477.
46. Howard K. Beale, *The Critical Year: A Study of Andrew Johnson and Reconstruction* (New York: F. Ungar Publishing Co., 1958), 90-92; Cox and Cox, *Politics*, 195-200.
47. *Cong. Globe*, 39 Cong., 1 Sess., pt. 1, pp. 1679-1681.
48. *Ibid.*, pt. 2, pp. 1755-1761; McKitrick, *Johnson*, 291-292; Brodie, *Stevens*, 262.
49. New York *Times*, April 7, 1866.
50. *Illinois State Register*, April 6-11, 1866; Peoria *National Democrat*, April 7-14, 1866.
51. Philadelphia *Press*, April 5, 1866; Chicago *Tribune*, April 6, May 2, 1866; Peck to Trumbull, April 24, 1866, Trumbull MSS.
52. Charles Fairman, *Mr. Justice Miller and the Supreme Court, 1862-1890* (New York: Russell & Russell, 1966), 113; Joseph B. James, *The Framing of the Fourteenth Amendment* (Urbana: University of Illinois Press, 1956), 98; *Cong. Globe*, 39 Cong., 1 Sess., pt. 2, pp. 1776-1777.
53. Ellen Jayne to Gershom Jayne, April 7, 1866 in Trumbull, "Trumbull," II, ch. 3, pp. 8-9.
54. *Cong. Globe*, 39 Cong., 1 Sess., pt. 2, p. 1809.
55. *Nation*, II (March 1, 1866), 257.
56. Ellen Jayne to Gershom Jayne, April 7, 1866, in Trumbull, "Trumbull," II, ch. 3, pp. 8-9.
57. Lyman Trumbull to Julia Trumbull, May 8, 1866, Trumbull Family MSS; Lyman Trumbull to Julia Trumbull, May 29, 1866 in ibid.; White, *Trumbull*, 273; Krug, *Trumbull*, 243-244.
58. Trumbull to Jayne, July 2, 1866, Jayne MSS.
59. Trumbull, "Trumbull," II, ch. 3, p. 7; Donald, *Sumner & Rights*, 157-158.
60. C. H. Ray to Trumbull, January 15, 1866, Trumbull MSS.
61. *Cong. Globe*, 39 Cong., 1 Sess., pt. 1, pp. 160, 207, 208, 913.
62. J. Medill to Trumbull, July 1, 1866, Trumbull MSS; E. C. Larned to Trumbull, July 2, 1866, ibid.; Horace White to Trumbull, July 5, 1866, ibid.
63. Oquawka *Spectator*, February 22, 1866; McKitrick, *Johnson*, 375.
64. *Cong. Globe*, 39 Cong., 1 Sess., pt. 4, pp. 3313, 3315.
65. *Ibid.*, 3788.

66. *Ibid.*, pt. 3, pp. 2193, 2218.
67. *Ibid.*, pt. 5, p. 4080.
68. Record Group 46, Records of the U.S. Senate, Minutes of the Judiciary Committee, February 21, 1866.
69. Horace E. Flack, *The Adoption of the Fourteenth Amendment* (Gloucester, Mass.: P. Smith, 1965), 30; McKitrick, *Johnson*, 348.
70. White, *Trumbull*, 284; McKitrick, *Johnson*, 349; John W. Burgess, *Reconstruction and the Constitution, 1866-1876* (Westport, Conn.: Negro Universities Press, 1970), 74-78.
71. *Cong. Globe*, 39 Cong., 1 Sess., pt. 2, p. 1285; pt. 4, pp. 2893, 2894, 2901, 2902.
72. *Ibid.*, pt. 3, p. 2699; pt. 4, p. 2900.
73. James, *Fourteenth Amendment*, 195-196; Chicago *Tribune*, August 2, 1866.
74. Baltimore *American*, March 2, 1866 as clipped in Trumbull, "Trumbull," II, ch. 5, p. 3.
75. *Cong. Globe*, 39 Cong., 1 Sess., pt. 5, p. 3987.
76. *Ibid.*, 3982.
77. Record Group 46, Records of the U.S. Senate, Minutes of the Judiciary Committee, July 21, 1866.
78. *Cong. Globe*, 39 Cong., 1 Sess., pt. 5, p. 3987.
79. *Ibid.*, 3988.
80. *Ibid.;* Lyman Trumbull to Julia Trumbull, July 22, 1866, Trumbull Family MSS.
81. *Cong. Globe*, 39 Cong., 1 Sess., pt. 5, pp. 3996-3997; McKitrick, *Johnson*, 361.
82. *Cong. Globe*, 39 Cong., 1 Sess., pt. 5, pp. 3997, 4003.
83. *Ibid.*, 4007.
84. Richardson, ed., *Messages and Papers*, VI, 395-396; Rembert W. Patrick, *The Reconstruction of the Nation* (New York: Oxford University Press, 1967), 82.
85. Maurice Baxter, *Orville H. Browning, Lincoln's Friend and Critic* (Bloomington: University of Indiana Press, 1957), 183.
86. David Davis to O. H. Browning, May 13, 1866, Orville H. Browning MSS, Illinois State Historical Library; *Senate Executive Journal*, XIV, pt. 2, pp. 824-1043; Phillips to Trumbull, January 7, March 5, June 29, 1866, Trumbull MSS.
87. *Cong. Globe*, 39 Cong., 1 Sess., pt. 3, pp. 2420, 2427, 2449, 2450, 2559; Lyman Trumbull to Julia Jayne Trumbull, May 8, May 13, 1866, Trumbull Family MSS; McKitrick, *Johnson*, 383-387; Ernest McKay, *Henry Wilson, Practical Radical: Portrait of a Politician* (Port Washington, N.Y.: Kennekat Press, 1971), 204.
88. Jonesboro (Ill.) *Gazette*, December 15, 1866.
89. Oglesby to Trumbull, January 27, 1866, Trumbull MSS.
90. Chicago *Tribune*, October 1, 1866; Hugh Craig, *Biography of John A. Logan* (New York: H. S. Goodspeed & Co., 1884), 361-514; Dell, *Lincoln and the War Democrats*, 33, 50, 57-59, 63, 71, 81, 82.
91. See the letters of John Logan to Mary Logan, August-December 1865 in John A. Logan MSS, manuscripts division, Library of Congress.
92. Mary Dearing, *Veterans in Politics: The Story of the G. A. R.* (Baton Rouge: Louisiana State University Press, 1952), 83; D. G. Hay to Trumbull, May 9, 1866, Trumbull MSS.
93. John H. Bryant to Trumbull, January 8, 1866, ibid.; Phillips to Trumbull, January 16, 1866, ibid.
94. Phillips to Trumbull, January 16, June 10, August 23, 1866, ibid.; Brown to Trumbull, September 25, 1865, ibid.; Bryant to Trumbull, January 8, 1866, ibid.; C. M. Hawley to Trumbull, July 1, 1866, ibid.
95. Dearing, *Veterans in Politics*, 82; J. W. Crampton to Trumbull, June 24, 1866, Trumbull MSS.
96. Dearing, *Veterans in Politics*, 76-77.
97. *Cong. Globe*, 39 Cong., 1 Sess., pt. 5, p. 4242.
98. Beale, ed., *Diary of Welles*, II, 564.

99. Ebenezer Peck to Trumbull, April 24, 1866, Trumbull MSS; William H. Brown to Trumbull, April 26, 1866, ibid.; John Evans to Trumbull, July 7, 1866, ibid.; Anson S. Miller to George T. Allen, May 14, 1865, ibid.; D. G. Hay to Trumbull, May 9, 1866, ibid.
100. Trumbull to Jayne, July 2, 1866, Trumbull Family MSS.
101. Medill to Trumbull, July 17, 1866, Trumbull MSS.
102. Chicago *Tribune*, May 26, 1866.
103. William H. Underwood to Trumbull, January 15, 1866, Trumbull MSS.
104. N. B. Judd to Trumbull, July 11, 1866, ibid.; John Cook to Trumbull, July 19, 1866, ibid.; John M. Palmer, *Personal Recollections of John M. Palmer: The Story of an Earnest Life* (Cincinnati: The R. Clarke Co., 1901), 278-280.

Notes to Chapter Fourteen

1. C. M. Hawley to Trumbull, July 24, 1866, Trumbull MSS; Leonard Swett to David Davis, August 8, 1866, copy in Leonard Swett MSS, Illinois Historical Survey, Urbana, Ill.; Lyman Trumbull to Julia Jayne Trumbull, July 26, 1866, Trumbull Family MSS.
2. Chicago *Republican*, August 2, 1866; Trumbull, "Trumbull," II, ch. 5, pp. 5-6; John Drury, "Old Chicago Houses," in Chicago *Daily News*, June 16, 1939, p. 26, cols. 1-2.
3. Philip D. Swenson, "Illinois Disillusionment with State Activism," in Jones C. Mohr, ed., *Radical Republicans in the North: State Politics during Reconstruction* (Baltimore: Johns Hopkins University Press, 1976), 108.
4. *Illinois State Register*, August 9, 1866.
5. Brown to Trumbull, August 16, 1866, Trumbull MSS.
6. Koerner to Trumbull, August 18, 1866, ibid.; William Jayne to Trumbull, August 12, 1866, Trumbull Family MSS; Trumbull to William Jayne, August 19, 1866, ibid.; Lyman Trumbull to Julia Jayne Trumbull, August 22, 1866, ibid.; Lyman Trumbull to Julia Jayne Trumbull, August 24, 1866, ibid.
7. D. G. Hay to Trumbull, May 9, 1866, Trumbull MSS.
8. Chicago *Republican*, September 1, September 20, 1866; Chicago *Tribune*, October 3, 1866; Hay to Trumbull, September 2, 1866, Trumbull MSS.
9. Chicago *Tribune*, October 11, 17, 26, 1866; Lyman Trumbull to Julia Jayne Trumbull, October 31, 1866, Trumbull Family MSS.
10. Chicago *Tribune*, November 2, 1866; Lyman Trumbull to Julia Jayne Trumbull, October 31, 1866, Trumbull Family MSS.
11. Dearing, *Veterans in Politics*, 101, 105, 110.
12. John M. Palmer, Sr., to John M. Palmer, Jr., November 10, 1866, Palmer MSS; McKitrick, *Johnson,* 447; Patrick, *Reconstruction,* 89.
13. Trumbull, "Trumbull," II, ch. 6, p. 2.
14. Ibid.; Jesse W. Fell to Trumbull, August 29, 1866, Trumbull MSS; Trumbull to S. W. Lawrence, September 10, 1866, copy in ibid.
15. See Logan MSS for November 1866.
16. D. J. Pinckney to Logan, November 14, 1866, ibid.
17. See ibid. for November 1866.
18. P. G. Clemens to Logan, November 14, 1866, ibid.; H. Green to Logan, November 11, 1866, ibid.
19. John Logan to Mary Logan, December 1, 1866, ibid.
20. See Palmer MSS for November-December 1866.
21. J. D. Ward to Palmer, December 22, 1866, ibid.
22. Trumbull, "Trumbull," II, ch. 6, p. 3.
23. Trumbull to W. C. Flagg, December 24, 1866 in "Trumbull Correspondence," *The Mississippi Valley Historical Review*, I (June 1914), 105; Trumbull, "Trumbull," II, ch. 6, p. 3.
24. Chicago *Tribune*, November 1866-January 1867.

25. *Illinois State Journal*, January 12, 1867.
26. Franklin William Scott, *Newspapers and Periodicals of Illinois, 1814-1879 (Collections of the Illinois State Historical Society*, VI) (Springfield: The Trustees of the State Historical Library, 1910), 85.
27. Charles Warren, *The Supreme Court in United States History*, II (Boston: Little, Brown, and Co., 1926), II, 418-454; Stanley I. Kutler, *Judicial Power and Reconstruction Politics* (Chicago: University of Chicago Press, 1968), 90-94; Krug, *Davis*, 248-256.
28. Chicago *Tribune*, January 7, 1867.
29. Trumbull, "Trumbull," II, ch. 6, pp. 5-6.
30. Ibid., 6-7.
31. Ibid., 7-8; Trumbull to Jayne, January 6, 1867, Trumbull Family MSS.
32. John Logan to Mary Logan, January 11, 1867, Logan MSS.
33. Cole, *The Era of the Civil War*, 404-405; Jonesboro (Ill.) *Gazette*, December 15, 1866.
34. John Logan to Mary Logan, January 11, 1867, Logan MSS; New York *Times*, January 14, 1867.
35. Trumbull, "Trumbull," II, ch. 6, pp. 10-11; Jacksonville (Ill.) *Daily Journal*, January 8, 1867; Cole, *The Era of the Civil War*, 404-405.
36. Trumbull, "Trumbull," II, ch. 6, p. 11; Moses, *Illinois Historical and Statistical*, II, 767.
37. Blaine, *Twenty Years of Congress*, II, 12-13; Chicago *Tribune*, January 15, 1867.
38. Blaine, *Twenty Years of Congress*, II, 13-15.
39. *Ibid.*, 15; Washington *Chronicle*, January 15, 1867; There is a slightly variant vote total in Moses, *Illinois, Historical and Statistical*, II, 767.
40. Illinois *House Journal*, 25 Gen. Ass., 1 Sess., 157, 177; Illinois *Senate Journal*, 25 Gen. Ass., 1 Sess., 113-115; New York *Times*, January 16, 1867.
41. Trumbull, "Trumbull," II, ch. 6, p. 20.
42. Ibid., 9.
43. *United States Statutes at Large*, XIV, 377.
44. *Cong. Globe*, 39 Cong., 2 Sess., pt. 1, pp. 159-160; Chicago *Tribune*, December 20, 1866.
45. *United States Statutes at Large*, XIV, 428-429.
46. *Cong. Globe*, 40 Cong., 1 Sess., pt. 1, p. 171; Record Group 46, Records of the U.S. Senate, Minutes of the Judiciary Committee, March 12, 1867, in the National Archives.
47. *Cong. Globe*, 40 Cong., 1 Sess., pt. 1, p. 94.
48. *Ibid.*, 171.
49. Trumbull, "Trumbull," II, ch. 4, pp. 9-10; *United States Statutes at Large*, XV, 14-15.
50. Ibid., 9-10; *Cong. Globe*, 40 Cong., 1 Sess., pt. 2, p. 357.
51. Trumbull, "Trumbull," II, ch. 4, pp. 9-10; *United States Statutes at Large*, XV, 14-15.
52. White, *Trumbull*, 292; Edward L. Pierce, ed., *Memoirs and Letters of Charles Sumner*, I (Boston: Roberts Brothers, 1881), 228.
53. White, *Trumbull*, 294-295.
54. Myron Ellis to Trumbull, May 31, 1867, Trumbull MSS.
55. Chicago *Tribune*, June 26, 1896.
56. White, *Trumbull*, 421. See also Joseph Brown to Trumbull, January 24, 1863, Trumbull Family MSS; B. C. Eastman to Trumbull, September 23, 1863, ibid.
57. Trumbull to Gilman, Son & Co., July 3, 1866, Trumbull Family MSS; Gilman, Son & Co. to Trumbull, January 2, 1867, ibid.; Julia Jayne Trumbull to Lyman Trumbull, May 20, 1867, ibid.
58. Gilman, Son & Co. to Trumbull, January 2, 1867, ibid.; Gilman, Son & Co. to Trumbull, April 19, 1867, ibid.; Julia Jayne Trumbull to Lyman Trumbull, May 20, 1867, ibid.
59. Lyman Trumbull to Julia Jayne Trumbull, July 24, 1867, ibid.
60. Julia Jayne Trumbull to Lyman Trumbull, May 20, 1867, ibid.
61. Ibid.; Thomas S. Mather to Trumbull, October 26, 1865, ibid.; Virgil Hickox to Trumbull, December 10, 1864, ibid.

62. *Cong. Globe*, 39 Cong., 2 Sess., pt. 2, p. 1862.
63. *Ibid.*, 977-978.
64. John B. Ellis, *The Sights and Secrets of the National Capital* (New York: United States Publishing Co., 1869), 438-441; *Congressional Directory*, 40 Cong., 2 Sess., II, 102.
65. *Cong. Directory*, 40 Cong., 2 Sess., II, 59.
66. Ellis Paxson Oberholtzer, *A History of the United States Since the Civil War* (New York: Negro University Press, 1969), 54-56; Patrick, *Reconstruction*, 113-114.
67. *Cong. Globe*, 40 Cong., 2 Sess., pt. 2, pp. 1288-1292.
68. *Ibid.*, 1417.
69. Henry Stanbery to U. S. Grant, December 21, 1867, Record Group 94, Records of the Adjutant General, R. P. No. 670220, National Archives.
70. Grant to Trumbull, January 8, 1868, ibid.
71. Trumbull to Grant, January 11, 1868, ibid.
72. Pease and Randall, eds., *Diary of Browning*, II, 65.
73. Trumbull to Stanton, January 20, 1868, Record Group 94, R. P. No. 670220.
74. Chicago *Tribune*, January 15, 20, 22, 1868.
75. *Cong. Globe*, 40 Cong., 2 Sess., pt. 1, pp. 707-711.
76. E. Bruce Thompson, *Matthew Hale Carpenter: Webster of the West* (Madison, Historical Society of Wisconsin, 1954), 94.
77. Ex parte McCardle, 6 Wallace, 321-322; Washington *Chronicle*, February 8, 1868.
78. Ex parte McCardle, 6 Wall., 327-328.
79. Thompson, *Carpenter*, 97.
80. Washington *Chronicle*, March 5, 1868; *Argument of Hon. Lyman Trumbull in the Supreme Court of the United States, March 4, 1868, in the matter of Ex parte William H. McCardle, appellant*, 29 pp. (Washington, 1868), copy in possession of Mrs. James L. Worrall, Indianapolis, Ind.
81. *Cong. Globe*, 40 Cong., 2 Sess., pt. 1, p. 489.
82. *Ibid.*, pt. 2, p. 1204; *Nation*, VI (February 20, 1868), 142.
83. *Cong. Globe*, 40 Cong., 2 Sess., pt. 2, p. 1428.
84. Kutler, *Judicial Power*, 78; Warren, *The Supreme Court*, II, 474, 475. See the account of the bill's amendment in the House in *Nation*, VI (March 19, 1868), 221.
85. Thomas Ewing to Browning, March 18, 1868, Browning MSS; Baxter, *Browning*, 208.
86. Richardson, ed., *Messages and Papers of the Presidents*, VI, 646-648; Pease and Randall, eds., *Diary of Browning*, II, 191-192.
87. *Cong. Globe.*, 40 Cong., 2 Sess., pt. 3, pp. 2096, 2128.
88. Beale, ed., *Diary of Welles*, III, 320; Pease and Randall, eds., *Diary of Browning*, II, 191-192. Kutler thinks the court was not routed by Congress, but rather it beat a strategic retreat. See *Judicial Power*, 84-85.
89. Ex parte McCardle, 7 Wall., 511-512; White, *Trumbull*, 329-330.
90. Ex parte McCardle, 7 Wall., 515; Kutler, *Judicial Power*, 84.
91. Secretary of War Robert Todd Lincoln to J. H. Chalmers, March 15, 1884, Record Group 94, R. P. No. 670220; New York *Times*, September 12, 1872; White, *Trumbull*, 330-332.
92. New York *Times*, September 12, 1872; White, *Trumbull*, 330-332.

Notes to Chapter Fifteen

1. Dr. H. Schroder to Trumbull, December 23, 1865, Trumbull MSS.
2. Michael Les Benedict, *The Impeachment and Trial of Andrew Johnson* (New York: W. W. Norton & Co., Inc., 1973), 16-36; Arthur M. Schlesinger, *The Imperial Presidency* (Boston: Houghton Mifflin Co., 1973), 73-74.
3. *Cong. Globe*, 39 Cong., 2 Sess., pt. 1, pp. 319-321.
4. House *Report* No. 7, 40 Cong., 1 Sess., passim.
5. *Cong. Globe*, 40 Cong., 2 Sess., pt. 3, p. 1964; Benedict, *Impeachment*, 77-78.

6. *Cong. Globe*, 39 Cong., 2 Sess., pt. 3, p. 1964; *United States Statutes at Large*, XIV, 430; McKitrick, *Johnson*, 495-497.
7. *Cong. Globe*, 39 Cong., 2 Sess., pt. 3, p. 1966.
8. *Ibid.*, 40 Cong., 2 Sess., pt. 6, supplement, 51.
9. *Ibid.*; Edward McPherson, ed., *The Political History of the United States during the Period of Reconstruction* (Washington: Solomons & Chapman, 1875), 262.
10. Beale, *Diary of Welles,* III, 259-262; Pease and Randall, eds., *Diary of Browning*, II, 173-175; William B. Hesseltine, *Ulysses S. Grant, Politician* (New York: F. Ungar Publishing Co., 1957), 103-111.
11. Trumbull, "Trumbull," II, ch. 7, p. 4; Pease and Randall, eds., *Diary of Browning*, II, 182.
12. McPherson, ed., *Reconstruction*, 262-263; Benjamin P. Thomas and Harold M. Hyman, *Stanton: The Life and Times of Lincoln's Secretary of War* (New York: Alfred A. Knopf, 1962), 587.
13. Pease and Randall, eds., *Diary of Browning*, II, 181, 187, 188; Thomas and Hyman, *Stanton*, 587-594.
14. *Cong. Globe*, 40 Cong., 2 Sess., pt. 2, pp. 1329-1330, 1336.
15. *Ibid.*, 1355-1358, 1396.
16. McPherson, ed., *Reconstruction*, 266; Trumbull, "Trumbull," II, ch. 7, p. 5.
17. *Cong. Globe*, 40 Cong., 2 Sess., pt. 2, pp. 1616-1618, 1642.
18. *Ibid.*, pt. 6, supplement, 3-5; Schlesinger, *Presidency*, 73-74; Raoul Berger, *Impeachment: The Constitutional Problems* (Cambridge: The Harvard University Press, 1973), 171-180.
19. *Cong. Globe*, 40 Cong., 2 Sess., pt. 2, p. 1619; Benjamin F. Butler, *Autobiography and Personal Reminiscences* (Boston: A. M. Thayer & Co., 1892), 927; Brodie, *Stevens*, 340-341.
20. *Cong. Globe*, 40 Cong., 2 Sess., pt. 6, supplement, 8.
21. Trumbull, "Trumbull," II, ch. 7, p. 9; Berger, *Impeachment*, 267; Pease and Randall, eds., *Diary of Browning*, II, 189.
22. David F. Hughes, "Chief Justice Chase at the Impeachment Trial of Andrew Johnson," *New York State Bar Journal*, XLI (April 1969), 224-225.
23. Benedict, *Impeachment*, 137; Van Deusen, *Seward*, 480; Pease and Randall, eds., *Diary of Browning*, II, 185.
24. Washington *Chronicle*, March, 1868; Chicago *Tribune*, February-March 1868; Chicago *Republican*, February-March 1868.
25. Trumbull, "Trumbull," II, ch. 7, pp. 5-12; James Fishback to Logan, February 28, 1868, Logan MSS; M. J. Clerihan to Yates, March 2, 1868, Yates MSS.
26. Trumbull, "Trumbull," II, ch. 7, pp. 5-12.
27. Butler, *Autobiography*, 927; *Cong. Globe*, 40 Cong., 2 Sess., supplement, 29-57; Benedict, *Impeachment*, 144-145; Howard P. Nash, *Andrew Johnson: Congress and Reconstruction* (Rutherford, N. J.: Fairleigh Dickenson University Press, 1972), 148-149.
28. *Cong. Globe*, 40 Cong., 2 Sess., supplement, 63, 175; Benedict, *Impeachment*, 129.
29. Trumbull to William Jayne, March 29, 1868 in Trumbull, "Trumbull," II, ch. 7, p. 14.
30. Thomas Ewing, Sr., to Hugh Ewing, April 6, 1868, Thomas Ewing MSS, manuscripts division, Library of Congress; Chicago *Tribune*, April 6, 1868; King, *Davis,* 268.
31. See Chicago *Tribune*, late March-early April 1868.
32. Shelby M. Cullom, *Fifty Years of Public Service: Personal Recollections of Shelby M. Cullom* (Chicago: A. C. McClurg & Co., 1911), 155; Philadelphia *Press*, March 12, 1868; Krug, *Trumbull*, 261.
33. Trumbull, "Trumbull," II, ch. 7, p. 14.
34. Ibid.; Fessenden, *Fessenden*, II, 186, 207-208.
35. Nashville (Tenn.) *Republican Banner*, April 26, 1868.
36. *Cong. Globe*, 40 Cong., 2 Sess., pt. 6, supplement, 78-90, 173.
37. *Ibid.*, 349.
38. Nashville (Tenn.) *Republican Banner*, April 26, 1868.

39. New York *Tribune*, May 2, 1868; Joseph Logsdon, *Horace White, Nineteenth Century Liberal* (Westport, Conn.: Greenwood Publishing Co., 1971), 153.
40. Pease and Randall, eds., *Diary of Browning,* II. 187-188, 189, 194; John M. Schofield, *Forty-six years in the Army* (New York: The Century Co., 1897), 404, 413-419.
41. Bendict, *Impeachment*, 137-138, 180; David Miller De Witt, *The Impeachment and Trial of Andrew Johnson: Seventeenth President of the United States* (New York: Macmillan Co., 1903), 546-547.
42. Trumbull's opinion in *Cong. Globe*, 40 Cong., 2 Sess., pt. 6, supplement, 417-421; Trumbull to William Jayne, May 15, 1868 in Trumbull, "Trumbull," II, ch. 7, p. 20; Trumbull to William Jayne, May 20, 1868 in ibid., ch. 8, p. 7; Trumbull to Koerner, May 20, 1868 in Belleville (Ill.) *Advocate* as reprinted in the New York *Times*, June 5, 1868.
43. Philadelphia Sunday *Dispatch*, May 10, 1868; Chicago *Tribune*, April 21, May 2, 1868; Trumbull to C. H. Ray, May 17, 1868, C. H. Ray MSS, Henry F. Huntington Library; Trumbull, "Trumbull," II, ch. 7, pp. 1-2; Trefousse, *Wade*, 300-301.
44. Cornelius Cole, *Memoirs of Cornelius Cole, Ex-Senator of the United States from California* (New York: McLaughlin Bros., 1908), 167; Trumbull to Ray, May 17, 1868, Ray MSS; Trumbull, "Trumbull," II, ch. 7, pp. 1-2.
45. New York *Times*, May 12, 1868; Nashville (Tenn.) *Republican Banner*, May 13, 1868; New York *World*, May 12, 1868; Jonesboro (Ill.) *Weekly Gazette*, May 16, 1868; Cullom, *Fifty Years*, 154.
46. Wilmington (Del.) *Commercial*, May 12, 1868.
47. *Ibid*.; New York *Tribune*, May 13, 1868; Boston *Evening Transcript*, May 13, 1868; Pittsburgh *Commercial*, May 13, 1868.
48. Nashville (Tenn.) *Republican Banner*, May 15, 1868; Philadelphia *Press*, May 12, 1868; De Witt, *Trial of Johnson*, 529.
49. New York *Times*, May 16, 1868.
50. Trumbull, "Trumbull," II, ch. 7, p. 20; Chicago *Tribune*, May 15, 1868.
51. Chicago *Tribune*, May 12, 1868. White had visited Washington in early May and decided to defend Trumbull. See Longsdon, *White*, 154.
52. Chicago *Tribune*, May 12-27, 1868.
53. Trumbull to Ray, May 22, 1868, Ray MSS.
54. Ralph J. Roske, "Republican Newspaper Support for the Acquittal of President Johnson," *Tennessee Historical Quarterly*, XI (September 1952), 262-273.
55. Jonesboro (Ill.) *Weekly Gazette*, May 16, 1868; Peoria *National Democrat*, May 14, 1868; Louisville *Democrat*, May 18, 1868.
56. John B. Henderson, "Emancipation and Impeachment, *Century*, LXXXV (December 1912), 207; De Witt, *Trial of Johnson*, 542-543; Benedict, *Impeachment*, 169-173; Baltimore *Gazette*, May 14, 1868.
57. New York *Times*, May 16, 1868; New York *Tribune*, May 16, 1868; Baltimore *Sun*, May 13, 1868; Benedict, *Impeachment*, 7.
58. Indianapolis *Journal*, May 14, 1868; De Witt, *Trial of Johnson*, 529-530.
59. Trumbull, "Trumbull," II, ch. 7, p. 20.
60. Edmund G. Ross, "A Previous Era of Popular Madness and its Lessons," *The Forum*, XIX (July 1895), 604-605; Edmund G. Ross, "Historic Moments: The Impeachment Trial," *Scribner's Magazine*, XI (April 1892), 521.
61. New York *World*, May 11, 1868; New York *Times*, May 18, 1868; Richmond (Va.) *Enquirer and Examiner*, May 19, 1868; Nashville (Tenn.) *Republican Banner*, May 17, 1868.
62. *Cong. Globe*, 40 Cong., 2 Sess., pt. 6, supplement, 411; Benedict, *Impeachment*, 173-178.
63. Trumbull to Ray, May 17, 1868, Ray MSS.
64. Benjamin C. Truman, "Anecdotes of Andrew Johnson," *Century*, LXXXV (January 1913), 438; James A. Rawley, *Edwin P. Morgan, 1811-1883, Merchant in Politics* (New York: Columbia University Press, 1955), 228-229.

65. *Cong. Globe*, 40 Cong., 2 Sess., pt. 6, supplement, 411; Donald, *Sumner & Rights*, 337; De Witt, *Trial of Johnson*, 549; Trumbull, "Trumbull," II, ch. 8, p. 9; Patrick, *Reconstruction*, 130; William A. Dunning, *Reconstruction, Political and Economic, 1865-1877* (New York: Harper & Bros., 1907), 107.

66. Chicago *Tribune*, May 21, 1868; New York *Times*, May 21, 1868.

67. New York *Tribune*, May 13-18, 1868.

68. Chicago *Tribune*, May 14, 15, 18, 1868.

69. Chicago *Republican* as reprinted in Peoria *National Democrat*, May 19, 1868; Logsdon, *White*, 155, 158.

70. Chicago *Tribune*, May 22, 1868; Logsdon, *White*, 155.

71. Trumbull to Koerner, May 20, 1868 in Belleville (Ill.) *Advocate*, as reprinted in the New York *Times*, June 5, 1868.

72. Trumbull to Ray, June 3, 1868, Ray MSS.

73. *Cong. Globe*, 40 Cong., 2 Sess., pt. 6, supplement, 414.

74. *Ibid.*, 415.

75. *Ibid.*

76. Emmet John Hughes, *The Living Presidency: The Resources and Dilemmas of the American Presidential Office* (New York: Coward, McCann & Geohagen, 1973), 169; Schlesinger, *The Imperial Presidency*, 76.

77. New York *World*, May 16, 1868; Louisville *Democrat*, May 26, 1868; *Frank Leslie's Illustrated Newspaper*, XXVI (May 30, 1868), 161, 163.

78. *Nation*, VII (September 24, 1868), 241.

79. Logsdon, *White*, 156; Trefousse, *The Radical Republicans*, 399-400.

80. Trumbull to Ray, May 22, 1868, Ray MSS.

81. *Nation*, VI (June 4, 1868), 241; Thomas and Hyman, *Stanton*, 608.

82. *Cong. Globe*, 40 Cong., 2 Sess., pt. 3, pp. 2514, 2858, 2859.

83. Trumbull to Ray, May 22, 1868, Ray MSS; Trumbull to Ray, June 3, 1868, ibid.

84. *Nation*, VI (May 21, 1868), 402. On Wade's poor relationship with Trumbull before Johnson's acquittal, see Trefousse, *The Radical Republicans*, 398 and Trefousse, *Wade*, 307.

85. Trumbull to Koerner, May 20, 1868, Belleville (Ill.) *Advocate* as reprinted in the New York *Times*, June 5, 1868. See also the Chicago *Tribune*, June 26, 1868 and Trumbull, "Trumbull," II, ch. 8, p. 13.

Notes to Chapter Sixteen

1. *Cong. Globe*, 40 Cong., 2 Sess., pt. 3, pp. 2514, 2858, 2930-2931, 3029, pt. 4, p. 3466.

2. See the miscellaneous papers of Trumbull Family MSS.

3. *A Sketch of the Life of Mrs. Lyman Trumbull*, 3-3; Mrs. Sibyl Slater Jayne to Mrs. William Jayne, June [?] 1868, then in private collection of Perry Jayne, Springfield, Ill.

4. *Sketch*, 7.

5. Ruth Painter Randall, *Lincoln's Sons* (Boston: Little, Brown and Company, 1955), 255-256; Randall, *Mary Lincoln*, 416.

6. Trumbull to Jayne, July 30, 1868, Trumbull Family MSS; *Sketch*, 4-5; Chicago *Tribune*, August 17-18, 1868.

7. *Illinois State Journal*, October 19, 1868; Chicago *Tribune* as reprinted in New York *Times*, October 21, 1868.

8. Chicago *Tribune*, October 21, 1868.

9. *Ibid.*

10. *Ibid.*, October 27, 1868.

11. *Ibid.*, October 28, 1868.

12. Stanwood, *A History of the Presidency*, 328; McPherson, ed., *Political History of Reconstruction*, 499.
13. Dennett, ed., *Diaries and Letters of John Hay*, 297; *Congressional Directory*, II, 113.
14. *Congressional Directory*, II, 58.
15. *Cong. Globe*, 40 Cong., 3 Sess., pt. 1, p. 293.
16. *Ibid.*, pt. 1, pp. 378, 543, pt. 2, pp. 1318, 1440-1441, pt. 3, pp. 1539, 1623-1633, 1638-1641.
17. *Ibid.*, 1641.
18. *Congressional Directory*, II, 58, 59.
19. Norton, ed., *History of Madison County*, 114; Alton *Daily Democrat*, June 10, 1880.
20. Brown to Trumbull, May 19, 1869, Trumbull MSS.
21. Norton, ed., *History of Madison County*, 114; Alton *Daily Democrat*, June 10, 1880.
22. *Congressional Directory*, II, 58, 59.
23. Richardson, ed., *Messages and Papers of the Presidents*, VII, 11-12; Trefousse, *The Radical Republicans*, 427.
24. Ben:Perley Poore, *Perley's Reminiscences of Sixty Years in the National Metropolis*, II (Philadelphia: Hubbard Bros., 1886), 207; David M. Jordan, *Roscoe Conkling of New York: Voice in the Senate* (New York: Cornell University Press, 1971), 90, 128-130. For Hacker's division into "old" and "new" Radicals, see Louis M. Hacker, *The Triumph of American Capitalism* (New York: Columbia University Press, 1940), 380, 383.
25. *Cong. Globe*, 41 Cong., 1 Sess., pt. 1, pp. 653-654.
26. *Ibid.*, 656.
27. Nathaniel Pitt Langford, *The Discovery of Yellowstone Park, 1870*, 2nd ed. (St. Paul: J. E. Haynes, 1923), 31.
28. Brown to Trumbull, May 19, 1869, Trumbull MSS; Brown to Trumbull, August 23, 1869, ibid.; James Fergus to Trumbull, August 28, 1869, ibid.
29. Jos. P. Root to Trumbull, October 8, 1869, ibid.; Trumbull to Root, October 12, 1869, copy in ibid.
30. *Cong. Globe*, 41 Cong., 2 Sess., pt. 1, p. 419.
31. *Ibid.*, 418-420.
32. *Ibid.*, 636-644.
33. *Ibid.*
34. *Ibid.*, 644.
35. *Ibid.*, 1166.
36. *Ibid.*, 41 Cong., 2 Sess., pt. 1, p. 17.
37. *Ibid.*, 18.
38. *Ibid.*, pt. 2, pp. 1078-1079; Ari Hoogenboom, *Outlawing the Spoils: A History of the Civil Service Reform Movement, 1865-1883* (Urbana: University of Illinois Press, 1968), 71.
39. Robert T. Lincoln to Trumbull, April 7, 1870, copy in Trumbull Family MSS; *Cong. Globe*, 41 Cong., 2 Sess., pt. 4, p. 3088; King, *Davis*, 243.
40. Trumbull to William Jayne, August 5, 1870, copy in Trumbull Family MSS.
41. Swenson, "Illinois: Disillusionment with State Activism," in Mohr, ed., *Radical Republicans in the North*, 108-115.
42. Trumbull to Jayne, August 5, 1870, copy in Trumbull Family MSS; personal interview with Judge Frances E. Wilson, Chicago, November 28, 1948.
43. Trumbull to Jayne, October 9, 1870, Trumbull Family MSS.
44. See Trumbull MSS for September-October 1870.
45. *Nation*, XI (November 10, 1870), 306-307.
46. Trumbull to Jayne, November 18, 1870, Trumbull Family MSS.
47. Ibid.
48. Claude M. Fuess, *Carl Schurz, Reformer, 1829-1906* (New York: Dodd, Mead & Co.,

1932), 1-153; Hesseltine, *Grant*, 58-59; Matthew Josephson, *The Politicos, 1865-1896* (New York: Harcourt, Brace & Co., 1938), 21, 22, 154.
49. Hesseltine, *Grant*, 200; Thomas S. Barclay, *The Liberal Republicans in Missouri, 1865-1871* (Columbia: The State Historical Society of Missouri, 1926), 15-172.
50. Trumbull to Jayne, November 18, 1870, Trumbull Family MSS.
51. *Cong. Globe*, 41 Cong., 3 Sess., pt. 1, p. 292.
52. *Ibid.*, 458.
53. *Ibid.*, 459, 667, 690, 782; Hoogenboom, *Outlawing the Spoils*, 86; Washington *Chronicle*, January 24, 1871.
54. *Cong. Globe*, 41 Cong., 3 Sess., pt. 3, p. 1997.
55. Hesseltine, *Grant*, 252; Hoogenboom, *Outlawing the Spoils*, 86; Paul P. Van Riper, *Civil Service*, 69-70.
56. Fuess, *Schurz*, 162-163; Hesseltine, *Grant*, 151-253; Van Riper, *Civil Service*, 69-70.
57. Trumbull to Jayne, January 8, 1871, Trumbull Family MSS; Richard Oglesby to William C. Flagg, December 12, 1870, William C. Flagg, MSS, Illinois State Historical Survey, Urbana, Ill.
58. See Logan MSS for August 1870, to January 1871.
59. Trumbull to Jayne, January 8, 1871, Trumbull Family MSS; White, *Trumbull*, 430-431; Chicago *Tribune*, June 28, 1896; Chicago *Inter-Ocean*, June 28, 1896; Chicago *Chronicle*, June 28, 1896.
60. Trumbull to Jayne, March 24, 1871, Trumbull Family MSS.
61. *Cong. Globe*, 42 Cong., 1 Sess., pt. 1, pp. 49-50; Donald, *Sumner & Rights*, 496.
62. White, *Trumbull*, 297, 420.
63. *Senate Executive Journal*, XVIII, 108-109.
64. New York *Times*, July 6, 1871.
65. Carl Schurz to E. L. Godkin, March 31, 1871 in Frederick Bancroft, ed., *Speeches, Correspondence, and Political Papers of Carl Schurz*, II (New York: Negro Universities Press, 1969), 252-253.
66. *Cong. Globe*, 42 Cong., 1 Sess., pt. 1, p. 224.
67. *Ibid.*, 579.
68. *Ibid.*, 817-818; George, *Chandler*, 191.
69. New York *Times*, July 6, 1871.
70. *Ibid.*, September 25, 1871.
71. Lyman Trumbull to Henry Trumbull, December 26, 1871 (when consulted, in possession of Perry Jayne, Springfield, Ill.); Lyman Trumbull to Henry Trumbull, November 6, 1871, ibid.

Trumbull, November 6, 1871, then in possession of Perry Jayne, Springfield, Ill.; *Congressional Directory*, II, 67, 121.
73. New York *Times*, December 6, 1871.
74. Trumbull to Flagg, January 10, 1872, copy in Trumbull Family MSS.

Notes to Chapter Seventeen

1. New York *Sun*, January 26, 1872; Martin B. Duberman, *Charles Francis Adams, 1807-1886* (Boston: Houghton Mifflin, 1961), 353.
2. Trumbull to Roeliff Brinckerhoff, March 20, 1872, copy in Trumbull MSS; Trumbull to Jesse W. Fell, April 11, 1872, copy in Jesse W. Fell MSS, Illinois Historical Survey, Urbana, Ill.
3. See Trumbull MSS for December 1871-April 1872.
4. Joseph Brown to Trumbull, December 12, 1871, ibid.
5. Ross to Trumbull, February 21, 1872, ibid.
6. O. P. Fitzgerald to Trumbull, January 4, 1872, ibid.
7. James H. Hill to Trumbull, February 3, 1872, ibid.

8. Carlton L. Lewis to Trumbull, February 26, 1872, ibid.; Jonesboro (Ill.) *Gazette*, February 10, 1872; E. L. Merritt to Trumbull, February 26, 1872, Trumbull MSS; James Hall to Trumbull, May 1, 1872, ibid.; Napa *Register*, March 30, 1872.
9. New York *Sun*, November 30, 1871-March 8, 1872.
10. *Nation*, January 1872-April 1872.
11. See the Trumbull MSS for January 1872-April 1872.
12. See the Carl Schurz MSS, manuscripts division, Library of Congress, December 1871-April 1872.
13. *Cong. Globe*, 42 Cong., 2 Sess., pt. 6, appendix, 82-87; Jordan, *Conkling*, 176-178.
14. New York *Times*, April 30, 1872; Cincinnati *Enquirer*, April 26, 1872.
15. Trumbull to Fell, April 11, 1872, copy in Fell MSS.
16. Trumbull to Koerner, March 9, 1872, Trumbull MSS.
17. Washington *Homestead Champion*, April 1872.
18. Palmer, *A Conscientious Turncoat*, 240-241; Palmer, *Personal Recollections*, 459.
19. A. W. Scharit to Trumbull, April 29, 1872, Trumbull MSS; New York *Tribune*, April 30, 1872.
20. Trumbull to White, April 24, 1872, copy in Trumbull MSS.
21. McCormack, ed., *Memoirs of Koerner*, II, 549; Chicago *Tribune*, April 30, 1872.
22. White to Trumbull, May 8, 1872, Trumbull MSS; Henry Watterson, "The Tragedy and Humor of the Greeley Campaign," *Century*, LXXXV (November 1912), 35.
23. McCormack, ed., *Memoirs of Koerner*, II, 544-545, 549; Cincinnati *Enquirer*, April 30, 1872.
24. John Wentworth to Frank Orme, May 2, 1872, copy of telegram in David E. Davis MSS, Illinois State Historical Library; Cincinnati *Enquirer*, May 1, 1872.
25. White, *Trumbull*, 378; Duberman, *Adams*, 359-360; Chicago *Tribune*, May 9, 1872.
26. Harry E. Pratt, "David Davis, 1818-1886," MSS doctoral dissertation, 1930, University of Illinois, 137; White, *Trumbull*, 380-381; Bingham Duncan, *Whitelaw Reid, Journalist, Politician, Diplomat* (Athens: University of Georgia Press, 1975), 42.
27. Donald Bruce Johnson and Kirk H. Porter, *National Party Platforms, 1840-1972* (Urbana: University of Illinois Press, 1973), 44-45.
28. Watterson, "The Tragedy and Humor of the Greeley Campaign," 36-39; White, *Trumbull*, 382-383; Duberman, *Adams*, 362-363; Duncan, *Reid*, 42-43.
29. Cincinnati *Enquirer*, May 4, 1872; New York *Tribune*, May 4, 1872.
30. Cincinnati *Enquirer*, May 4, 1872; White, *Trumbull*, 383.
31. Cincinnati *Enquirer*, May 4, 1872; New York *Tribune*, May 4, 1872.
32. *Ibid*.
33. *Ibid*.
34. *Ibid*.
35. White to Trumbull, May 8, 1872, Trumbull MSS; Koerner to Trumbull, May 24, 1872, *ibid*.
36. David A. Wells to Trumbull, May 8, 1872, ibid.; Wentworth to Fell or Orme, May 2, 1872, Davis MSS.
37. New York *Tribune*, May 4, 1872; Cincinnati *Enquirer*, May 4, 1872.
38. McCormack, ed., *Memoirs of Koerner*, II, 555.
39. New York *Tribune*, May 4, 1872; Cincinnati *Enquirer*, May 4, 1872. The traditional view of the Brown-Greeley deal is stated in Earle Dudley Ross, *The Liberal Republican Movement* (Seattle: University of Washington Press, 1970), 102 and disputed by Matthew T. Downey, "Horace Greeley and the Politicians," *The Journal of American History*, LIII (March 1967), 727-750.
40. Cincinnati *Enquirer*, May 4, 1872; McCormack, ed., *Memoirs of Koerner,* II, 556.
41. New York *Tribune*, May 4, 1872.
42. *Ibid*., May 4, 1872.
43. Schurz to Godkin, May 20, 1872, copy in Schurz MSS.

44. Ibid.
45. Trumbull to Greeley, May 20, 1872, copy in Trumbull MSS.
46. Greeley to Trumbull, May 21, 1872, ibid.
47. Henry D. Lloyd to Trumbull, June 6, 1872, ibid.
48. White to Trumbull, June 13, 1872, Trumbull MSS.
49. White, *Trumbull*, 392; New York *Tribune*, June 21, 1872.
50. Oberholtzer, *A History of the United States*, III, 27; Logsdon, *White*, 243-244.
51. George T. McJimsey, *Genteel Partisan: Manton Malone Marble, 1834-1917* (Ames: Iowa State University Press, 1971), 160-161; Lawrence Grossman, *The Democratic Party and the Negro: Northern and National Politics, 1868-1892* (Urbana: University of Illinois Press, 1976), 34.
52. New York *Tribune*, June 26, 1872; White to Trumbull, May 13, 1872, Trumbull MSS.
53. John A. McClernand and Charles Lamphier to Trumbull, May 3, 1872, ibid.
54. White to Trumbull, May 13, 1872, ibid.
55. McCormack, ed., *Memoirs of Koerner*, II, 561; New York *Tribune*, June 27, 1872.
56. McCormack, ed., *Memoirs of Koerner*, II, 562.
57. Thompson, *Carpenter*, 161-165; James A. Rawley, "The General Amnesty Act of 1872: A Note," *The Mississippi Valley Historical Review*, XLVII (December 1960), 480-484.
58. Nevins, *Fish*, 600.
59. George S. Kimberly to Cyrus H. McCormick, July 19, 1872, Cyrus McCormick MSS, then in McCormick Agricultural Library, Chicago, Ill.; form letter sent out by Ozias Hatch, July 21, 1872, ibid.; a speech by McCormick to the Democratic State Central Committee, August 27, 1872, draft in ibid.
60. Chicago *Tribune*, July 19, 1872.
61. New York *Tribune*, July 26, 1872.
62. Chicago *Tribune*, August 17, 1872.
63. *Ibid.*, August 31, 1872, September 3, 1872.
64. *Ibid.*, September 4, 5, 1872.
65. *Ibid.*, September 10-20, 1872.
66. Duff, *A. Lincoln: Prairie Lawyer*, 376.
67. Chicago *Tribune*, September 10-20, 1872.
68. *October 1-4, 1872.*
69. *Ibid.*, October 10-16, 1872.
70. Robert Selph Henry, *The Story of Reconstruction* (Gloucester, Mass: Peter Smith, 1963), 470; Bradley, *Militant Republicanism*, 412-415.
71. Chicago *Tribune*, November 2, 4, 1872.
72. Sam C. Parks to Jesse Dubois, May 27, 1872, McCormick MSS; Sam C. Parks to Ozias Hatch, May 29, 1872, ibid.; D. L. Phillips to Trumbull, May 16, 1872, Trumbull MSS.
73. Chicago *Times*, October 21, 1872 as reprinted in New York *Times*, October 23, 1872; Chicago *Tribune*, October 15, 1872.
74. *Congressional Quarterly's Guide to U.S. Elections* (Washington: Congressional Quarterly, Inc., 1975), 235; Stefan Lorant, *The Presidency: A Pictorial History of Presidential Elections From Washington to Truman* (New York: Macmillan Co., 1953), 320.
75. Chicago *Tribune*, November 18, 19, 1872.
76. *Ibid.*, November 23, 1872; Illinois *House Journal*, 28 Gen. Assembly, 1 Session, 89, 103.
77. New York *Times*, November 18, 1872.
78. Chicago *Tribune*, November 7, 1872.
79. *Ibid.*, December 4, 1872.
80. *Cong. Globe*, 42 Cong., 3 Sess., pt. 1, p. 366.
81. Henry, *Reconstruction*, 476-483; Thompson, *Carpenter*, 183.
82. *Cong. Globe*, 42 Cong., 3 Sess., pt. 1, p. 366.

83. Trefousse, *Butler*, 225-226; Hesseltine, *Grant*, 313-314; Jordan, *Conkling*, 190-191; Nevins, *Fish*, 612.
84. *Cong. Globe*, 42 Cong., 3 Sess., pt. 3, pp. 2173, 2179, 2184.
85. Hesseltine, *Grant*, 314; Trefousse, *Butler*, 225-226.
86. Chicago *Tribune*, March 12, 1873, January 11, 1877. Trumbull had voted for and accepted retroactive pay raises in 1856 and 1866; see Milwaukee *Sentinel*, June 27, 1873, but the climate of the times was different.
87. Chicago *Tribune*, March 13, 1873.

Notes to Chapter Eighteen

1. White, *Trumbull,* 407.
2. E. J. Church to Thomas Shirley, September 27, 1876, McCormick MSS.
3. See the letterheads in the Trumbull Family MSS.
4. Chicago *Tribune,* September 21, 1876.
5. New York *Times,* November 8-12, 1876; Ian Polakoff, *The Politics of Inertia, Election of 1876 and the End of Reconstruction* (Baton Rouge: Louisiana State University Press, 1973), 39-93.
6. Chicago *Times,* November 11, 1876.
7. Ralph J. Roske, " 'Visiting Statesmen' in Louisiana, 1876," *Mid-America: An Historical Review,* XXXIII (April 1951), 92.
8. Chicago *Times,* November 28, 1876.
9. New York *Times*, December 6, 1876.
10. Franklin, *Reconstruction,* 213; Patrick, *Reconstruction,* 259-260.
11. McJimsey, *Genteel Partisan,* 198-199; Polakoff, *Inertia,* 274-276; *Congressional Record,* 44 Congress, 2 Session, part 2, pp. 913, 1051.
12. Cincinnati *Enquirer,* February 13, 14, 15, 1877; *Proceedings of the Electoral Commission* in *Cong. Record,* 44 *Cong. Record,* 44 Cong., 2 Sess., pt. 4, pp. 57-119.
13. *Proceedings of the Electoral Commission* in *Cong. Record,* 44 *Cong. Record,* 44 Cong., 2 Sess., pt. 4, pp. 178, 179, 192, 193.
14. John Bigelow, *Retrospections of an Active Life,* V (New York: The Baker & Taylor Co., 1909-1913), 299.
15. See scattered references in Trumbull Family MSS, 1877-1881.
16. Giles Blague to author, January 19, 1952; notes of Walter Trumbull to author, January 14, 1952; clipping of Chicago *Times,* February 23, 1892, Trumbull Family MSS; clipping of Chicago *Herald,* October 22, 1893, ibid.
17. White, *Trumbull,* 431.
18. Pease, *Illinois,* 266; Milwaukee *Sentinel,* June 12, 1880; James W. Neilson, *Shelby M. Cullom: Prairie State Republican, Illinois Studies in History,* LI (Urbana: University of Illinois Press, 1962), passim.
19. *Rock Islander* as reprinted in *Illinois State Journal*, August 2, 1880; *Greenback Signal* as reprinted in Champaign County *Gazette,* August 11, 1880; Streater, *Monitor-Index* as reprinted in *Illinois State Journal,* October 28, 1880; Chicago *Tribune,* November 10, 1880; Chicago *Inter-Ocean,* November 11, 1880.
20. Chicago *Tribune,* November 10, 1880; Chicago *Inter-Ocean,* November 11, 21, 1880.
21. Lyman Trumbull to Mary Ingraham Trumbull, November 2, 1880, Trumbull Family MSS.
22. Herman Kogan, *The First Century: The Chicago Bar Association, 1874-1974* (Chicago: Rand McNally, 1974), p. 38.
23. Edson R. Sunderland, *History of the American Bar Association and Its Work* (Ann Arbor, Mich.: [n.p.], 1953), 3-4.
24. Walter Trumbull to Lyman Trumbull, July 2, 1881, Trumbull Family MSS; Walter Trum-

bull to Lyman Trumbull, July 3, 1881, ibid.; Lyman Trumbull to Mary Ingraham Trumbull, July 8, 1881, ibid.; Lyman to Mary Ingraham Trumbull, July 9, 1881, ibid.; Lyman Trumbull to Lewis B. Parsons, November 9, 1881, Lewis B. Parsons MSS, Illinois State Historical Society; Lyman Trumbull to Parsons, May 29, 1884, ibid.

25. Interview with Judge Francis E. Wilson, Chicago, November 28, 1948; Perry Trumbull to Lyman Trumbull, October 9, 1877, Trumbull Family MSS.

26. Notes of Walter Trumbull, January 10, 1950; White, *Trumbull,* 431.

27. Trumbull to Grover Cleveland, May 26, 1885, Grover Cleveland MSS, manuscripts division, Library of Congress; Trumbull to S. W. Moulton, January 7, 1885, ibid.; Melville W. Fuller and others to Cleveland, September 28, 1885, ibid.; "Bayardism," undated and manuscript in handwriting of Walter Trumbull, then in possession of Edward Trumbull, Seattle, Wash.; notes on "Differences of the Republican and Democratic Parties in their Attitudes toward Former Liberal Republicans," undated and unsigned in handwriting of Walter Trumbull, ibid.

28. Lyman Trumbull to Mary Ingraham Trumbull, September 27, 1888, Trumbull Family MSS; Paxton Hibben, *The Peerless Leader, William Jennings Bryan* (New York: Farrar & Rinehart, Inc., 1929), 94-95; Charles Morrow Wilson, *The Commoner: William Jennings Bryan* (Garden City, N. Y.: Doubleday, 1970), 64-65.

29. Joseph Kirkland, *The Story of Chicago,* II (Chicago: Dibble Publishing Co., 1892-1894), 293; Hibben, *The Peerless Leader,* 93-94.

30. Hibben, *The Peerless Leader,* 94; Paolo E. Coletta, *William Jennings Bryan, Political Evangelist,* 1860-1908 (Lincoln: University of Nebraska Press, 1964), 93-94.

31. Hibben, *The Peerless Leader,* 95; notes of Walter Trumbull, January 9, 1950.

32. Charles McDaniel Rosser, *The Crusading Commoner: A Close-up of William Jennings Bryan and his Times* (New York: Putnam, 1971), 42-43.

33. Genealogical table in handwriting of Walter Trumbull; Trumbull to Parsons, May 29, 1884, Parsons MSS.

34. Notes of Walter Trumbull, January 14, 1950; Interview with Mrs. George Cragg, Chicago, November 29, 1948; Mary Ingraham Trumbull to Julia Trumbull (?), May 16, 1881, Trumbull Family MSS; Lyman Trumbull to the Ingrahams (?), August (?) 1884, draft in ibid.

35. White, *Trumbull,* 431.

36. Notes of Walter Trumbull, January 10, 1950; White, *Trumbull,* 425, 426, 431; Interview with Donald McWilliams, Chicago, November 28, 1948.

37. Lyman Trumbull, Diary, 1894, Trumbull Family MSS; Mary Ingraham to Mrs. A. W. Ingraham, August 19, 1894, ibid. See the many letters of condolence in ibid.

38. Trumbull to William Jayne, January 20, 1895, William Jayne MSS; Lyman Trumbull, Diary, 1894, Trumbull Family MSS; Mary Ingraham to Mrs. A. W. Ingraham, August 19, 1894, ibid.

39. Lyman Trumbull, Diary, 1894, Trumbull Family MSS; Diary of Mary Ingraham, 1882-1885, ibid.

40. Trumbull to Mary Jane Ingraham, September 23, 1877, ibid.

41. "At the Commencement of St. Ignatius College, June 25, 1890," manuscript in handwriting of Lyman Trumbull; when consulted, in possession of Edward Trumbull, Seattle, Wash.

42. Chicago *Legal News,* XXC (August 12, 1893), 429.

43. Koerner to Carl Schurz, April 18, 1872, Schurz MSS.

44. Allan Nevins, *Grover Cleveland: A Study in Courage* (New York: Dodd, Mead & Co., 1948), 620-624; Stanley Buder, *Pullman: An Experiment in Industrial Order and Community Planning, 1880-1930* (New York: Oxford University Press, 1969), 187. See the contemporary record as chronicled by Chicago *Tribune,* July 4-10, 1894.

45. Trumbull to Conners, January 16, 1894, Trumbull MSS; White, *Trumbull*, 413.

46. St. Louis *Globe-Democrat,* October 5, 1894.

47. Chicago *Herald,* October 6, 1894; Chicago *Tribune*, October 8, 1894; the Champaign County *Gazette,* October 10, 1894; Chicago *Times,* October 6, 1894.

48. Chicago *Tribune*, October 6, 1894.
49. Chicago *Times*, October 6, 1894; Chicago *Herald*, October 8, 1894; Chicago *Tribune*, October 8, 1894; Alton Weekly *Sentinel-Democrat*, October 11, 1894; Albion (Ill.) *Weekly Journal*, October 18, 1894; Champaign County *Gazette*, October 10, 1894; Council Bluffs (Io.) *Nonpareil*, October 10, 1894; Indianapolis *Sentinel*, October 9, 1894; New York *Journal of Commerce* as reprinted in Chicago *Tribune*, October 14, 1894.
50. Chicago *Times*, October 8, 1894; Denver *Rocky Mountain News*, October 11, 1894; Omaha *Bee*, October 11, 1894.
51. Chicago *Times*, December 27, 1894. The *Times* printed the resolutions as modified by the Populist party leaders.
52. Chicago *Tribune*, December 28, 1894; Cincinnati *Times-Star*, December 27, 1894.
53. Edwin C. Walker to Attorney General Richard Olney, December 29, 1894, Record Group 60, General Records of the Department of Justice, No. 16-123, National Archives; Arnold M. Paul, *Conservative Crisis and the Rule of Law: Attitudes of Bar and Bench, 1887-1895* (New York: Harper & Row, 1969), 153-154; Lawrence M. Friedman, *A History of the American Law* (New York: Simon and Schuster, 1973), 488.
54. Clarence S. Darrow, *The Story of My Life* (New York: C. Scribner's Sons, 1932), 67; White, *Trumbull*, 414.
55. *In Re Debs*, 158 *United States Reports*, 573-577; New York *Times*, March 26, 1895; Chicago *Tribune*, March 26, 1895.
56. New York *Times*, March 26, 1895.
57. *Ibid.*, March 27, 1895; Chicago *Tribune*, March 27, 1895.
58. New York *Times*, March 27, 1895.
59. *In Re Debs*, 158 *United States Reports*, 573-600; Chicago *Tribune*, May 28, 1895.
60. Henry James, *Richard Olney and His Public Service* (Boston: Houghton Mifflin, 1923), 57.
61. Eugene V. Debs, *Debs: His Life, Writings, and Speeches* (Girard, Kans.: The Appeal to Reason, 1908), 327-328.
62. Charles Johnson, "Personal Recollections of Some of the Eminent Statesmen and Lawyers of Illinois," *Illinois State Historical Library No. 9* (1904), 47; White, *Trumbull*, 418.
63. Brooklyn (N. Y.) *Eagle*, June 25, 1896; Chicago *Tribune*, June 25, 1896.
64. *Hurd* v. *Hodge*, 334 *United States Reports*, 24.
65. *Jones v. Mayer Co.*, 392 *United States Reports*, 409.
66. *Runyon* v. *McCrary*, 427 *United States Reports*, 160-214.
67. *McDonald* v. *Santa Fe Trail Company*, *ibid.*, 273-296.

Index